IMMIGRATION THE EASY WAY

Howard David Deutsch, Esq.

BARRON'S

All inquiries should be addressed to:
Barron's Educational Series, Inc.
250 Wireless Boulevard
Hauppauge, New York 11788

Library of Congress Catalog Card No. 92-27054

International Standard Book No. 0-8120-4798-2

Library of Congress Cataloging-in-Publication Data

Deutsch, Howard David, 1944–
    Immigration the Easy Way/Howard Deutsch.
        p.   cm.
    ISBN 0–8120–4798–2
    1. Emigration and Immigration law—United States—Popular works.
2. Emigration and immigration law—Canada—Popular works.
I. Title.
KF4819.6.D48   1993
342.73'082—dc20
[347.30282]   92-27054
                                                                    CIP

PRINTED IN THE UNITED STATES OF AMERICA
 345 100 98765432

Contents

APPENDICES

ACKNOWLEDGMENTS

I would like to thank my children, Jeremy and Rebecca, for their encouragement; my invaluable and irreplaceable law partner Libby Salberg; Marlene Stanger for her skillful research and editing; and the staff at Barron's for their encouragement and support.

LETTER TO THE READER

America prides itself as a "Nation of Immigrants" with a "Light at the Golden Door" welcoming newcomers to our land. That is still our heritage, and one for which all Americans can take pride.

But today's welcome mat can be daunting.

Working one's way through the labyrinth of American immigration law and policy to come to the United States, either as an immigrant or nonimmigrant, or for study, business, or trade, can pose extraordinary challenges. Some don't try; many more fail at the effort.

This guide to U.S. immigration in the 1990s is a comprehensive review of American immigration law and practice that will help many to overcome these hurdles. Prepared by Howard D. Deutsch, it will be an invaluable companion to anyone—practitioner and petitioner alike—who seeks to enter, or to help someone enter, the United States. In considerable detail, and with thorough explanations and illustrations, it will help answer most questions, mundane or profound, that immigrants may have about the processes and requirements of American immigration law.

As many have noted, the U.S. Immigration and Nationality Act is one of the longer and more complicated statutes on our law books—perhaps just behind the United States tax code! But this book will help bring it down to size, to make it more manageable to the uninitiated, and more comprehensible to the outsider.

> Jerry M. Tinker
> Staff Director
> Subcommittee of Immigration and Refugee Affairs
> United States Senate

AUTHOR'S NOTE

The U.S. Immigration and Nationality Act of 1990 radically transformed the landscape of the U.S. immigration process. Practitioners and their clients have not yet fully absorbed all of the far-reaching changes that have occurred.

Although the statute was passed in the final days of 1990, most regulations were not published until almost a year later. Some regulations and forms have yet to become final and other modifications to policy will certainly occur. Throughout the text, I have made every effort to present the most up-to-date information available, and for the most part, I believe I have succeeded. Where this was not possible, I have alerted readers to pending changes.

The publisher and I suggest that readers keep these facts in mind as the book is read; seek competent legal advice if more detailed answers are required.

Comments and recommendations from readers are encouraged. They may be sent to Barron's, and will be kept for use as appropriate in later editions.

Howard David Deutsch
New York City, 1993

Introduction

HOW TO USE THIS BOOK

Your interest in this book obviously comes from a wish to immigrate to the United States. People from every continent of the world have had this same wish and millions have acted upon it. This book was written to guide you through the process of immigration and to give you the skills for making this wish a reality.

You first have to decide exactly what your goal is. Maybe you first want to go to the United States as a tourist so you can decide if you really want to live there. Or you may want to find a job there and decide about immigrating at a later stage. You may, however, have already made up your mind, and you want to get permanent residence as quickly as possible. Once you know what you want to achieve, you are ready to begin on the road to immigration. Remember that each step towards immigration has its own rules and if you break these rules, you decrease your chances of success.

This book presents the immigration picture in full. A lot of the information will not apply to you, but, nonetheless, forms an integral part of the whole. However, as you read, you will identify information that applies to you. To some of you, it may seem as if you are not eligible for any visa categories, or, if you are, the wait might be too long (this is the case if your United States citizen sibling sponsors you for immigration). But don't lose hope. Remember that the law often says one thing, but, in practice, it is not always the case. Therefore, even if you think you may not succeed in getting a green card because of a legal stumbling block, there are often loopholes in the law and you may be able to squeeze through. Or you may be able to take steps that will make you eligible to get a United States visa, as you will read.

Once you understand the laws and you feel confident about your decision to immigrate, you must decide if you are going to attempt the process alone, or with the help of an immigration lawyer. If you are not completely comfortable, and feel that your case is complicated, you are best off consulting a lawyer. If your case is straightforward, you will probably succeed without a lawyer. On the other hand, you may decide to do part of the process alone and hire a lawyer at a later stage. If you represent yourself, this book will be your guide along the way, providing information on the various visa categories, showing you sample forms, and telling you what to expect along the way. If you use a lawyer, this book will make you a smarter client by informing you of all the steps to immigration and pointing out the pitfalls and problems that could occur. The goal of this book is to help you fulfill your wish to live, work, and settle in the United States, with as few bumps along the way as possible.

At the beginning of Part One, the background and history of immigration is described, and this will help you understand the context of immigration law as it exists today. In addition, Part One explains the different government departments involved in immigration and outlines the different steps that one has to follow in order to immigrate, starting with getting into the country and the need—in most cases—for a visa. However, it only details those steps involved in getting nonimmigrant visas and gives a breakdown of all these visas and their requirements. It also deals with procedures involved in the immigration process, such as extending your stay once you are in the country as a nonimmigrant, and changing nonimmigrant visa categories. This section also explains who may enter the United States without a visa and on what terms they may do so, and who may not enter at all! Included in the section on nonimmigrant visas is a detailed discussion of the Canada-United States Free Trade Agreement (FTA), which makes it easy for Canadian citizens to cross the border to do business, work, or make investments in the United States. This subject is also covered briefly earlier on, in discussing who may enter the United States without visas.

Part Two deals with how to get a green card, as the United States permanent residence visa is known. This part is divided into the different components of immigration—family-sponsored, employment-sponsored, and all other ways of becoming a permanent resident, including the recently-created diversity program. All those with qualifying family relationships or job prospects in the United States are eligible for permanent residence, as are those people willing to invest one million dollars in the country to set up new businesses that employ at least ten American workers. Apart from these groups, other groups have been targeted for immigration, depending on their nationalities, their political statuses, or their relationship with the United States. All these special immigrants, diversity immigrants, or transitional diversity immigrants, as they are called in immigration law, are also discussed.

Part Three deals with the process of naturalization in which a legal permanent resident can become a United States citizen. The rules and regulations governing this procedure are discussed, as are the forms needed and steps to follow to acquire citizenship status. As you will read, even naturalized United States citizens are subject to rules and conditions and this section outlines the requirements for ensuring that once you become a citizen of the United States, you are able to remain a citizen.

Part Four covers Canadian immigration, which will be of interest to many people planning to immigrate to North America and who have not yet pinpointed exactly where they wish to live. For many, climate and geography is a consideration of where to live. For others, investment opportunities play a big role in this decision. And for some people, a major issue might be the health and education system. On all these issues, Canada and the United States differ—in some cases, considerably. This section, will not outline these differences, but will extend your knowledge of immigration and give you the opportunity to compare the systems in Canada and the United States.

THE ROLE OF THE IMMIGRATION LAWYER

How to Represent Yourself and Win

If you are serious about immigrating to the United States and if this is important to your future, you should think long and hard before trying to get a green card on your own. You should only consider representing yourself in a visa application if you understand all the requirements for getting a visa and you think you can do this without making a mistake. If you have any doubts that you can do this, or are confused by the instructions for obtaining a visa, you should go to an immigration attorney. Usually, it is easier to represent yourself in cases of family-sponsored immigration where the family relationship is uncomplicated (that is, it does not involve adoption, divorce, stepchildren, or any other relationship in which slightly different rules apply). If you are planning to immigrate using work as your means of entry into the country, the process could be tricky. Some companies with large numbers of foreign staff employ human resources personnel who specialize in immigration matters, and others retain immigration lawyers to act on their behalf. If you are going to work for a company that has helped other foreign employees get their non-immigrant visas and/or green cards in the past, some of your problems will be solved. However, if you are going to work for a company that is not interested in your long-term goal to immigrate, merely in its own short-term goal of using your skills, you will probably have to arrange your own visa. This will involve dealing with the Immigration and Naturalization Service (INS), probably the Department of Labor (DOL), and, if you are applying for your visa from your home country, the Department of State (the United States consulate nearest your home).

After reading this book, you should be able to judge your chances of success in representing yourself, because you will know if you are eligible for your chosen visa category. If you decide to go ahead on your own, you must stick to the rules and regulations at each step along the way. Your main task, in representing yourself, will be filling in forms and gathering documentary proof of your eligibility in support of your application.

The art of completing bureaucratic forms lies in consistency. From the beginning, make copies of every form you ever submit to the INS and make sure that you give them consistent information throughout the immigration procedure. You should also take care to answer every question. This is extremely important when completing United States visa application forms because, if you leave an empty space in an application form, the INS might assume you forgot to fill it in and send it back to you. This could cause a major delay in your visa application, because your application will go back to the bottom of the pile when you resubmit it. Therefore, you must always write "Not Applicable" or N/A in spaces where the question does not apply to you rather than leave it blank.

The issue of consistency has hampered many a prospective immigrant, particularly those who are immigrating to the United States through job sponsorship. Many people claim to have certain skills, but the jobs they are offered in the United States need either higher or lower skills levels. There are many situations that relate to finding a job and getting a visa in which you might be faced with a dilemma. For example, you may want to be consistent in filling in forms, and yet feel the need to choose information selectively to increase your chances of success. For example, when you reach the point of applying for permanent residence based on a job, you will realize that your employer has to have a sound reason for employing you rather than an American worker. You will, therefore, try to represent yourself and your skills as being unique, to reduce the chances of anyone else getting your job. This could be difficult, especially in times of high unemployment in the United States, and unless you are confident of your chances, you would do well to hire a competent immigration lawyer. Even if you obtained your own visa to enter the United States as a nonimmigrant, you might consider consulting a lawyer when you apply for permanent residence.

Getting a nonimmigrant visa is not always easier than getting permanent residence. There are many areas that have been disputed for years, such as the issue of who is a professional, and the Immigration Act of 1990 created several new visa categories to add to the confusion. If your skills and qualifications clearly fit the specific visa category for which you plan to apply, you are likely to succeed in getting this visa without the help of a lawyer. Apart from being eligible for a visa category, your ability to obtain this visa on your own will depend on your literacy in the English language and your ability to follow instructions. There are also unspoken rules that many State Department officials follow when they decide whether or not to grant a visa application—and this applies to tourist visas as well.

The consuls will consider four things:

1. Will you be returning to a job?
2. Do you have money or other investments?
3. Do you own property?
4. Do you have family who will remain behind?

If the answers to these questions are mainly "no," you can be reasonably sure that you will not get a visa to visit the United States. If the consul suspects that you will not be returning to your country he or she will conclude that you are not an authentic visitor, as stated on your visa application, but an intending immigrant. People from strife-torn countries find it particularly difficult to obtain United States visas because it is widely believed that they do not plan to return.

You should always be prepared for hitches along the way, because sometimes the least expected things can cause obstacles. For example, failure to provide suitable or adequate documentation is often the reason why visa applications are denied the first time. You must ensure that you have documents to back up all your visa applications and to prove your eligibility in the category for which you apply. It is often possible to appeal a visa denial, but this requires experience and, again, even if you've represented yourself to this point, this is the time for legal intervention. You should avoid incompetent attorneys as well as immigration consultants who may pose as lawyers or notaries and are not entitled to represent you legally.

When applying for a work-related visa, you will have to provide proof of your educational qualifications. If a degree is part of the qualifications for the job, you will have to provide a notarized copy of your degree and have it evaluated before your visa will be granted. Evaluating your degrees is essential and in order to do this, you must send your degree/s to one of the organizations in the United States that specialize in providing this service. These organizations make sure that the courses you studied for your degree are equivalent to qualifying courses for the equivalent degree at United States universities or colleges. This process helps to eliminate fraudulent applications by people claiming to have the qualifications for a job, but not really having them. It also protects your prospective employer, who wants to be sure that the person he/she is hiring is capable of doing the job.

If you are applying for a green card based on your family relationship with either a United States citizen or permanent resident, you will have to prove the relationship on which this application is based. You or your family member can submit this application and there should be no legal hitches, provided you complete all the questions and follow all the instructions.

A final word of caution. At one time, immigration was a fairly straightforward procedure, with rules and regulations that were open to a certain amount of interpretation, but that, by and large, were understood. Over the years, as new laws have been passed, more complexities have arisen and more issues are unclear. Immigration is now a minefield of information and the rules in many cases are so new that not even INS or State Department officials are clear about how they all work. Therefore, you must expect that there will be bumps along the way. Read this book, plan your strategy for immigration, then sit down and think about how you will put this strategy into action.

How to Use an Attorney if You Need One

During the past ten years, more and more lawyers have specialized in immigration. Other lawyers once looked down on immigration lawyers, but tougher laws and a higher standard of practice that many immigration lawyers have had to adopt to attract business, has ended this discrimination.

Whether or not you need an attorney depends on how you see your chances of successfully reaching your goal of immigration. If you are confident of reaching this goal, or if you cannot afford the services of a good immigration lawyer, you may choose to represent yourself. If you know that you qualify in a specific category, there should be no problems. But, where your eligibility is in doubt, or if you are not sure how to go about applying, you would be better off consulting an immigration lawyer.

Although no lawyer can guarantee success, he/she will have a clear picture of your chances. Many people believe that immigration lawyers cannot fail and that they have special government connections that can speed up the process. This is not the case in the United States. Therefore, if any lawyer claims that he/she can guarantee your success in a visa application, you should be cautious. Most immigration lawyers know from experience that different INS officials may respond differently to the same application. Even among different immigration lawyers, if you ask the same question to all of them, you are likely to get several different answers. Some people employ various immigration lawyers before they get their green cards. Many of these people compare their situations to those of their friends or colleagues who may have got their visas sooner. But you should not compare your situation to anyone else's. No two cases are identical so do not assume that your application should take the same length of time to process as your friend's. There are many factors that affect the length of time it takes to get a visa, as you will read in Part One. Do not think that changing your lawyer will make your green card arrive sooner. What your lawyer *can* and *should* do to help you, however, is prepare your application as thoroughly as possible to increase your chances of success. Based on his/her experience, it should be clear whether or not you are likely to get the visa for which you are applying. Based on this knowledge, your lawyer's skill and experience in approaching your case should count a great deal.

But remember, your immigration lawyer is human and could make a mistake. This is not impossible, if you consider all the new information and changes in the laws. If this happens, you may be aware of it, and immediately look for another lawyer to represent you. You are perfectly entitled to do so. But you may not even know, and, being none the wiser, may simply have to wait a while longer for your visa. Because you are paying a lawyer for his/her services, you must expect complete honesty in your dealings with this person and, in turn, be prepared to be completely honest with him or her in return. It will be impossible for any lawyer to represent you unless you provide him or her with all the details pertaining to your application. Ask what is happening with your visa application at each step along the way, and expect answers to any questions you have regarding your fears. It is natural to be anxious during a green card application. You are usually unable to leave the country while your application is being processed and this could leave you feeling fragile and isolated. Your immigration lawyer is aware of this and should be sympathetic to your needs. Your lawyer takes on a very personal role in your life, not only because he/she is dealing with you at a turning point in your life—when you decide to immigrate—but also because he/she is helping you realize your wish to live in the United States. Therefore, it helps to have a good working relationship.

The cost involved in hiring an immigration lawyer may be the reason you choose to represent yourself. But usually lawyers are prepared to come to a financial arrangement with you. You should investigate the market before starting the process. Possibly your friends, relatives, colleagues, or others from your country who are already settled in the United States can recommend a good immigration lawyer to you. If you need the lawyer for moral support as well as for his/her legal expertise, you will probably pay a higher fee, because in most cases, the higher the fee, the greater the personal contact. Some lawyers who charge lower fees will not see you directly but will assign a paralegal in his/her office to your case.

Many lawyers charge fixed fees for specific services. When an attorney gives you a set price for a specific service, he or she is, to some extent, taking a gamble. If your case goes smoothly and the attorney takes less time on it than anticipated, he/she will make money from you. But in more complicated cases, where your lawyer takes more time than anticipated, this costs both time and money. Although you may be paying a set price, any additional services, such as appealing a visa denial or organizing to have your university degree evaluated, will cost extra. Disbursements, which are all out-of-pocket costs incurred by the attorney, are usually extra as well. If your attorney has to send faxes on your behalf, for example, or uses his/her own money when submitting your visa application, these expenses will be added to your bill. Before hiring an immigration lawyer, you must be sure you understand his/her billing structure. If you are quoted a set fee, you understand that this may be the minimum fee and does not necessarily include extra costs. Once you have come to an agreement with your lawyer about costs and services, you should ask him/her to prepare a retainer statement that outlines all the details on which you agreed and you should both sign it.

It may be possible for you to consult with a lawyer on an hourly basis if you want to represent yourself, but need advice in a specific area. You should call various immigration lawyers to see if any are prepared to see you on this basis. This could be a useful strategy if you understand what you are doing, but sometimes need a professional backup.

Now move to Part One which begins by giving the background and history of immigration to the United States and continues with an explanation of rules and regulations governing the immigration process.

PART ONE

PREPARING THE WAY FOR IMMIGRATION

CHAPTER 1

The Immigration Arena

BACKGROUND

New possibilities in a new land: this has been the attraction for people coming to the United States from the earliest days of immigration. Immigrants have been drawn by the success of others and over time the United States has become known, worldwide, as the "land of opportunity." However, with each new flood of immigrants, restrictive laws were passed to control the flow of immigration and these laws have made it increasingly difficult for people to enter the country unchecked. These restrictions on immigration have resulted in a situation where there are millions more people wanting to immigrate to the United States than there are green cards available.

As one of millions of people wanting to live in the United States, you must expect to wait some time before you get your visa. The immigration process has certain steps that you will have to follow in order to get a green card, or whatever nonimmigrant visa you require, and the rules state that you may only proceed to the next move once you have completed the previous one. How long you will have to exist in a state of limbo—from the time you apply for a visa until the time you get it—depends very much on the visa you require and the number of people who have applied before you. As you will learn from this book, immigration may at first appear to be a straightforward process, but it often presents many complications along the way.

Immigration is a complicated subject because when laws are passed by Congress, the Immigration and Naturalization Service (INS) has the job of applying these laws as it believes Congress intended. This causes many problems, especially where United States employers may suffer, thereby hurting the economy, or where families may be split up, contrary to what the government tries to avoid doing—or so it claims. Because different interpretations are applied to the laws, there has been a great deal of confusion surrounding immigration for decades. The nineties has produced yet another batch of laws to control immigration to the United States. The Immigration Act of 1990 was passed to reform legal immigration. It will take a long time to assess the success of this legislation, which will benefit mostly those people who are skilled and educated, or have money to invest in the United States. It strikes a blow to unskilled workers, particularly from those countries from where immigration has been the highest during the past decade. Current laws make it much more difficult for these people to get immigrant visas.

It is important that you understand the limitations to immigration. It is only by realizing that the American dream cannot be a reality to everyone and that the process of selection is extremely strict that you will appreciate why the green card has become such a precious commodity to so many people.

SEEKING THE AMERICAN DREAM: A BRIEF HISTORY OF IMMIGRATION

Since the 1400s, people from all over the world have been coming to the United States for many different reasons. First there were the explorers, then, as many critics have noted, the exploiters. Following early foreign settlement, waves of immigrants settled and became assimilated in the American way of life. By the time the next wave arrived, the early settlers were no longer immigrants but part of the settled population who resented the arrival of new immigrants. This pattern still exists today.

The first immigrants were landowners, slaves, merchants, indentured servants, victims of religious persecution, and fortune seekers. The political development of this country gave rise to the Constitution and the Bill of Rights, neither of which made any distinction between citizens and non-citizens. In the nineteenth century, the United States politicians viewed immigration as a cheap and plentiful source of labor and, from 1860 for approximately 60 years, more than 28 million immigrants came to America. Their labor was valued. Their presence in the country was not. The political and social conflict that resulted from immigration led to the passing of the first general immigration law in 1882. This law required every immigrant to pay a head tax of 50 cents to the Treasury Department. It also denied entry to "idiots, lunatics, convicts, and persons likely to become public charges."

In 1888, a federal law placed a one-year limit on foreign contract workers in the United States. Workers were drawn to the United States to work, knowing that they had to leave after one year. Within a 20-year period, the legal restrictions placed on immigrants had been extended to exclude "paupers," "anarchists," people who had entered the country illegally, and those who could not earn a living because of physical or mental handicaps. These restrictions still apply.

At the turn of the century, when emigration from Europe was growing, an English literacy test was imposed to restrict entry to the United States. The racist nature of immigration law became more obvious in 1917, when, despite President Wilson's veto, Congress passed a law that incorporated an "Asiatic Barred Zone," excluding most Asians from the country. Only in 1952 did Japanese immigrants become eligible for United States citizenship. Other exclusion tactics were used during the 1920s recession, when American workers were threatened by the influx of foreign labor and demanded laws to protect their jobs from foreigners. The Quota Act of 1921 limited annual immigration of foreigners from any one country to 3 percent of the number of foreigners from that country already in the United States in 1910.

Racism has always played a part in immigration law, in spite of the fact that exclusion on racial grounds was abolished in 1952, and political expediency has been behind most of the changes in the laws. In the mid-sixties, Congress abolished the national origin quota system. This law removed all restrictions on Asian immigration and divided immigrants into those from the Western Hemisphere and those from the Eastern Hemisphere. This 1965 act established visa preferences, addressed family unity and labor needs, and provided an avenue for professionals to enter the country. Although it ostensibly removed the quota system, a quota system is still in place today and determines how many people from which countries may immigrate each year.

In spite of legal immigration laws, hundreds of thousands of immigrants enter the United States illegally every year. Illegal immigration peaked in the eighties, when Congress passed the Immigration Reform and Control Act of 1986 (IRCA) to try to control this problem. IRCA targeted employers, making it a punishable offense to employ illegal residents. It made employers responsible for keeping written records of all employees they hired after this act was passed, with documented proof of their work authorization. On the other hand, IRCA also made it an offense to discriminate against workers based on their national origin or citizenship. This was necessary because people realized that many employers would find it too much trouble to keep records for all their workers, particularly foreign workers, so they would avoid hiring anyone foreign looking or sounding. This law is still confusing to American employers, many of whom know little or nothing about immigration.

The lottery system became a popular way of distributing visas in the eighties and early nineties and millions of people from all over the world swamped the United States mail system to get their applications in first. The Immigration Act of 1990 has had to allocate visas to people who were promised green cards through the IRCA lottery, but who did not get them.

Whereas illegal immigration was the issue of the eighties, legal immigration is the issue of the nineties, as reflected by the Immigration Act of 1990. Analyzing the history of immigration shows that each law has been in response to previous ones—either implementing them more thoroughly or correcting some of the problems that the government thought they created.

THE SHIFTING PICTURE: WHY THE LAWS KEEP CHANGING

Many would argue that immigration laws are interpreted widely and changed according to political expediency. For example, when the Immigration Act of

1990 was still in its Senate bill phase, it was nicknamed the "Irish Immigration Bill." This was because of the known interests of Senator Ted Kennedy, who was one of the architects of this new law. Irish nationals benefitted from the recent OP-1 lottery and stand to benefit from the current AA-1 lottery more than any other group. Apart from the benefits to any national group, the current immigration laws were the result of political and economic pressures exerted on American politicians for many years. IRCA was also in response to issues that affected the political and economic life of Americans.

The Civil Rights Act of 1964 increased people's political awareness and one year later, the national origins quota system, a feature of immigration law since 1910, was abolished. The liberal political climate gave rise to laws to abolish this obviously racist system.

There have also been international causes for changes in United States immigration laws. Wars, impoverishment, political anarchy or oppression, and other upheavals in various parts of the globe have left millions of people without homes. This problem still exists. Some are forced out of their countries and others have chosen to leave because of conditions there. United States immigration law allows many of these people to enter by granting them political asylum or refugee status, or in other ways.

No laws have been powerful enough to keep out foreigners excluded by legal channels. Some estimates say that more people immigrate to the United States illegally every year than legally. IRCA attempted to put a stop to this, but illegal immigration continues to flourish. Employers are not particularly interested in enforcing employer sanctions, which makes them responsible for checking whether or not their employees are authorized to work in the United States. This is because, in many cases, the illegal workers fill a void created by American workers who are not willing to do certain types of labor. One example of this is domestic workers. Many American citizens complain about the high rates of immigration but do not realize that immigrants, many of them illegal, provide essential services.

The Immigration Act of 1990 takes into account the increased demands for immigrant visas as well as existing backlogs in many visa categories. As more people have gained immigrant status, more people have become eligible to immigrate, based on their family relationships. This increased pressure on the INS forced the government to adopt a new strategy. The new act makes thousands more visas available each year. It also takes into account America's need to compete more aggressively on an international market and makes a significantly higher number of visas available to professionals, business people, and investors.

If you look at immigration from a national and global perspective, you will understand that, as long as the political and economic picture changes, the laws will have to keep changing too.

OUTLOOK FOR THE NINETIES: UNDERSTANDING THE IMMIGRATION ACT OF 1990

The Immigration Act of 1990 is about three things: reuniting families, allowing people to come and work in the United States by bringing their skills and/or money, and giving a more diverse selection of people the chance to immigrate. It seems a straightforward policy but these laws are no less complicated than immigration laws have been in the past.

Until this act was passed, 270,000 immigrant visas were available annually, excluding immediate family members of United States citizens. From now until the end of the 1994 fiscal year, 700,000 immigrant visas are available annually and, after this, 675,000 visas will be available each year. Of the 700,000 visas, 520,000 are for family-sponsored immigration—including, for the first time in immigration history, immediate family members, plus 55,000 visas for the spouses and children of newly-legalized aliens. There are 140,000 work-related visas and 40,000 are for "transitionals" who have job offers in the United States. From October 1, 1994, there will be 480,000 visas for family-based immigration—including immediate family of United States citizens, 140,000 for employment-based immigration, and 55,000 "diversity" visas.

There are more visas available to skilled workers and investors coming to the United States, but significantly fewer visas available to unskilled workers. In fact, current legislation has restructured the employment-based immigration category to get rid of the specific subcategory that catered to unskilled workers, and has grouped them with other workers. This has resulted in significantly fewer immigrant visas for those without skills, which, many argue, is part of the racist legacy of immigration law, because the majority of unskilled visa applicants come from Third World countries.

There is no restriction on how many immediate family members, defined as minor children, spouses, and parents of United States citizens, may immigrate in any year. However, the law guarantees 226,000 family preference visas each year. There are four family preferences: the first preference for the adult, unmarried children of United States citizens; the second preference for the spouses and unmarried children of permanent residents; the third preference for the married sons and daughters of United States citizens; and the fourth preference for the adult siblings of United States citizens who are, themselves, over the age of twenty-one. If the demand for immediate relative visas is so high that it reduces the available number of preference visas below the "floor" level of 226,000, additional visas will be taken from the currently available visas for amnesty beneficiaries. There is a fairly simple mathematical formula employed to keep tabs on this situation, based on a current annual 6 percent increase in demand for immediate relative visas. This will be explained fully in Chapter 8.

The 140,000 employment-linked visas will be allocated within five subsections. "Priority Workers," including people of "extraordinary ability," those at the top of their professional or academic fields, and some executives and upper management of multinational corporations, will receive 40,000 first preference visas. The same number of visas will be allocated to professionals with advanced degrees and those with "Exceptional Ability" in the second preference. Another 40,000 visas are for "Other Workers," including skilled workers, professionals with baccalaureate degrees, and unskilled workers who are all in the third preference. Unskilled workers will only be eligible for a quarter of this annual allocation. The fourth and fifth preferences respectively consist of "Special Immigrants" who will get 10,000 visas, and "Investors," who will get another 10,000. Investors willing to start their businesses in areas of high unemployment will receive 3,000 of these visas and will be able to make a smaller investment than those setting up in urban areas where the shortage of jobs is not as acute. Either way, investors will have to provide ten jobs for American workers, excluding their own family. Investors will obtain conditional residence status that the government will review after two years to ensure that the investment is legitimate. Employment-based immigration is discussed in detail in Chapter 9, with a special focus on investors.

The rest of the visas are for people from countries that have been underrepresented in United States immigration during the past five years. People from underrepresented countries who have job offers from United States employers will be eligible for 40,000 "transitional" visas. From the 1995 fiscal year, there will be 55,000 diversity immigrant visas available to people from countries that have provided the least number of immigrants during the preceding five years. This will be covered in Chapter 10.

To sum up, the Immigration Act of 1990 gives more opportunities to those without family connections in the United States who plan to immigrate using their academic, professional, business, or economic skills to gain access to permanent residence. On the contrary, those without skills will find it extremely difficult to immigrate. This law increases the overall number of family-linked immigrant visas, but reduces the number of fourth preference visas. Some people have estimated that the wait in the fourth preference family category could be at least 15 years, and probably longer.

CHAPTER 2

A General View of Immigration

GOVERNMENT DEPARTMENTS: THE BUREAUCRACIES BLOCKING THE BORDERS

The Immigration and Naturalization Service (INS) falls under the Department of Justice and is responsible for the approval of all immigrant visas and most nonimmigrant visas, notably, those permitting work or study in the United States. However, other branches of government are also involved in immigration, namely, the State Department and the Department of Labor (DOL).

United States consular officials abroad have been issuing entry visas to foreigners for more than a century. The Act of July 5, 1884 gave foreign service officials of the State Department the authority to issue visas to certain people. Since 1917, everyone entering the United States has needed a visa to do so. There are now approximately 230 United States consular or embassy posts throughout the world that issue these visas. The Immigration Reform and Control Act of 1986 (IRCA) relaxed these laws slightly and the nationals of Britain, France, Germany, Italy, Japan, the Netherlands, Sweden, and Switzerland may enter the United States without visas if they are coming on vacation for not more than 90 days. This program was extended by the Immigration Act of 1990 and more countries have been added to this visa waiver list. When you read about the different categories of visas, both immigrant and nonimmigrant, and how to obtain them, you will understand the current role of the different government departments in the immigration process.

The Department of Labor plays a significant role in the immigration procedure of most people entering this country on work-related visas. The function of the DOL is to ensure that United States employers are not giving jobs to aliens without first conducting an intensive search for American workers. In addition, it ensures that neither the working conditions nor the wages paid to American workers are jeopardized by the employment of aliens. This process is called either labor attestation or labor certification, depending on the visa category for which you are applying.

The DOL and Board of Alien Labor Certification Appeals (BALCA)—the agency that reviews appeals after the DOL has denied labor certification applications—have become extremely strict in recent years. Employers sponsoring foreign employees have to present strong cases to show that there are no American workers qualified or available for the position being offered.

The Department of State could ruin your plans to come to the United States by refusing to stamp a visa in your passport, even if the INS approves your visa petition—if one was needed. If a State Department official thinks that your application for a visa is based on incorrect information, he/she may deny your visa. Or, you may get your visa quite easily from the consulate or embassy abroad, but an INS official at the airport could turn you away if he/she finds any inconsistencies. For example, before the new laws came into effect, you had to maintain a foreign residence if you came to the United States on certain nonimmigrant visas. When this was the case, many people were questioned when they arrived in the country and turned away if the INS found that they did not meet the eligibility requirements.

HOW THE SYSTEM OPERATES: NUMBERS, QUOTAS, AND WAITING PERIODS

Most people planning to enter the United States need a visa to do so. In order to qualify for a visa, you have to meet the conditions for the particular visa category that you require. This is true whether you are applying for a nonimmigrant visa or an immigrant visa (green card). A nonimmigrant visa will give you legal access to the United States on a temporary basis and may, depending on the visa category, enable you to study, work, or both. An immigrant visa will enable you to live and work permanently in the United States and to apply for citizenship at a later stage. The immigration system allocates visa numbers to different visa categories and processes applications within these categories on a first-come, first-served basis. Certain visa applications are relatively problem-free. For example, if your spouse is a United States permanent resident, he/she can petition on your behalf for a family second preference visa (in this case, second preference, 2A—see Chapter 8) and must simply supply the necessary information proving your status as spouse. Once your petition is approved, you submit your application for a visa, then you sit back and wait. If any problems exist, they would only be in the area of time delays, because how soon you obtain your visa depends on how many people are ahead of you in the particular category. If people apply for more visas than are available in a particular category in any given year, this category is said to be oversubscribed and applications that are not processed are carried over to the following year, reducing the number of available visas for that year.

If you are applying for an immigrant visa based on your job, the procedure is more complicated because, in most cases, you will first have to get clearance from the DOL. This process of labor certification could hold up your visa application for many months and, in some cases, even years. (Chapter 9 covers this subject in detail.)

Many people do not try to immigrate because they do not think they are eligible. But there are many ways of immigrating to the United States and it may just be a case of trying to figure out where you fit into the picture. For example, if you work in a certain field but do not have a degree, it may be worth your while to go back to the university and get a degree in that particular field. This would then make you eligible in an employment preference category and increase your chances of finding a job in the United States by raising your skills level. If you do not have a university degree, but have substantial experience in a field that usually requires the minimum of a bachelor's degree, you can still be eligible for immigration provided you have the experience that is considered by immigration officials to be equivalent to a United States degree in your particular field. A figure often given by immigration officials is that you need to have three years of experience for each year of a university degree. Therefore, if the minimum requirement for a job in your field in the United States is a four-year bachelor's degree and you have 12 years of experience, the chances are good that you will qualify for a visa to work in your field. If you are in business, you might consider opening a branch in the United States in order to qualify for a visa that would enable you to work there first as a nonimmigrant and then as an immigrant. There are many strategies to adopt when you consider immigration, because, although the rules are strict, the options are many. It may be worth your while to contact an immigration lawyer at this point, especially if you are starting to despair of your chances of immigrating. Try to get a recommendation before consulting with a lawyer. It makes good sense to use a lawyer with whom other people from your country have had success because he/she will, therefore, be familiar with the conditions in your country and might be able to suggest a strategy that has worked for others in your situation.

TEMPORARY OR PERMANENT RESIDENCE: MAKING THE LEGAL CHOICE

Any person who applies for a visa to enter the United States or for any other benefits under the immigration and naturalization laws falls into either the immigrant or nonimmigrant category. An immigrant is a person who relocates permanently. A nonimmigrant is a person who, for whatever reason, relocates temporarily and intends returning home after a certain period.

Current laws enable certain nonimmigrants to apply for immigrant status, while maintaining lawful nonimmigrant status. Previously, and currently in some categories, it was considered fraudulent to apply for a nonimmigrant visa with the intention of remaining permanently in the United States. This is known as dual intent.

If you apply abroad for a nonimmigrant visa to enter the United States, you can expect a certain amount of difficulty, because State Department officials will often assume that you intend to remain permanently. A large percentage of immigrants started out as nonimmigrants, so the officials are wary of this. Some people have even been denied tourist visas on this ground. Therefore, you must have proof of returning to your own country, unless you are applying for a visa that permits you to live and work in the United States without maintaining your home abroad. The conditions of entry into the United States are strict, despite the high number of people who enter the United States illegally every year by slipping across the borders in the night and evading the INS patrols, or by entering the country, presumably as tourists, with no intention of leaving, or with fraudulent documents.

All visas can be issued abroad and some first need INS-approved petitions before they can be granted. If your visa needs prior INS approval (in the form of an approved petition submitted to the INS in the area where you will be working, studying, or living—depending on the circumstances), the consulate or embassy nearest you will notify you when this is granted and you can go there to get the visa stamped in your passport.

Most immigrants who do not have family members to sponsor them first come to the United States as tourists or on other nonimmigrant visas, and then begin the immigration process. If you apply for immigrant status while in the United States as a legal nonimmigrant, this is called applying for *adjustment of status*. If you arrive as a tourist and change to another nonimmigrant status, for example, one that permits you to work, this is called *changing status*. These terms are often confused and some people use them interchangeably. However, they both mean specific things in immigration and, because they will be referred to very often in this book, you should make sure you understand the difference between them.

These and other issues are discussed in the following chapters, which deal with different procedures in immigration and how to obtain the visa you want. In the next chapter the various ways of entering the United States and why it is important to follow all the rules along the way are considered.

Entering the United States of America

NONIMMIGRANT VISAS AND VISA WAIVERS

Apart from a few exceptions, anyone entering the United States on a temporary basis needs a visa to do so. If you are applying for a tourist visa, you will need to provide information to the United States State Department office in your area showing that you have a return ticket to your country and, in some cases, you will have to provide proof that you have sufficient funds to support yourself while in the United States. Similarly, if you are applying for another visa category that does not permit study or employment, you will have to provide information to support the basis for your claim in that particular category. In applying for a nonimmigrant visa for a temporary visit to the United States, you are undertaking to fulfill the conditions of that visa, namely, that you will not live there illegally or enter into any employment. Even if you are entering the United States on a B-1 business visa, which will enable you to conduct business in the form of making investments, buying merchandise, attending conferences, or carrying out a business transaction or fulfilling a contract on behalf of a non-United States employer, you will be restricted to all business activities that will not result in your being paid in the United States.

The Immigration Reform and Control Act of 1986 (IRCA) launched a Visa Waiver Pilot Program, which permits the nationals of Britain, France, Germany, Holland, Italy, Japan, Sweden, and Switzerland to enter the United States without a visa provided they are coming as tourists and staying a maximum of 90 days. The Immigration Act of 1990 has extended this visa waiver program until 1994 and has given the Immigration and Naturalization Service (INS) the go-ahead to extend this program to the nationals of Belgium, Denmark, Finland, Iceland, Luxembourg, Norway, and Spain. In these situations, the airlines transporting tourists from the qualifying countries to the United States have to screen passengers for their eligibility before they are allowed to board the United States-bound aircraft. Even if you qualify in terms of this program, you are not obligated by it and are still eligible to apply for an entry visa. Your options will be greater with a visa if you have any intention of extending your visit, for whatever reason, because, without a visa, you cannot obtain an extension of stay or change to another visa category. All those people entering the United States on the visa waiver program will have to complete Form I-94W, the nonimmigrant visa waiver arrival and departure form.

If you are applying for a nonimmigrant visa that permits employment in the United States, you must first submit a visa petition to the INS in the area where your employment will take place. Once the INS has approved this petition, it will notify the State Department post from which you will be obtaining your visa. The consulate or embassy concerned will then notify you and you will then have to take your passport to be stamped with this visa. If you are a student or involved in a cultural, scientific, business, or professional exchange program, the institution where you will be studying or sharing your expertise must first approve your application and once it sends you notice of your acceptance, a visa can be issued to you at your nearest United States consular or embassy post. Schools, universities, medical facilities and other organizations that offer courses of study or skills-training/sharing programs have been accredited by the INS or by the United States Information Agency (which, in turn, has been given INS approval) to approve the applications of those who are eligible and, therefore, facilitate getting their visas.

In many cases, other people will take care of organizing a visa for you. Foreign media representatives and employees of international organizations, including government and consular officials, obtain their visas through their employers or governments. Also, if you are the fiancé or fiancée of a United States citizen, your future spouse will petition for an entry visa on your behalf. All this will be covered in greater detail in Chapter 5, which deals with all the nonimmigrant visa categories, including the new ones created by the Immigration Act of 1990.

There is no limit to the number of nonimmigrant visas that are issued in any year and any person qualifying in a particular visa category has an excellent chance of getting it. Only those who do not meet the criteria for obtaining a nonimmigrant visa or who are not admissible based on grounds of excludability will be denied access to the United States.

PAROLE, ASYLUM, REFUGEE, AND TEMPORARY PROTECTED STATUS (TPS)

Certain categories of people fall outside the visa system. These are refugees or those seeking political asylum (asylees) who are fleeing their countries, or have already done so, on account of persecution, or people who are already in the United States on a temporary basis, who are nationals of countries where either natural or political disasters have prevented them from returning. The latter are given temporary protected status (TPS).

Each year, the United States President determines the number of refugees who will be admitted into the United States and the regions from which they will be selected. Economic hardship does not make a person eligible for obtaining refugee status. Refugees must be able to substantiate a claim that they are being persecuted on account of their race, religion, nationality, political opinions, or membership of a particular group. Those applying for political asylum are subject to the same criteria of eligibility, but the differences between them and refugees are that they are already in the United States and they are not subject to an annual numerical quota. Another important difference between refugees and asylees is that refugees have to have financial sponsorship before they will be considered eligible for coming to the United States and have to be able to pay for their own transportation. Political asylees, on the other hand, are already in the United States and are not required to have sponsorship. Usually political or church groups, individuals, often family members, and, occasionally, the United States government itself, act as sponsors for refugees.

If any people who otherwise qualify for refugee status have been "firmly resettled" in another country, they are no longer eligible for consideration. One of the obstacles for refugees is that they have to apply in person to an INS Overseas Office and there may not be such an office in their countries. These offices only exist in 13 countries: West Germany, Russia, Greece, Italy, India, Austria, Philippines, Korea, Singapore, Thailand, Hong Kong, Mexico, and Panama. Refugees from any of these countries can travel to the cities where these offices operate and submit their applications. Refugees from other countries have to travel to one of these countries to make their applications. This may mean they have to flee from their own countries and wait in their host countries until their applications are approved. However, they must be careful not to become resettled in the interim, because they could forfeit their eligibility.

People who have not suffered past persecution in a country are still eligible as refugees or asylees if they have a genuine belief that they will be subject to persecution in the future. Also, if they belong to a group and a pattern or practice exists of persecuting people who belong to similar groups, this constitutes grounds for acceptance by the United States. There is no need for people to prove that they would be singled out from the group and individually persecuted.

It may be possible for some refugees to gain entry into the United States as parolees if the annual refugee quota has been filled. Given that many more people qualify as refugees each year than there are refugee quotas available, many go on lengthy waiting lists. Parolees are permitted to enter the United States without a visa and must have their status renewed annually. They may live and work here for as long as their parolee status is valid. However, a parolee's status may be revoked at any time and parolees are not guaranteed permanent residence in the United States. Therefore, being paroled into this country has fewer long-term benefits and is usually the last resort of those who are desperate to leave their sources of hardship and misery.

Both refugees and those applying for parole must submit Form I-131 plus a filing fee of $65.

During the nineties to date, the nationals of five countries—El Salvador, Kuwait, Lebanon, Liberia, and Somalia—as well as the nationals of Bosnia, Hercegovina—have qualified for temporary protected status (TPS). In order to qualify for TPS, the nationals of these countries must have been living temporarily in the United States since the date that the INS determined to be significant in terms of the upheaval taking place in their countries of birth or last previous residence. The INS has the liberty to extend TPS status if and as it sees fit, both to those who already qualify and to nationals of other countries that are afflicted with disasters in the course of time. Applicants for TPS must submit form I–82 ($50 filing fee). They must also submit form I–765; if they wish to work in the United States, this form must also be accompanied by a filing fee of $60.

As with the applicants for all visas to enter the United States, those people who are generally excludable, will also be excluded from obtaining refugee, asylee, or TPS status. They can apply for a Waiver of Excludability and, provided they have not committed a serious crime, participated in persecuting others, or been involved in any subversive activities that could threaten the security of the United States, the chances are high—for humanitarian reasons—that they will be admitted.

IMMIGRANT VISAS—"GREEN CARDS"

People who qualify for permanent residence status in the United States every year fall into two groups: those who adjust their status in the United States and those who wait in their own countries for their green cards to be issued. You will have to determine your ultimate goal and decide whether or not it is in your best interests to go to the United States as a nonimmigrant and then try to immigrate, or to go as an immigrant and wait out the processing period in your home country. If you will be able to obtain immigration within a time frame that suits your needs, nothing could be smoother than remaining put until your green card arrives in the mail—or at least, until notification of its approval arrives—and you can set your move in motion.

ILLEGAL ENTRY: WHAT ARE THE CONSEQUENCES?

You hear stories of millions of people who have disappeared into the huge melting pot of people in the United States after entering as tourists. You also hear stories of how so many people have been given amnesty—rewarded for being illegal with permanent residence! The recent amnesty program that was part of the Immigration Reform and Control Act of 1986 is over, but many people are still under the wrong impression that they can come to the United States illegally and eventually get green cards. However, if you enter or remain in the United States illegally, you must expect trouble. At some point you are going to have to face the fact that what may have seemed easy at the beginning, may not be easy in the long term. Some people do not find it easy to enter the United States illegally, even if they have this intention. Many international airports have INS officials waiting to check your visa, and possibly, your personal papers. If any evidence is found that you are not complying with the terms of your visa, for example, you may be entering as a tourist and an INS official may find your resumé among your papers, you could be denied entry. If this happens you will be put on the next plane back to where you came from. The terms used by the INS for this procedure are excludability and deportation. The INS uses electronic surveillance devices along the borders of Canada and Mexico and there is also extensive policing of the Mexican border posts. Videotapes recorded from helicopters and photographs by land patrols are used to catch and apprehend people crossing the borders illegally. The INS uses radio equipment to inform its officials of illegal traffic heading towards them. Thousands of people manage to evade these border patrols. Thousands more do not.

Apart from the issue of visa fraud, which means that you got your visa under false pretenses and had no intention of maintaining eligibility for this visa, you will also be punished if you try to enter the country using false documents. It is probable that the INS has computerized all the disclosed information about everyone who enters this country. Therefore, trying to enter the United States using false papers or under false pretenses could result in your being ineligible to enter the United States for many years and is not advisable for anyone seriously considering immigration. If your situation is desperate and you have a political motive for moving away from your country, it is better to arrive with no documents at all and claim political asylum.

If you overstay your welcome as a tourist and decide to apply for a change of status to a visa permitting you to work in the United States, you can forget about your chances of success. And if you have worked in the United States illegally, you may not adjust your status to that of permanent resident but, instead, will have to leave the country to obtain a green card. Whatever your immigration strategy, your position of strength will always be in maintaining legal status. The alternatives are costly appeals, travel back and forth out of the country in order to obtain your new status and enable you to have flexibility, and generally, a major headache.

Apart from obvious grounds for denying you entry into the United States, such as no papers, false documents, or visa fraud, there are other grounds on which the INS can prevent you from entering the country. These are called the *grounds of excludability*. The Immigration Act of 1990 has streamlined the criteria for excludability to five categories, two of which relate to immigration: status violations and falsification of documents. The others relate to health, crime and national security, and finances. For example, if you have tuberculosis, a criminal record, belonged to the Nazi party, or do not have the means of supporting yourself and are likely to become a public charge, you will not be admitted into the country! The INS has a detailed list of which types of people will not be permitted into the country.

NO VISAS NEEDED

Citizens of the contiguous countries to the United States—Canada and Mexico—and of certain islands in close proximity, do not need visas to enter the country. However, they do need other travel documents to prove their identity and eligibility.

Canadians can enter the United States without visas for almost all purposes, provided they have proof of their reasons for entering. For example, a Canadian coming to study in the United States need only show his/her Canadian passport (or other form of identity that proves citizenship) and certificate of eligibility from the United States school (the approved Form I-20/I-20 ID) in order to be admitted across the border as a student. Free travel back and forth is allowed.

In January 1989, the Canada-United States Free Trade Agreement (FTA) came into effect, making a significant impact on immigration practice between the two countries. The FTA was designed to foster trade between America and its largest trading partner and to make it easy for the nationals of both countries to have access back and forth across the borders to conduct trade and business. For the first time, Canadians became eligible to obtain E treaty trader and investor status in the United States (see Chapter 5) and a new nonimmigrant category, TC visas, was created to allow Canadian professionals easy access into the United States. Other nonimmigrant visas that allow business activity or employment (the B-1, H, L, O, P, Q, and R categories) are all available to Canadians who can, in most cases, obtain these visas from the INS border officials. Provided Canadians coming to work or do business in the United States have with them all the documentary evidence that is normally required in any of these visa applications, and they can prove that they are Canadian citizens, the INS border official will issue them border crossing I-94 cards which show their nonimmigrant status and the terms of their stay. They have to pay application fees at the border and can either pay in cash or by check. Those entering on E visas have to apply in advance at the United States consulate, as do non-Canadian spouses and children of Canadian citizens granted entry in terms of the FTA's immigration rules. The FTA as it affects immigration to the United States will be discussed in detail in Chapter 6.

Mexican nationals who have an I-186 Border Crossing I.D. Card do not need a visa to enter the United States. If they are crossing the border as tourists or to conduct business for which they are being paid in Mexico (in other words, for purposes which would require a B visa), their I-186 card will give them permission to be in the United States for 72 hours. If they wish to stay for longer or will be leaving the border city, they will receive an I-94 or I-444—a Mexican Border Visitors Permit.

Foreigners from countries that own islands adjoining the United States, who live on these islands—for example, French nationals on Martinique—as well as Bahamian nationals, or British nationals living in the Bahamas, the Cayman Islands, or the Island of Turks and Caicos, do not need visas to enter the United States. They must, however, have passports and papers proving that they are otherwise eligible to enter the country. One necessary form of proof is police clearance from their places of residence.

TRAVELING TO CANADA OR MEXICO

There is a certain amount of reciprocity with United States contiguous neighbors, Canada and Mexico, with regard to crossing the borders north and south. United States citizens and permanent residents can come and go across the border without a visa. They need simply present their passports or green cards to immigration officials on their return. Nonimmigrants also have a certain amount of freedom to travel across the border, provided they are in status and their I-94 cards, or the blue approval notices reflecting extensions of stay, are valid. If you are traveling to either Canada or Mexico for less than 30 days and do not leave the country, you will be readmitted into the United States by showing INS border officials your I-94 card and your blue approval notice showing an approved extension of stay in situations where your underlying visa has expired. However, if you leave either country to travel to a third country, you will not be permitted to return to the United States without a valid visa as well. If you have applied for a change of nonimmigrant status but this is not reflected in your passport stamp, you may be lucky and be able to return to the United States if you travel across the border, but there is no guarantee this will work, because an INS official at the border could deny you return access based on a suspicion that you do not intend to leave the United States at the expiration of your temporary status. Many people who change status in the United States travel to Canada to have their new visas stamped into their passports. This is easier and cheaper than traveling to their home countries, but only works for some people. The safest bet is to remain in the United States if there is a discrepancy between your I-94 and your visa. The rules state that you can get away with it. In reality, unfortunately, this is not always the case.

The next chapter looks at some of the rules governing immigration and provides various options for meeting the test of eligibility.

CHAPTER 4

Following the Rules

When you begin the immigration process, remember that your plans may change along the way and you may have more options than you realize. However, in the same way as you need to meet various eligibility requirements in order to gain entry into the United States, you also need to fulfill certain basic visa requirements before you put your plan into action, particularly if this plan involves changing status along the way. In the next chapter, you will read about all the nonimmigrant visa categories and find out the terms of eligibility for each one. In this chapter, the basic principles of immigration that you need to know will be discussed.

MAINTAINING STATUS

When you enter the United States as a nonimmigrant, you are given a rectangular, white card to complete and this is stapled into your passport. Once you are in the country, this Form I-94 is your most important document in terms of the immigration process, because it indicates your legal entry into the country and your eligibility to remain there. This card determines how long you are allowed to remain in the United States in the visa category in which you gained entry. It states whether or not you are allowed to work and gives an expiry date. You are not allowed to remain in the United States beyond this date, unless you have an extension of stay and this is reflected on a blue approval notice. If you need an extension of stay, you must send the INS a copy of your I-94 plus whatever documentation is needed, and if it is approved, the INS will send you this approval notice, which you must keep with your I-94. If you violate the conditions of your I-94 or approval notice (whichever one is current), you will not be able to get a green card in the United States by adjusting your status and will have to start the process again from abroad. Your I-94 or your approval notice (whichever is current) has to be submitted in all visa procedures.

Many people fail to realize that your I-94, not your visa, determines how long you may stay in the United States and whether or not you are in status. For example, you may get an L-1 visa abroad that is valid for one year, determined by reciprocity that your country may have with the United States.

However, when you enter the country, the INS official may stamp your I-94 card for a three-year stay. If you are willing to remain in the country for three years without leaving, you will be legally entitled to do so. However, if you leave the country during this period and your visa has expired, you will not be entitled to reenter unless you have your visa renewed abroad. Similarly, if you obtain a change of nonimmigrant status while in the United States and you travel abroad, you will have to go to the United States consulate or embassy to have your new visa stamped into your passport before you will be allowed to return.

The most important thing you must remember when you come to the United States with the intention of becoming an immigrant once you are there, is that you must remain in status at all times. If you are in the United States you may not continue to travel, work, study, or whatever it is that you came to do, once the date of expiration on your I-94 or extension approval notice has passed. If you change to a nonimmigrant status that permits such an activity, you may not begin working, training, or whatever else your new visa status permits, before this has been approved. An exception is made for students: if you entered as a B-2 tourist and changed to an F-1 student, it may happen that school starts before you have received approval of your new status. You will not be considered out of status if you begin your studies before receiving this approval. If you violate either the time limit given on your I-94 card (extension approval notice) or the terms of your nonimmigrant visa, such as, by working illegally, you will be out of status and will not be permitted to pursue any other visa options unless you leave the United States. If you become out of status and cannot apply for a different visa in the United States, this does not mean that you cannot apply for that visa abroad. But, if you are in a situation where it would be financially or politically difficult for you to travel back and forth to your home country, you should take extra care to keep in status throughout the immigration process.

If you have applied for a visa that permits you to work in the United States, you may not start working until your visa petition has been approved. If you do, it means you worked illegally in the United States and will, therefore, be prevented from adjusting your status to permanent residence. Instead, you will have to go to your home country to get your green card. The INS has made provision for its inefficiency by allowing certain people who have applied for employment authorization or visas permitting employment to start working if they have not received a response to their applications within 60 days. Typically, you may work for three months on a temporary employment authorization card, and if you still have had no word from the INS, you must stop working and either re-apply, in which case your temporary work authorization will be reinstated after another 60 days, or you will, hopefully, have obtained the status for which you applied. This applies fairly consistently, whether or not you have applied for a nonimmigrant visa permitting employment, or whether you have applied for employment authorization (Form I-765).

It is important to remember that you will not be eligible to change your nonimmigrant status if you are out of status already.

CHANGING FROM ONE NONIMMIGRANT VISA CATEGORY TO ANOTHER

Which Visa Categories May Not Be Changed?

Before discussing this procedure, you must be aware that nonimmigrants in the following visa categories may *not* change status under any circumstances: C (transit), D (crew members), K (fiancés/fiancées), J (exchange visitors/students), B–1/B–2 business visitors or tourists on the visa waiver pilot program, TWOV's (people in transit without visas), and M–1 to F–1 (vocational to academic student). J visa holders can only change nonimmigrant status if they obtain a waiver of the two-year foreign residence requirement affecting them, or if they are not subject to this requirement or if they are changing to A or G visas, which are both government-related. (See Chapter 5 in the section on J visas.)

It is highly likely that, for the vast majority of you without close enough family ties to guarantee you immigrant status, your path to immigration will be tied to employment. Typically, the higher skilled and more illustrious you are, the greater your chances of successfully finding work in the United States. However, there are various ways and means of obtaining your goal and you may find yourself first contemplating a visit to the United States to see if you really want to live there or not.

Entering on a B-2 Tourist Visa

Tourist visas are the earliest entry into the immigration game for most people. Although it is illegal and considered fraudulent to enter the United States on a tourist visa and look for a job or enroll in a school or training program, an overwhelmingly high number of people do so. There are many countries in this world facing political and economic upheaval and the nationals of these countries know that if they apply for temporary nonimmigrant visas to work in the United States, the chances are that they will be denied. This is because State Department officials realize that there is a slim chance of these people returning to their homes once their nonimmigrant status expires. Thousands of people enter the United States ostensibly to visit, and do not leave again until they have their green cards. This scenario has been played out countless times. However, there are certain steps that everyone who uses this strategy has to follow. The first step is changing nonimmigrant status.

Overcoming Obstacles at the Port of Entry

The tourist visa has been chosen as the starting point because it is the one most commonly used to enter the United States. A first and most important word of warning: if an INS official at the port of entry in the United States suspects or discovers anything to contradict the fact that tourism is your only motive, you will be denied entry into the country. Therefore, if you are carrying copies of your degrees and educational certificates, as well as copies of your resumé, and you get caught, that's it, for the foreseeable future! If you are planning to look for work, be sure to mail all your work-related papers to the United States ahead of time. It is necessary to offer this warning because most of the change of nonimmigrant status cases involve changing from a B-2 tourist visa to other nonimmigrant categories.

Avoiding Being Caught on "Preconceived Intent"

If you entered the United States on a tourist visa, you should be careful not to apply for a change of nonimmigrant status too soon after arriving, because the INS will interpret your motives as "preconceived intent." This means, they will assume you had no intention of leaving the United States after your so-called vacation, but planned to find a way of remaining—either by becoming employed or becoming a student. Because most tourist visas are given for six months, and you may not apply for a change of nonimmigrant status unless your underlying status is still valid, you would do well to wait at least four months—and even still, the INS may refute your credibility. One strategy that has proved successful for many, if funds and circumstances allow, is to apply for an extension of stay on your tourist visa (the following section covers extension of stay) and then to apply for a change of status, once this is secured. That way, you can avoid the issue of becoming out of status while waiting for your new nonimmigrant status to be approved.

Changing Status *Not* Visas

You must realize that, if you apply for a change of nonimmigrant status, you will get just that and *not* a new visa. Therefore, if, you succeed in finding a job and you get an approved H-1B petition, you can only get H-1B status in the United States, not an H-1B visa. Because your visa is the travel document that allows you to enter any country, if you leave the United States for any reason with your change of status recorded, you will not be allowed to reenter unless you have a valid visa that reflects this change. This means you will have to go to the United States consulate or embassy in your country, or the country where you are traveling, and apply for a visa. In the case of an II-1B, this should be fairly routine, because you will already have an approved petition, and need only submit this. However, for the reasons cited earlier, you may find that your visa application is denied. This can be very traumatic, when you have a family and home in the United States, but this is a reality you must consider. Therefore, when applying for any change of nonimmigrant status, remember, the INS may approve this status, but, if you ever have to leave the United States, you will have to deal with the State Department to obtain your new visa before you will be allowed to return. And, there are no guarantees that this will be approved if there are any doubts that you may not return home. Whereas it was once necessary for both H-1B and L visa applicants to maintain a foreign residence before being granted their visas, this is no longer the case. Neither will O or P visa applicants be required to have a foreign residence in order to be eligible for these visas. Therefore, there is now less chance of having a visa denied abroad in any of these visa categories if you cannot show foreign residence.

Planning for Future Obstacles

Before you file for a change of nonimmigrant status, you must consider the criteria for getting a visa in the category for which you are applying. For example, if you are applying for a J-1 visa and your program sponsor has approved your credentials and issued you with an IAP-66, you must realize that this visa comes with its own set of obstacles. If you will be working in a government sponsored program—and many research institutes fall into this category—you will be subject to a two-year foreign residency requirement. This means that, if you wish to adjust your status to permanent residence, you will first have to leave the United States for two years. In certain circumstances, you can apply for a waiver (medical doctors are not eligible for this waiver), and this is simply another bureaucratic step along the way.

Eligibility to Change Status

In order to change to another nonimmigrant visa category, you will have to be eligible for this category. It is not enough to make a personal decision to work in the United States and, therefore, decide that you need a visa status that authorizes employment. You have to first make sure that new visa status is available to you, either by committing yourself to a job offer or by accepting entry into a course of study or a training program, or whatever other circumstances apply. To give you an idea of what is involved in changing status, consider a hypothetical case of changing from a B-2 to an H-1B visa. Assume you are a professional engineer who comes, with your family, to the United States as a tourist on a B-2 visa. You meet someone who offers you a job and you need to change your nonimmigrant status to get employment authorization as a professional (H-1B category). How do you go about changing your status so that you can remain in the United States legally and work there? Your employer will have to go through the rigorous procedure of making an attestation to the Department of Labor and obtaining approval to petition on your behalf. Once this is organized, you may submit this petition, which includes a change of nonimmigrant status application, together with a filing fee of $150.

New Application Forms and Fees

Those people who use Form I-129 (undergoing revision at press time) to obtain nonimmigrant visas that authorize employment in the United States must use the same form for changing their nonimmigrant status. All other nonimmigrants must use Form I-539. Nonimmigrants with visas authorizing them to work in the United States must also use Form I-129 for filing extensions of stay. All other nonimmigrants must use Form I-539. This includes students, who formerly used Form I-538, and exchange visitors, who formerly used Form IAP-66.

The filing fee for either a change in nonimmigrant status or an extension of stay where no employment is involved (Form I-539) is $70, with a $10 additional fee for each co-applicant. If you are applying for a change of status to a work visa, you must submit Form I-129, checked off in the appropriate box, plus the supplement for the appropriate category (H, L, and so on), and a filing fee of $150. If you are employed and applying for an extension of stay, you must also submit Form I-129, checked off in the appropriate box, plus a filing fee of $120. Based on the hypothetical case above, if you, your spouse, and two children come to the United States as tourists and you get a job offer, you must submit Form I-129 plus $150 to change status to a category that authorizes employment, and Form I-539 plus $90 for your spouse and children to change status to a category enabling them to remain in the country with you.

Submitting Supporting Documentation

The first step in putting together a change of nonimmigrant status application is photocopying the I-94 card that is stapled in your passport. You must submit this with your change of status application form, filing fee, and all the papers and documentation needed to prove your eligibility for the new nonimmigrant visa category. If you are a student or exchange program participant (F-1 or J-1 visa holder) this will be clear-cut. You need only to submit your certificate of eligibility that your school or employing organization will supply—in this case, Form I-20/I-20 ID and Form IAP-66, respectively. If your change of status application is approved, you will receive a blue approval notice giving you the date to which you are legally permitted to remain in this country and indicating your new visa status. You must keep this blue form with your I-94 card, so it is best for you to attach it to your passport as well.

When you read the next chapter explaining all the nonimmigrant visa categories and their criteria of eligibility, you will get a clearer picture of what is required when you apply for a change of status to a new visa category. You will then be able to prepare the necessary documentation. If you plan on changing status to an L or E visa, it is strongly advised that you consult with an immigration lawyer. Whereas it may have been possible in the past to compile your own application or to do so with the assistance of a specialist corporate member who had a basic knowledge of immigration law, recent changes in the law have rendered previous information invalid and proving eligibility could be more complex than you realize. *Therefore, unless you are completely familiar with the workings of the law, it would best serve your interests to consult with a lawyer.*

Evaluation of Educational Credits

If you are applying for an H-1B visa, you will have to provide proof of your professional qualifications in the form of an educational credits evaluation. There are certain organizations in the United States that specialize in checking the educational credentials of foreigners to make sure that their degrees or diplomas are equivalent to similar United States qualifications. (For a list of these organizations, see Appendix 7, page 270.) This enables the INS to confirm that you are suitably qualified for the job for which your employer is submitting your petition. By the same token, it enables the INS to judge whether or not you may be too qualified for the job, in which case, your petition will be denied.

Appealing Against Denials

If the INS denies your application to change status, you may not appeal against this finding. However, there are certain options available to you if your application was denied for reasons that you are able to counter with additional information or documentary evidence. The most commonly exercised option is the Motion to Reopen, which involves resubmitting your application together with Form I-290A and a filing fee of $110, and any additional information you can provide to support the basis for your application. If you are eligible, there should be few problems and this Motion to Reopen should result in an approval of your application. If, however, this is not successful, your only other recourse is to file an appeal through the United States District Court. However, this is a costly and lengthy procedure and, in the face of a double denial, is unlikely to be successful. It is advisable to consult an immigration lawyer, if you have not already done so, before filing a Motion to Reopen. You can probably negotiate a fee for this procedure only.

Where to Submit Your Application

When changing your nonimmigrant status to one that permits employment in the United States (requiring the submission of Form I-129), you must submit your application by mail to the Regional Service Center of the INS that has jurisdiction over the area where you will be working. In its bid to achieve consistency and reduce bureaucratic delays, the INS has determined that all such visa applications in the Southern Service Area must be sent either to the Eastern Service Center (for the Atlanta and Miami districts) or the Northern Service Center (for other districts). This does not apply when making applications for visas that do not involve Form I-129.

REVALIDATING YOUR VISA

Once your change of status has been approved, the INS will send you a blue approval notice, which reflects your new status and gives a new expiry date. You must attach this notice to your I-94 card. At this point, the visa stamp in your passport is invalid and, if you leave the United States, you will not be readmitted without obtaining a new visa first. In certain cases, where you have obtained a change of status or an extension of status, you will be able to apply for a new visa without leaving the United States. This procedure is called revalidation or is available to those who hold or have recently changed to an A, E, G, I, or L visa. Your I-94 card must be valid (which in these situations it obviously will be, because this is the reason for seeking revalidation), and your passport must be valid for six months beyond the date shown on the new expiry date on your I-94. As with all procedures in the immigration process, the vital issue here is being in status. If your status expires during the course of your application for visa revalidation, that's it! But, given that you are applying after extending your status or changing your status, this should not affect you. You may apply for a visa revalidation by doing the following:

1. Complete Form OF-156 (application for nonimmigrant visa), ensuring that the information you supply is identical to the information supplied on your underlying visa application. This highlights the importance of keeping copies of all your immigration papers.

2. Write a letter explaining why you need your visa and any hardships or inconveniences you will experience if you have to leave the United States to have this visa stamped into your passport by the United States consul in your country.

3. Submit Form I-94 to prove that you are in status.

4. Attach a passport-size photograph to your visa application.

5. Inquire from the Office of Diplomatic Liaison in Washington D.C. whether or not a filing fee is required, and, if so, send a check or money order.

6. Submit proof of your eligibility for the visa category that you want stamped in your passport. This should be in the form of employment contracts, business transactions, tax returns, annual reports, or whatever other relevant materials are available.

A separate application package must be made for each member of your family.

DUAL INTENT WHEN YOU ALSO SEEK PERMANENT RESIDENCE

If you apply for a green card once you have changed to a nonimmigrant status that will facilitate this adjustment of status, you will, ideally, need to remain in the United States until this has been approved, unless your current nonimmigrant visa has been stamped into your passport and is valid for multiple entry. If you have obtained a change of status and, soon after, applied for an adjustment of status, your life could become complicated when you travel abroad to have your new nonimmigrant visa stamped into your passport. You will have to admit that you have a permanent residence application pending and this will raise suspicions about your intent in terms of your nonimmigrant visa. Clearly, you will be demonstrating what the INS terms "the doctrine of dual intent." This doctrine states that, even though a nonimmigrant must demonstrate that his or her genuine intent is to remain in the United States temporarily, he or she may have both the short-term intent to leave and a long-term intent to immigrate. The Immigration Act of 1990 specifically provides for this doctrine in the case of H-1, L, O, and P visa holders who obtained changes in their nonimmigrant status before their most recent departures from the United States. If you are traveling to Canada or Mexico for a period of less than 30 days and you do not leave these countries to travel abroad to a third country during this time, this is not an issue. You do not need a visa stamp to re-cross the borders, as long as you are in status. If you are traveling on an F or J visa, you will also be permitted to travel to the islands adjacent to the United States if your visa has expired, as long as you are traveling for less than 30 days with your I-20 ID or IAP-66 card, and your I-94 card is still valid.

EXTENSIONS OF STAY

Regardless of the time limits stated on the visa stamp in your passport, your length of legal stay in the United States is determined by the expiry date stamped on your I-94 card, which you get from the INS when you enter the country as a nonimmigrant. Your ability to exercise options in the immigration process from within the United States depends on your remaining in status at all times. This means, you may not exceed the time limit imposed by the I-94 card. Certain nonimmigrant visas are legally available for longer periods than the one initially granted to you. In the case of executives entering the country on L-1 visas, for example, they may have obtained these visas for only one year, with a similar time period granted by the INS on the I-94 card. Because the law permits executives and managers on L-1 intracompany transfer nonimmigrant visas to work in the United States for up to seven years (five, for specialized employees), they are clearly eligible to extend their stay. This is true for almost all nonimmigrant visa holders (except for C, D, and K visa holders, who may not apply for extensions or any other visa changes), whose initially-granted visas are generally for portions of the full, legally-sanctioned time periods permitted by their visa categories.

Because all nonimmigrant visas are, by definition, temporary in nature (some more temporary than others), you must supply information supporting your application for an extension of stay, and, where necessary, prove that the conditions of eligibility are still being met. Say, for example, you are in the United States on a B-1 business visa (B visas are generally available for a maximum of one year) and you need to remain in the country longer than the six months initially granted to you. Your employer will have to support your application for an extension of stay by describing your remaining duties and will also have to confirm that your salary is being paid abroad—thereby indicating that you are still meeting the eligibility requirements for this visa. If you are a tourist on a B-2 visa, planning a strategy that involves a change in nonimmigrant status, you may want to extend your stay to ensure that you do not become out of status during your change in nonimmigrant status procedure. Or, you may want to buy extra time to avoid suspicion by the INS that you had "preconceived intent" to change your status.

You must be able to prove you are still eligible for this B-2 visa, by submitting letters from friends or family inviting you to extend your vacation and undertaking to support you while you are in the United States, or by confirming that you have enough cash left to cover your expenses for the additional time period.

In the case of H-1B visa holders, it is fairly routine to obtain extensions for up to six years, usually requiring two extension of stay applications. Your employer will have to write a letter explaining why the company needs your continued services or skills, taking care not to stress the company's long-term requirements. E visas can be extended annually for long periods of time, because there is no upper limit to the time imposed. And, in the case of all study and training program visas, extensions are determined by the length of the course of study or program—or, in certain cases, what the INS considers to be a reasonable length for such pursuits.

When you file an application for an extension of stay and your underlying visa permits employment in the United States (E, H, I, L, O, P, Q, R), you must submit Form I-129, with a filing fee of $120, together with supporting documentation or letters explaining the need for this extension. When your underlying visa does not permit work, or is one that binds you to a specific training or exchange program, you must submit Form I-539, plus a filing fee of $70 (plus $10 per co-applicant), and all the necessary documentation or letters needed to explain your need for an extension. In all cases, you must also submit a copy of your I-94 card, and your passport must be valid for at least six months beyond the date to which you have requested an extension.

If your application is approved, you will receive a blue approval notice with a new expiration date stamped on it. This date now becomes your legal time limit for remaining in the United States. If your status expires during the time your application for an extension of stay is being processed, and you are employed, you are not legally entitled to work until your extension of stay has been approved, because this is a violation of your status. You may not apply for an extension of stay more than 60 days or less than 15 days before your status expires. This application must be mailed to the Regional Service Center of the INS that has jurisdiction over the area where you are visiting, working, or studying.

STRATEGIES FOR SUCCESS

In this chapter, some of the options available to you as a nonimmigrant in the United States have been examined. You may notice a pattern in the way this process works: the pivotal points of the entire process of immigration are legal status and eligibility and these issues arise at every step along the way—from getting your first visa to naturalization. In the next chapter, you will read about the nonimmigrant visa categories and their criteria of eligibility. You will then be able to assess whether or not your qualifications and/or skills meet these requirements. Before you are granted a visa, however, you will also have to meet the rules of excludability. These rules pertain to your political, social, and moral attitudes and your mental and physical health, as well as to your immigration history, as discussed in Chapter 3.

Do not despair if you feel you have little hope of success. You cannot change the immigration system, but, in some cases, you can change your chances. For example, some of you may have been a few credits short of a university degree and dropped out for a number of reasons. Perhaps your current financial situation will allow you to complete your degree in a certain field, thereby enabling you to fulfill the minimum requirements for your profession. Or, you may be able to open a United States branch of your business, fulfilling the requirements to obtain either an L-1 or an E-1 visa. With understanding and planning—and, if necessary, obtaining the help of a good lawyer—you probably have a better chance of getting a United States visa than you think.

When you apply for a visa, the key to success—ensuring that everything runs as smoothly as possible until your visa is approved—lies in reading and understanding the instructions and following them precisely. For example, a simple instruction such as "Answer all the questions" could be interpreted as "Answer all the questions that apply to my situation." This is not the case. If you leave a blank on a form, the INS may think you left out an answer and are likely to mail your forms back for completion. Therefore, in filling out forms, complete all questions, even if you have to write N/A—Not Applicable—in some spaces. Send checks or money orders when paying application fees, not cash, because cash can easily get lost and you will have no record of having sent it. Keeping records of all the forms you submit is essential and you must know exactly what you have written on all forms. You never know what might happen along the way and if you have to appeal a denial, you must have a copy of your original application to refer to. Therefore, make copies of all forms and documents you submit to the INS or State Department and keep them together in one file.

All reports and documents sent in support of a visa application within the United States should be translated into English. If you apply abroad at a United States consulate or embassy, these papers do not need to be translated, as long as they are in the language of the country where you are applying. In Japan, however, all papers in support of visa applications must be translated into English. At the end of each translation, the translator must write the following:

> *"I hereby certify that I have translated this document from...(fill in the appropriate language) to English. This translation is accurate and complete. I further certify that I am fully competent to translate from...(state language) to English."*

Recently, the INS relaxed its requirement that all documents and personal papers in support of visa applications had to be submitted in their original form. It is now permissible to submit photocopies of most documents. If you are applying for a visa at a United States consulate abroad, the photocopies you submit in support of your application must be government certified. Notarized copies are not acceptable. Translations must be signed but do not have to be notarized or certified. You will not have to provide government certified copies of documents when you submit an application to the INS from within the United States, although you have to be willing to show the original documents if requested to do so. When you submit an application in the United States that contains photocopied papers, you must include the following written statement:

> *"All documents submitted are exact photocopies of unaltered original documents and the Petitioner and Beneficiary understand that it may be necessary to submit the original documents to an immigration or consular official at a later date."*

Although the Immigration Reform and Control Act of 1986 (IRCA) made it an offense to photocopy personal documents pertaining to nationality and status (such as passports, green cards, I-94 cards), the latest legislation has relaxed this law in terms of the application process. The reason it was enacted at all was because employers have to check the eligibility of their employees to work in the United States and it was feared that, if photocopied documents were admissible as proof of this employment authorization, it could lead to a high incidence of fraud.

OBTAINING WAIVERS OF EXCLUDABILITY

It is easier to obtain a waiver of excludability if you are a nonimmigrant than if you are an immigrant, because the rigorous standards of testing that are administered when you apply for a green card, are not administered when you apply for a nonimmigrant visa. The Immigration Act of 1990 gives greater leniency in the waiver program, making it possible to obtain a waiver against excludability in far more cases than previously. For example, you can now get a waiver for a criminal offense of prostitution, or of drug possession where less than 30 grams of marijuana was involved, and this did not result in prosecution. Also, if you are a Communist or supporter of other totalitarian government systems, it is possible to obtain a waiver. If you violated the terms of your nonimmigrant status in the past, you can get a waiver to enter the United States as long as your prior offense happened at least ten years ago. Relaxation of waivers of excludability available for political/nonharmful criminal/INS-related grounds is not extended to other areas. Nazis, saboteurs, and subversives are excluded without recourse.

You may only apply for a Waiver of Excludability if you are judged to be excludable after you have submitted your application for a visa. Once this has been established, you may submit Form I-724 (Application to Waive Exclusion Grounds) and a filing fee of $90.

The next step along the way is to determine which nonimmigrant visa category is suitable for your needs. The following chapter will provide this information.

CHAPTER 5

Nonimmigrant (Temporary) Visa Categories

THE IMMIGRATION ACT OF 1990: UNSCRAMBLING THE CODES

The major changes to the nonimmigrant visa categories brought about by the Immigration Act of 1990 relate to those categories that permit professionals, artists, scientists, athletes, performers, cultural exchange visitors, and religious workers to live and work in the United States. Until this legislation, the H-1B nonimmigrant visa category more or less encompassed the full range under the banner "professionals and people of exceptional ability in the arts and sciences." However, now certain people who would previously have qualified for an H-1B visa are eligible for their own visa category. The Immigration Act of 1990 has added to the alphabetical visa list the O, P, Q, and R categories, each of which will be explained in detail in the individual visa category breakdown.

Apart from creating new visa categories, this act has modified the H-1B category, placing a ceiling on the number of visas available each year and giving the employer a greater role in the processing procedure by adding additional requirements. Theoretically, there will have to be greater commitment on the part of any employer intending to sponsor an H-1B worker, because this foreign employee now has greater protection in terms of both salary and fair treatment in the workplace. However, this does not necessarily mean that it will be more difficult to get an H-1B visa; it's simply a matter of following procedure.

The new legislation gives some foreigners more options and reduces the options of others. For example, cultural exchange visitors who would have been eligible for a J-1 visa, can opt for a Q-1 visa instead and avoid the two-year foreign residence clause should they decide to adjust their status to permanent residence at a later stage. By the same token, however, certain categories of people will be adversely affected, such as people in business who have extensive experience, which previously might have enabled them to get H-1B visas, but who are not acclaimed by others within their field. The confusion and debate that has always raged around H-1B issues is likely to rage on. For this reason, it is strongly recommended that those who intend to apply for a specialty occupation, H-1B visa, either make sure they are in complete compliance with the visa requirements, or consult with a reputable immigration lawyer.

A BREAKDOWN OF THE NONIMMIGRANT VISA CATEGORIES

At this stage, your most important concerns are likely to be which visas will enable you to work in the United States and which visas will assist you in gaining immigrant status. In this section, a simple breakdown of what visa categories enable what activities within the United States is provided. Following is a detailed account of each nonimmigrant visa category. First assess which category or categories apply to you, in terms of your current needs, then find the appropriate visa, according to its alphabetical listing, in the next section.

Visas for Business and Tourism: B-1 and B-2

The B visas are for people coming to the United States either on short-term business trips, during which they will be paid abroad, or on vacation, in which case they may not legally work or look for work.

Employment-based Nonimmigrant Visas: E-1, E-2, H-1A, H-1B, H-2A, H-2B, I, L-1, O-1, O-2, P-1, P-2, P-3, R-1

For the purposes of nonimmigrant visa allocation, work is defined in several different ways, depending on your employer and the nature of the job. Two categories, the E and the L visas, presuppose that you or your foreign company has an existing, viable business concern within the United States, whereas the H visa enables any foreign worker to work in the United States for any United States employer, provided they both fulfill the underlying requirements of the visa category. For an E-1 treaty trader visa, at least 50 percent of the trade conducted by you or the company that employs you, must be between the United States and your country of citizenship. There are fairly complex conditions governing this and the E-2 visa for treaty investors—in which substantial investment in a viable business operation is the key requirement, as are issues of nationality and ownership—as in the case of the E-1 visa. You should be warned against applying in this category without consulting an immigration lawyer first. Given that you will be able to live and work in the United States in E visa status for a lengthy period of time, it is worth the investment to obtain this visa with as few complications as possible. This advice also goes for the L-1 visa, which permits foreign executives, managers, or employees with specialized knowledge of a company to be transferred to the United States to work for that company's United States concern. The key issues here are eligibility of the company, vis-à-vis its relationship with the United States company where you will be working, and of you, in terms of your position within the company. Foreign nurses have their own H-1A category, whereas professionals in "specialty occupations" qualify for H-1B visas. These two categories differ from the H-2A category, for agricultural workers and loggers, and H-2B category, for all other skilled and unskilled temporary workers, because the jobs need not be temporary, only the positions being offered. In the case of the latter two categories, the jobs must themselves be temporary. Category I visas are for foreign media workers involved in either newspaper, television or radio journalism. Their visas are issued by their employers and are only valid for a particular employer. The O visa is for people of "extraordinary ability" in the arts, sciences, education, business, and sports and their support staff, whereas the P visa is exclusively for performing artists and athletes. The R visa is for religious workers who will be employed by United States organizations that are affiliated to their religious denominations abroad.

Visas for Study and Training: F-1, M-1, H-3, J-1

All these visas have slightly different terms and conditions, but, essentially, they enable foreigners to come to the United States to study, train, conduct research, and/or gain practical work experience in their fields of study. If you are an undergraduate or graduate student involved in an academic program, the F-1 category applies. In most postgraduate programs, the J-1 visa would be appropriate. For nonacademic and vocational courses, the M-1 visa is best, and the H-3 is for training programs where employment is incidental to the program and not a major component.

Visas for Cultural Exchange Visitors and Those Involved in Reciprocal Exchange Programs with the United States: J and Q Visas

These visas enable both employment and training in situations where the United States has a particular vested interest in the program, either for cultural, scientific, or educational benefits. Usually, there is a symbiotic relationship, whereby both the foreign country and the United States gain, such as where foreign doctors come to do postgraduate research, or academics come to teach at United States schools or universities, and then return to their own countries where they, in turn, can enrich the lives of others by their experiences in the United States. Or, in the case of participants involved in industrial programs, they can take their newly-acquired expertise and apply it in their jobs abroad. J visas are issued by the United States Information Agency (USIA) for approved programs sponsored by medical, research, academic, or business institutions in the United States. Q visas are only for cultural exchange programs that do not have to be pre-approved.

Medical Doctors

There are so many stories circulating internationally about how difficult it is for doctors to gain entry into the United States. Medical doctors may enter on J-1 visas or H-1B visas. A discussion of both categories in the next section gives more specific information regarding this profession. If you are a doctor of international fame, you will be eligible for an O-1 visa, but this will not apply to the majority of you!

Diplomats (A), Employees of International Organizations (G, NATO), Families of Certain International Employees (N), Fiancé/es of United States Citizens (K), Foreign Crew (D), and Transit Visas (C)

Each of the nonimmigrant visas in this miscellaneous group has its own terms and conditions, which will be described in the following section in the appropriate alphabetical listing.

The next section gives an alphabetical listing of all the nonimmigrant visas currently available. If you have been able to ascertain, from the brief outlines above, what visa category applies to you, you may turn directly to the listing. However, if you are reading this to gain a thorough knowledge of the subject before developing your immigration strategy, start with A and read on. Some categories will be described in great detail, where the terms and conditions for obtaining the relevant visas are complicated. Other visa categories are self-explanatory and will be described in less detail.

AN ALPHABETICAL LISTING: THE A TO R

Diplomats: A Visas

A-1—Purpose/Eligibility:

This visa is for foreign ambassadors, public ministers, and diplomats, and their immediate families.

A-2—Purpose/Eligibility:

This visa is for lower-ranked accredited officials or employees of foreign governments, such as consuls and trade attachés, and their immediate families.

A-3—Purpose/Eligibility:

This visa is for the personal employees, including valets, servants, chefs, of all A-1 and A-2 visa holders and their immediate families.

Special Limitations and Conditions:

The dependents of the primary visa holders in these categories are not entitled to work in the United States without obtaining special permission. They may complete forms supplied by the State Department and apply for an Employment Authorization Card (EAC), which the INS will grant at its discretion.

Application Procedures:

It is highly likely that your government will take care of all the paperwork necessary to obtain your visa. You will be told what you have to supply and, in most cases, will have no direct contact with the United States consulate or embassy. Visas are issued for the duration of the official assignment. A-3 visas are issued for one year, but can be renewed annually.

Other Considerations:

Visa holders in this category are generally entitled to diplomatic immunity. The higher the rank, the higher the level of immunity. Certain governments are not recognized by the United States. Diplomats and other government officials of these countries are not eligible for A visas and must travel in and out of the United States on B, C, or G visas.

Business: B-1 Visas

Purpose:

This visa allows you to enter the United States to attend business meetings or conferences, engage in buying or selling, oversee contracts on behalf of your foreign employer, or participate in other business ventures. You may also obtain this visa if you are coming to work as a volunteer, for example, for a religious organization. In addition, you may use this visa if you are coming to attend a training course being offered by a foreign company operating in the United States or if you are coming as an employee of a foreign-based company to provide consulting services to a United States company.

Eligibility:

You are eligible for this visa if you can demonstrate that any of the above situations apply in your case.

Special Limitations and Conditions:

Your salary must be paid abroad and you may receive no remuneration in the United States other than expense account payments, which can be made by a United States source. If you enter the United States on this visa and you want to obtain an extension of stay, you must get a letter from your foreign employer confirming that your salary is being paid abroad.

During the mid-1980s the International Union of Bricklayers brought pressure against the INS and succeeded in getting them to make construction workers ineligible for B-1 visas, even if their salaries were being paid abroad. Foreign companies involved in building projects in the United States are required to use labor on the domestic market.

Application Procedures:

This visa is only available from your nearest United States consulate or embassy. You may submit your application for a nonimmigrant visa (Form OF-

156), together with data pertaining to your reasons for requesting a business visa and filing fees, if applicable. Usually filing fees are based on reciprocity with other countries. For example, if a foreign government requires United States citizens entering that country for similar purposes to pay for a business visa, nationals of that country will be charged at a similar rate for a United States visa. You will have to provide details of any conferences or business meetings you will be attending, or correspondence to show that you are intending to fulfill the terms of a contract on behalf of your employer (for example, you may be going to service machinery that a United States company has purchased from your company). B-1 visas are usually issued for six months, with one six-month renewal available. The nationals of certain countries receive less time, also based on the reciprocity of those countries with the United States.

Other Considerations:

If you intend to come to the United States as an investor, either as an immigrant or an E-2 nonimmigrant, the INS will be looking out to ensure that the investment is sound and the project viable before granting you this status. Therefore, many immigration lawyers advise their clients to come to the United States on a B-1 visa, preceding their major move, to ensure that their investment is going ahead as planned and that the conditions for their proposed investor status applications are likely to be met.

Tourism and Travel: B-2 Visas

Purpose/Eligibility:

This visa is for bona fide tourists with nothing but pleasure on their agenda.

Special Limitations and Conditions:

The major limitation in this category is that employment is not permitted. Nevertheless, many foreigners enter the United States on B-2 visas and look for employment opportunities while they are here. Legally, this constitutes visa fraud, but it is a common abuse. However, if you are caught, you could be prevented from obtaining another visa to enter the United States for a long time. Many people apply for changes to their nonimmigrant status while in the United States on tourist visas. This, too, is technically visa fraud, because it suggests that you had other intentions when you applied for your tourist visa. There is a fine line to walk in this procedure: you cannot apply for a change in status too soon after arriving, because the INS will assume previous intent, but you must apply for this change before your status expires. You would do well to consult an immigration lawyer at this stage if it is important to you that a change of status is granted. You are allowed to come to the United States as a tourist and look for a school while you are here. If you intend doing this, you must tell the United States consul in your country when you apply for a visa. Your B-2 visa will have the words "prospective student" written on it and you may then apply for a change of status to an F-1 visa without any problems. Because student visas are only issued within 60 days of the beginning of the school year, anyone eligible for an F-1 visa who travels to the United States before this cut-off period will be issued a B-2 visa with the words "prospective student" and will have to apply for a change of status to an F-1 visa once they are here.

Application Procedures:

You can only apply for a tourist visa from your nearest United States consulate or embassy abroad. In submitting your application for a nonimmigrant visa, you will also need to show proof of your intention to return to your country, in the form of a return ticket, plus proof that you will be able to support yourself while in the United States. Often a letter of invitation from relatives or friends in the United States, stating that they will be supporting you while you are visiting, is sufficient proof of this, along with your bank statement indicating sufficient funds. Other documentation might be a letter from your employer to say your job is being kept for you while you are away. Fees and time limits are, like in the previous category, based on reciprocity with other countries.

A word of warning is necessary here. If the consul suspects that you will not be returning to your country, there is a strong possibility that even a tourist visa will be denied. Theoretically, all you need to get a tourist visa is to buy a return ticket to the United States and have the desire to travel there. But practically, it doesn't work like that. State Department officials do not apply an empirical test to determine whether or not to grant visas. They make their decisions on purely subjective grounds, using as guidelines information about family, work, property, and money or other investments that will ostensibly bring you home after your travels.

Other Considerations: The Visa Waiver Program

As discussed in Chapter 3, the United States implemented a visa waiver program in 1986 and this has been extended until 1994 by the Immigration Act of 1990. This means that the nationals of eight countries—Britain, France, Germany, Holland, Italy, Japan, Sweden, and Switzerland—may enter the United States without a visa provided they are coming as tourists and staying a maximum of 90 days. The INS will add more countries to this list in terms of the extension of this program and Belgium, Denmark, Finland, Iceland, Luxembourg, Norway, and Spain have been earmarked. The airlines transporting tourists from the qualifying countries to the United States have to screen passengers for their eligibility before they are allowed to board the United States-bound aircraft. Even if you qualify in terms of this program, you are not obligated by it and are still eligible to apply for an entry visa. Your options will be greater with a visa if you have any intention of extending your visit, for whatever reason, because, without a visa, you cannot obtain an extension of stay or change to another visa category.

People in Transit: C Visas

C-1—Purpose/Eligibility:

This category is exclusively for foreign travelers who are in direct transit through the United States and will not be breaking their flight schedule in any way, other than possibly transferring to another airport.

C-2—Purpose/Eligibility:

This visa is for qualified foreigners who are in transit from their own countries to the United Nations Headquarters in New York City.

C-3—Purpose/Eligibility:

This visa is issued on a reciprocal basis with other countries to foreigners from those countries who are in transit to and from their consulates.

Special Limitations and Conditions:

If you have a C visa, you may not apply for a change of status to any other category, nor may you apply for permanent residence.

Application Procedures:

You must submit form OF-156 at your nearest United States consulate or embassy and provide travel documents to show that you will be in continuous transit or fulfilling other criteria of eligibility. The visa covers both the forward and return parts of your journey and the fee is based on reciprocity with other countries. The maximum time limit in this category is usually less than one month.

Foreign Crew: D Visas

Purpose/Eligibility:

This visa is for paid crew members of foreign airlines or ships who will be arriving in the United States and departing on the vessels or aircraft of the same foreign employer.

Special Limitations and Conditions:

You are not allowed to work on any United States vessel or aircraft in the United States, nor may you be coming to the United States to take up employment in situations where strikes or labor disputes have created a temporary shortage of labor. If you are coming to work for a company where a strike or lockout is in progress, your employer must show documentary evidence that proves you have worked for him/her in the past and that you will be performing the same duties as you did previously—and not additional duties that would constitute strike-breaking behavior. If you are a crew member of a foreign merchant vessel, you may only perform longshore work that has been sanctioned by the United States Secretary of Labor. Your employer will have to make attestations to the DOL as to the nature of your work and the DOL will have to consult with and obtain the approval of trade union officials in the different cities in the United States where your ship will be offloading. You may not change to any other nonimmigrant status nor may you apply for an adjustment of status with a D visa.

Treaty Traders: E-1 Visas

Purpose:

This visa allows foreign business people to come to the United States to engage actively in the substantial trade of goods and/or services between the United States and the foreigner's country of nationality.

Eligibility:

E-1 visas are available to the citizens of countries that have Treaties of Trade and Commerce with the United States. (For a list of these countries, see Appendix 3, on page 252.) You are eligible for this visa if you are the national of a country with such a treaty and are coming to the United States solely to engage in substantial trade principally between the United States and your country. This means, over 50 percent of your business must be between the United States company and your country. You may either be the owner of the United States company, or an executive or key employee, but at least 50 percent of the foreign-based company must be owned by nationals of that country. At least half the shareholders must either live abroad or, if living in the United States, must themselves have E-1 visas. If, for example, some of the owners of your company are living in the United States and are permanent residents there, their shareholding cannot be counted towards the foreign-owned or controlled 50 percent.

Trade is defined as the import and export of goods, but can also be in services, including technical services. Among the services included in this category are banks, travel agencies, airlines, advertising agencies, high technology businesses, management consulting, project management, and law and accounting firms. You do not have to maintain a foreign residence in order to be eligible for an E visa, but you must undertake to return to your country at the expiration of E-visa status.

Special Limitations and Conditions:

You must be a citizen of a country having a Treaty of Trade with the United States in order to qualify for an E-1 visa. It is not sufficient to be a legal resident of that country. In fact, even if you are the legal resident of another country, you are still eligible for an E-1 visa if your country of birth has a treaty with the United States. The only exception is for nationals of the United Kingdom, who must also be residents there to be eligible.

The latest legislation has focused on the issue of how much trade is considered substantial. There is no minimum dollar tamount and, generally, this will depend on the nature of the business. For example, if your company imports and exports heavy machinery, the dollar value of the trade will be substantially higher than if it traded in dried flowers and fruits. The main criterion is that the business should be engaged in regular trade in volumes high enough to sustain a full-time business in the United States. The Department of State, in considering E-1 visa applications from abroad, must consult with various other government departments to determine whether or not the amount of trade meets the "substantial" requirement. The State Department's most recent definition of what constitutes "substantial trade" for E-1 purposes is a "continuous flow of trade items between the United States and the treaty country." Traditionally, the Department of State has issued visas where there has been "existing trade." However, the INS has recognized that in many new import-export companies, the foreign representative has to be present in the United States before the trade can be implemented. Therefore, provided all conditions are met, in the case of newly set-up companies, prospective trade may be a qualifying criterion.

It is becoming more and more difficult to obtain E-1 visas on behalf of essential employees, because the INS and State Department are in agreement that United States workers should be considered first. There is likely to be a great deal of future litigation regarding the admissability of nonexecutive or managerial E visa personnel and it is advisable for a company wishing to employ such a person to seek the advice of an immigration lawyer.

Application Procedures:

You must submit Form I-129 with the E visa supplement to the United States consulate or embassy abroad, together with your application for a nonimmigrant visa and extensive supporting documentary data that proves your eligibility and your company's. If you are in the United States and applying for a change of nonimmigrant status to an E visa, you must submit the Form I-129 with the E supplement, as well as an application to change nonimmigrant status, together with all the documentary evidence needed to prove eligibility. The filing fee for an E nonimmigrant application is $70. A change in nonimmigrant status application also has a filing fee of $70. E-1 visas are indefinitely renewable, either on an annual basis, or every few years, depending on the length of the underlying visa. It is possible to remain in the United States for a very long time on an E nonimmigrant visa.

Other Considerations:

Spouses and children do not have to be of the same nationality as the E-1 visa holder. They will also be granted E-1 visas, but will not be permitted to work in the United States. The INS has noted that, if these people do work, they will not be subject to deportation, but they will become ineligible to adjust their status to permanent resident or to change their nonimmigrant visa status. In other words, if your spouse has an E-1 visa and you want to work, it is best to try to obtain your own change in nonimmigrant status to another category that does permit you to work.

Treaty Investors: E-2 Visas

Purpose:

This visa allows foreigners who have made substantial investments in the United States to live and work in the United States in order to develop and direct the business operation established by their investments.

Eligibility:

You are eligible for this visa if you are the investor, or if you are an executive, manager, or essential employee of a foreign company that made the investment, and you and the major shareholders of your company are the nationals of a country that has a Treaty Investor agreement with the United States. (For a list of countries that have Treaty Investor Agreements with the United States, see Appendix 3, on page 252.) Half the shareholders in the business must either live abroad or, if they live in the United States, must themselves be E-2 visa holders.

Special Limitations and Conditions:

In the case of executives and corporate personnel, only nationals from the same country as the corporation are eligible. You do not have to live in your country of birth in order to be eligible for Treaty Investor status, unless you are a citizen of the United Kingdom. In this case, you must also be a resident there in order to qualify for E-2 status.

You will have to show that an investment has already been made in the United States or that you or your company is close to closing a deal, before an E-2 visa will be granted. Immigration lawyers often advise their clients intending to invest in this country to come here on a B-1 visa first to ensure that plans are going smoothly before applying for their E-2 visas. This is to satisfy the criteria of the State Department and to place themselves in better positions to have their visas granted.

Both the INS and State Department will apply inverse sliding scales to determine what constitutes a "substantial investment" in terms of E-2 eligibility: the greater the value of the total investment, the lower the percentage that must already be invested in order for the foreign national to obtain E-2 status. For example, in a business investment valued at under half a million dollars, the investor is expected to have invested 75 percent of the total value before obtaining an E-2 visa. In an investment of $500,000 to $3 million, 50 percent of the investment must be made, and in investments above $3 million, the investor will qualify for E-2 status with an initial investment of 30 percent. These are not conclusive percentages, but, rather, form the basis for calculations of the INS and State Department on what constitutes "substantial." As is presently the case, applicants whose investments fall short of this ballpark range, will be able to argue their cases individually. Another criterion for obtaining an E-2 visa relates to the issue of marginality. This means, your investment has to generate a bigger return than simply providing a living for you and your family. You must be able to provide jobs for Americans through this investment and the capitalization must be large enough to ensure the viability of the business. Therefore, even if you are providing jobs for American workers, it will not counteract an inadequate investment.

It is becoming more and more difficult to obtain E-2 visas on behalf of essential employees, because, the INS and State Department are in agreement that United States workers should be considered first. There is likely to be a great deal of future litigation regarding the admissability of nonexecutive or managerial E visa personnel and it is advisable for a company wishing to employ such a person to seek the advice of an immigration lawyer.

Application Procedures:

You must submit Form I-129 with the E visa supplement to the United States consulate or embassy abroad, together with your approved petition for a nonimmigrant visa and supporting documentary data. If you are in the United States and applying for a change of nonimmigrant status to an E visa, you must submit the Form I-129 with the E supplement, as well as an application to change nonimmigrant status, together with all the documentary evidence needed to prove eligibility. The filing fee for an E nonimmigrant application is $70. A change in nonimmigrant status application has a filing fee of $70. E-2 visas are indefinitely renewable, either on an annual basis, or every few years, depending on the length of the underlying visa. Obviously, the criteria for eligibility must continue to be met in order to renew this, or any other, visa. It is possible to remain in the United States for a very long time on an E nonimmigrant visa.

Other Considerations:

Now that the Immigration Act of 1990 has added a permanent resident visa category specially for investors, many potential E-2 visa applicants with large enough sums to invest might opt directly for immigration and forgo the nonimmigrant choice completely. This is an important consideration given that the INS and State Department are purported to have become much more stringent in recent years in examining E-2 visa applications. This visa provided an avenue for wealthy foreigners to enter this country on a long-term basis without actually complying with the visa requirements.

As in the case of E-1 visas, spouses and children do not have to be of the same nationality as the E-2 visa holder. They will also be granted E-2 visas, but will not be permitted to work in the United States. The INS has noted that, if these people do work, they will not be subject to deportation, but they will become ineligible to adjust their status to permanent resident or to change their nonimmigrant visa status. In other words, if your spouse has an E-2 visa and you want to work, it is best to try to obtain your own change in nonimmigrant status to another category that does permit you to work.

Academic and Language Students: F Visas

F-1

Purpose:

This visa enables foreigners to study in the United States in full-time academic or language programs.

Eligibility:

You are eligible for this visa if you are an academic or language student enrolled in a full-time course of study that will lead to a degree or certificate. If you are coming to the United States with your family and your spouse or parent is an A, E, G, H, J, L or NATO visa holder, you will be able to enroll for a course of study on your existing visa and will not need to get a special student visa.

Special Limitations and Conditions:

You will be able to remain in the United States on your F-1 visa until you have completed your studies. The INS or State Department will usually specify that your duration of stay will be for the completion of your educational program, including practical training, plus an additional 60 days. You are eligible to work part-time on-campus and, if economically necessary, you may obtain permission from the INS to work part-time off-campus as well. You are also permitted to work off-campus in jobs that constitute practical training for your course of study. You may do your practical training at any point during your educational program, provided that this is endorsed by your Designated School Official (DSO). You must apply to do practical training by submitting Form I-538 to the DSO.

Before you can apply for an F-1 visa, you must be accepted into an accredited school and your visa will only be valid for the specific school through which your application was made. If you decide to transfer to another school or educational program, you must notify the DSO at your current school and complete the necessary forms and papers.

F-2

Purpose:

This visa is for the spouses and minor children of F-1 visa holders. You may not work in the United States with this visa.

Application Procedures:

You may apply for your F-1 visa once your school has issued you a Certificate of Eligibility. You must submit Form I-20 A/B together with either a nonimmigrant visa application form, OF-156 (if you are applying from abroad at a consulate), or change of nonimmigrant visa application Form I-506 (if applying to the INS). You will also have to submit a letter guaranteeing financial support for your course of studies. This can be in the form of a letter from your parents, lawyer, or bank manager, or through the completion of an INS form, I-134, which is an Affidavit of Support.

The State Department will only issue student visas within 60 days of the beginning of the school year. Therefore, if you plan on going to the United States sooner, or if you plan on looking for a school once you are there, you must tell them of your plans. In this case, you will receive a B-2 tourist visa marked with the words "prospective student." If you enter the United States in the visa waiver program, you may not apply for a change in nonimmigrant status to student or any other category, because you have no underlying visa.

You will receive a student identity card, Form I-20 ID, when your F-1 visa is approved. If you entered as a tourist and obtained your student visa while in the country, you will also receive a blue approval notice showing your change in nonimmigrant status. You must keep this paper with your I-94 form in your passport. The fee for an F-1 application is $70. The fee for a change of nonimmigrant status application is $35.

Other Considerations:

You may work on campus for a maximum of 20 hours a week while school is in session. During vacations, you may work full-time. You may work off-campus for a maximum of 20 hours a week only after you have completed your first year of studies and your DSO determines that you are in good academic standing. During holidays and school vacations, you may work full-time off-campus as well. These time restrictions apply to pre-completion practical training as well.

You may work for American companies who make attestations to the Department of Labor that they have recruited workers for 60 days and cannot find suitable United States workers to fill the positions. These companies must also attest that they will pay foreign students the same wages they pay local workers and that working conditions will be the same. If you will be working for an international organization, or if you can prove economic hardship, your employer will not have to make this attestation to the DOL. In order to prove economic hardship, you must be able to show that your circumstances were unforeseen. For example, the exchange rate of the currency in your country may go down, your sources of financial support may be experiencing their own economic hardship, or you may incur high medical expenses. In order to get off-campus employment authorization, your DSO must endorse your Form I-20. You must also submit Form I-538 to your DSO, who will certify your application to the INS.

Employees of International Organizations or Government Agencies: G Visas

Purpose:

G visas enable official representatives and foreign employees of international organizations to live and work in the United States, or to enter on official business. It also allows the nationals of foreign countries that have no diplomatic ties to the United States or are not members of international organizations (and, therefore, do not qualify for G-1 or G-2 status) to fulfill their government obligations in the United States.

Eligibility:

There are five subcategories, each with its own conditions for eligibility:

G-1:

This visa is for the chief representative of foreign governments employed by international organizations, their staff, and immediate family members.

G-2:

This visa is for other accredited representatives of foreign governments employed by international organizations and their immediate families.

G-3:

This visa is for representatives of foreign governments and their families who would normally qualify for G-1 and G-2 visas, but whose governments have no diplomatic relations with the United States and are not members of the international organizations that they will be visiting.

G-4:

This visa is for all other employees of international organizations and their immediate families.

G-5:

This visa is for the personal employees (attendants, servants) and their immediate families of all visa holders in the previous four categories.

Special Limitations and Conditions:

The spouses and children of G visa holders are not officially allowed to work in the United States. However, if they want to do so, they can apply to the INS for special permission. If this is granted, they will receive Employment Authorization Cards (EACs).

Application Procedures:

These visas are generally taken care of by foreign government representatives, so you will not be required to deal personally with the United States consulate or embassy. You will simply have to provide your personal travel documents and photographs of you and your family and whatever other documents are specified. G visas are usually granted for the duration of the assignment, except for G-5 visas, which are granted for one year, but can be renewed annually.

Professional Nurses: H-1A Visas

Purpose:

This category was created by the Immigration Nursing Relief Act of 1989 which became law in December 1989 and became effective in September 1990. It was enacted to counteract the critical shortage of professional nursing staff in the United States by making it easier for foreign nurses to obtain visas to work here and to become permanent residents.

Eligibility:

H-1A visas are available exclusively for professional foreign nursing staff employed by hospitals and other medical institutions or organizations.

Special Limitations and Conditions:

You or your employer may only file an H-1A visa petition after your employer organization has attested to the Department of Labor (DOL) that they will experience a "substantial disruption" if they do not employ foreign nurses; that neither the pay nor the working conditions of similarly employed American nurses will be affected by employing foreign nurses and that they are taking "significant steps" to recruit and train nurses who are either United States citizens or legal permanent residents. If you will be working for a nursing agency who will send you to various hospitals, both the agency and the hospitals that will be using your services or the services of other foreign nurses must make such attestations. If you have a job and are moving to another medical facility to relieve a shortage of staff, it is possible that the need for your new employer to submit another attestation on your behalf will be waived.

Application Procedures:

You or your employer must submit Form I-129 with a special H visa supplement, together with proof of attestation plus proof of professional nursing status, and a filing fee of $70 to the INS Regional Service Center that has jurisdiction over the area where you will be working. Once this petition is approved, you must submit this approved petition with your application for a nonimmigrant visa (if applying from abroad) or with an application to change nonimmigrant status (if applying from within the United States). Visas will be granted for an initial three-year period with one two-year renewal possible. A sixth year is possible under special circumstances.

Other Considerations:

The Immigration Nursing Relief Act of 1989 also made it possible for licensed professional nurses who had been employed in the United States in H-1 status for three years, at the date of enactment, to adjust their status to permanent residence. Adjustment of status will not allow members of your immediate family who are not already in the United States to gain automatic entry. They will have to apply for immigration through the family-linked channels.

However, if your immediate family is in the United States, they, too, will get permanent resident status. Filipinos, particularly, could benefit from this rule, because the current backlog for family first preference visas is seven years.

Employees in Specialty Occupations: H-1B

Purpose:

This visa is for professionals in specialty occupations who are coming to the United States to work in their fields of expertise.

Eligibility:

You are eligible for an H-1B visa if you have at least a bachelor's degree in the specific field in which you will be working—or whatever the minimum educational requirement is for the job—and you also have both the theoretical and practical knowledge for applying your highly specialized skills. If you do not have a degree, you will be considered eligible if you have the experience equivalent to the attainment of higher education as well as professional recognition in your field. The INS uses the simple formula of allotting one year of higher education to three years of experience. So, if your peers need five years of college to qualify in their "specialty occupation," you will be eligible with 15 years of practical experience and/or professional recognition. Most of the professions are covered in this category as is professional modeling, although the latter is not considered a specialty occupation. You will be expected to have your university degree evaluated in the United States by an organization that is qualified to do so. The names of organizations that evaluate foreign university degrees or certificates for foreigners coming to the United States on nonimmigrant visas that permit employment based on professional qualifications or on similarly-based employment-linked immigrant visas is supplied in Appendix 7 (see page 270). Unlike most other nonimmigrants applying for visas to enter the United States, you will not need to maintain a foreign residence, although your intention should still, theoretically, be to leave the United States once you have completed your job. The job itself can be permanent, but you must be coming to work in this job on a temporary basis.

Special Limitations and Conditions:

Before you or your employer is able to petition for an H-1B visa, your employer must have filed a "labor condition application" (LCA), or labor attestation, with the Department of Labor (DOL). This LCA must state how many foreign employees are being recruited, the occupational classification of each, and their wage rates and working conditions. Your employer must guarantee that you will be paid the higher of the actual or prevailing wage for your position and that other nonimmigrants employed in similar positions will be paid at the same rate. Your employer will also have to undertake that working conditions will be the same for both foreign and United States workers and that there are no strikes or lockouts in progress. Other staff members or union officials must have access to this LCA prior to petitioning for a foreign worker and they are at liberty to complain to the DOL if they feel that the employer is not revealing the true picture or is not meeting the conditions stated. If the DOL finds that an employer willfully and knowingly failed to comply with the LCA requirements, they are subject to a fine of up to $1,000 for each violation and may be prevented from recruiting foreign employees for 12 months or more. Also, if an employer has been underpaying you, the DOL can instruct him/her to raise your salary and award you back pay. The DOL is required to decide on an LCA within seven days of filing. If it does not approve an LCA, the INS will not suspend or revoke an approved H-1B petition. However, the employer must agree to meet the requirements of the LCA for as long as its foreign employee works there.

If you come to the United States to work for an employer on an H-1B visa and the employer dismisses you prematurely, this employer will have to pay the "reasonable costs" for your return transportation abroad. If you leave your job, you cannot expect your employer to pay such costs, nor will your employer be liable to do so. If you are dismissed, you will be expected to lodge an official written complaint with the regional service center of the INS where your H-1B petition was approved and they will instruct your employer to pay these costs.

If your employer does not pay these costs, he/she will not be fined, but could be jeopardized in any future petition applications for other foreign workers. Your H-1B visa only allows you to work for the employer who petitioned on your behalf. Therefore, if you leave your job to work somewhere else, your new employer must submit another H-1B petition for you and you can only start working at your new job once your new petition has been approved.

Application Procedures:

Obtaining Labor Condition Application (LCA) Approval (Labor Attestation): Your employer has to submit an LCA to the Department of Labor outlining all the conditions described above. Once this has been done, he/she can proceed to the next step and submit a visa petition on your behalf. Recent changes to the law make it possible to petition for a visa before the DOL has approved an LCA as long as employers can prove they have submitted it. This is also known as labor attestation.

Obtaining an H-1B Petition: You must submit to the INS proof of an LCA submission, together with form I-129-H and all the documentation required to prove the bona fide credentials of your company and your ability to fulfill the requirements of the specified job. This will require a validation of your university degree or other educational certification to show that your academic credentials meet the United States professional standards for the given job, based on the appropriate United States equivalent qualifications. There is a filing fee of $70.

Applying for an H-1B Visa or Status: You must submit your approved I-129-H Petition, which is Form I-797, or Notice of Action, together with either another I-129 form, to request change in nonimmigrant status and a filing fee of $70, or form OF-156, if you are applying for a nonimmigrant visa abroad. In addition, you must supply your personal travel documents, appropriate forms, as well as your personal credentials supporting your application. Visas are usually granted for a total of six years: an initial period of three years, with another three years available as extensions of stay. A maximum of 65,000 H-1B visas will be issued annually to those in specialty occupations who qualify in terms of the criteria for eligibility described above.

Other Considerations:

Dual Intent: If you apply for labor certification in support of an immigrant visa application while on an H-1B visa and you travel outside the country, you will not be prevented from returning on H-1B status because the rule of dual intent has been applied to this visa category. Nor are you required to maintain a home abroad when you apply for this visa.

Foreign Medical Graduates: Foreign physicians will be able to enter the United States on H-1B nonimmigrant visas if they are coming at the invitation of an educational or research institute to conduct research, teach, or do both. They will also be eligible for H-1B visas if they have passed the Federation Licensing Examination (FLEX) administered by the Federation of State Medical Boards of the United States; Parts I, II, and III of the National Board of Medical Examiners (NBME); or Steps 1, 2, and 3 of the new U.S. Medical Licensing Examination (USMLE). However, in December 1993 FLEX is being phased out; from 1995 only the USMLE will be recognized. This requirement also applies to Canadian doctors. Foreign doctors must also be proficient in oral and written English, or graduates from medical schools (either in the United States or abroad) accredited by the Education Department. Graduates of foreign medical schools will have to pass an English proficiency test given by the Educational Commission for Foreign Medical Graduates. If you graduated from a medical school in the United States, you must submit evidence of this to the INS when you apply for a visa. All applicants must also prove that they meet state licensing requirements if the state requires licensing or other authorization for direct patient care. **Note:** Although current law states that foreign medical doctors will be able to get H-1B visas to do clinical work in the United States if they meet all the necessary criteria, the Chief of Operations of the INS noted just before this book went to print that the INS may take an adverse position on this issue and see what happens on appeal.

Defense Contract Workers: Another 100 Defense Department visas will be available in the H-1B classification for foreigners of exceptional merit and ability coming to the United States to work in cooperative research, development and coproduction projects based on reciprocal agreements between foreign governments and the United States. This program, administered by the Secretary of Defense, will offer visas for a maximum of ten years. Unlike other H-1B visa applicants, those applying for this defense department visa will need to maintain a foreign residence as a criterion of eligibility.

Temporary Workers in Agricultural and Other Temporary Jobs: H-2A and H-2B Visas:

Purpose:

This visa is for temporary, skilled or unskilled workers who will be coming to the United States to work for employers who are unable to obtain sufficient or suitable United States workers during periods of heavy demand. H-2A visas are issued to those who will be doing temporary agricultural work and H-2B visas to those, either skilled or unskilled, who will be employed in any other fields.

Eligibility:

You are eligible for an H-2 visa if your skills and abilities meet the requirements of an employer who needs you to work on a temporary basis in a job that is itself of a temporary or seasonal nature. You will be eligible for an H-2A visa if you are a temporary agricultural worker and for an H-2B visa if you are either skilled or unskilled and you will be needed to meet a short-term requirement on the United States labor market. In both cases, your employer must be able to prove to the DOL that no qualified or suitable United States workers were available for the job. In the case of H-2B visas, the kinds of jobs that you may be coming to do are building jobs, where the project has a finite date for completion and there are not enough qualified artisans to complete the project; training, where you will be training others to perform a function and, once the training is over, your services will no longer be required; and entertainment, where you are not illustrious enough to qualify for an O or P visa and you are coming to work for an employer who operates, for example, a summer resort that offers live entertainment. These are by no means the only kind of jobs that require this visa, but these examples all demonstrate the temporary nature of the job itself. If, for example, you are coming to work for a company that employs temporary employees on a continuous basis, you will not meet the criteria for eligibility, because any ongoing need for temporary employees is seen by the INS as a permanent job.

Special Limitations and Conditions:

In order to confirm this labor shortage on the domestic market, employers first have to obtain temporary labor certifications from the DOL to state that their foreign H-2 employees will not be taking jobs away from American workers nor will they be adversely affecting the salary level paid to United States workers doing equivalent jobs. The INS requires employers to demonstrate to the DOL that their request for workers is a one time occurrence, a need to meet a temporary shortage of labor, a seasonal need, or an intermittent need, in order to be eligible to petition for foreign workers. If you work in the entertainment industry, your employer—who could be your agent if you are an individual or your personally formed United States corporation, if you are part of a group—must submit the application for temporary labor certification to a specially-designated office that was set up by the DOL to deal with applications for anyone in the entertainment industry, performers and nonperformers alike. These offices are listed in Appendix 7 (see page 270). In the case of H-2A agricultural workers, farmers have to comply with a 50 percent rule that states they will hire qualified United States farm workers who apply for their jobs until 50 percent of the total fee or contract period has been completed, before they will be permitted to bring in foreign agricultural workers. In the case of H-2B visas, there is an annual quota of 66,000 visas available in this category annually. The most common reasons for denying temporary labor certifications is that employers fail to demonstrate to the DOL that the jobs they are offering their H-2 foreign workers are of a temporary nature. If a temporary labor certification is denied, you may not appeal the decision of the DOL, and you may still apply for the visa. But you will have to convince the INS why the DOL was not correct in denying labor certification.

Application Procedures:

Temporary Labor Certification: Employers (other than those employing people in the entertainment industry) must submit form ETA-750, Part A in triplicate to the DOL, which will determine whether or not there is a need for foreign workers to do the job. You will also have to submit a positive recruitment plan to show exactly what steps you have taken to recruit local workers first. Although the forms themselves will ask questions about your qualifications or skills to meet the requirements of the job, it will be the INS rather than the DOL that determines if you are suitable for the job. The DOL will simply be determining whether or not there really is a shortage of workers that justify bringing in more foreign labor, and whether or not the job being offered is temporary. The DOL will make its assessment based on the information you provide, information received from the employment offices, and information obtained from relevant union organizations. In the case of entertainment workers, this form must be submitted to an office specially designated by the DOL and this office will decide on an employer's eligibility to bring in foreign workers. In the case of both H-2A and H-2B employees, employers must notify their local state employment services at the same time as they submit their applications for temporary labor certifications to the DOL. Employers may submit these applications 60 days in advance of the jobs, for H-2A workers, and 45 days in advance of the jobs, for H-2B workers. In the case of H-2A workers, farmers are required to look for local workers up to the date the foreign workers leave their countries to travel to the United States to fulfill their contracts. Farmers have to pay an application fee for every H-2A worker they bring into the United States. It is possible to bring in many workers on one application, with an overall fee of $100 plus $10 for each worker listed on the petition. It is possible to apply for labor certification for a large number of workers at the same time provided they will all be doing the same job and obtaining their visas from the same consulate abroad. There is a ceiling payment of $1,000 for a multiple-recipient certification. It is also possible to bring in large numbers of H-2B workers, under the same circumstances, but no fee is required. For example, a developer may need to recruit large numbers of bricklayers or other artisans to complete a project on time.

Petition for H-2A or H-2B Approval: Once labor certification has been approved, you or your employer must submit Form I-129 with the H supplement to the INS together with a filing fee of $70 and your notice of approval or denial of the temporary labor certification, plus all the documents you sent to the DOL in support of this application. Your employer will have to submit documentary evidence of the nature and viability of his/her business and you will have to supply documentary support of your credentials to do the job, if any are necessary. If you are an entertainer or athlete, you will also have to provide a written schedule of the dates and places where you will be performing. Employers or those acting on behalf of farmers, filing petitions for H-2A agricultural workers will have to agree to allow INS officials to inspect the places of employment to ensure compliance with the regulations. Farmers will be accountable to a certain extent for all foreign agricultural workers who leave their jobs before their contracts expire. Farmers will be liable for $200 fines for each worker who leaves their employ unless they can prove that these workers either left the United States or obtained authorization to be in the United States during the time they were working in H-2A status or within five days of their early termination, whichever date came first. Farmers are also required to inform the INS if any workers leave their employ or if their jobs are terminated more than five days before their visas expire. Unless farmers comply with this notification requirement, they face fines of $10 for each worker they fail to report. The INS will ensure that the jobs are commensurate with the requirements of the foreign workers and, in turn, that these workers are suitable for the jobs in question.

Applying for an H-2 Visa or Status: You must submit your approved I-129-H petition and your approved temporary labor certification together with the appropriate form and filing fee for obtaining either a change in nonimmigrant status or an application for a nonimmigrant visa, depending if you are applying for this visa or status change in the United States or abroad.

Visas are usually granted for up to one year, given that the jobs are required to be temporary or seasonal and presupposes that they will not last beyond one year. However, under special circumstances, it is possible to obtain two, one-year extensions, but these may be denied if the temporary nature of the job becomes suspect. In applying for extensions of stay for H-2 visas, your employer will have to reapply to the DOL for an extension of the temporary labor certification and ensure that all the criteria are still being met.

Other Considerations:

Now that the H-1B visa category has been restricted to those in specialty occupations, many people, not prominent in their fields, and therefore not eligible for the new O and P visa categories, may have to resort to the H-2B visa category. This category would apply to people whose skills are not considered professional, but who, nevertheless, want to find work in the United States. The main problem would be finding a job, itself temporary in nature.

Trainees: H-3 Visas

Purpose:

This visa enables people to further their careers in their home countries by participating in on-the-job training programs offered by United States companies. This training must be unavailable in their own countries and the programs designed to enhance the skills of trainees in their jobs abroad.

Eligibility:

You are eligible for an H-3 visa if your qualifications enable you to meet the requirements for participation in the training program. You must also maintain your home abroad and show your intention to return home once the training program is complete. The program itself must be a legitimate one, with a formal curriculum, study materials, and books. You must be invited or requested to participate in such a program and it must be aimed at furthering your career abroad; it cannot simply be any training program aimed at furthering your personal interests.

Special Limitations and Conditions:

You may only work in the United States if this is a minor component of the training program and is one of its requirements. You must be able to show that less than half your time will be spent working in order to justify obtaining an H-3 visa. Because one of the conditions of eligibility is that you will be going back to your home country to implement the knowledge you gained in your training program, you will be expected to provide evidence proving your intention of returning.

Application Procedures:

Petitioning for H-3 Approval: You must submit Form I-129 with its H visa supplement to the INS, together with a filing fee of $70. This must be accompanied by information regarding the training program in which you will be participating and documentary evidence showing that your education and/or training make you eligible to be a participant in such a program. All those petitioning on behalf of a foreign trainee will be asked whether or not they intend to employ this trainee once the program is complete, and, if not, why they wish to incur the costs of providing this training and what they hope to gain in return. This could be a difficult question to answer unless there was some kind of symbiotic relationship between the company for which you work abroad and the company offering the training program in the United States. For example, if you work for a company with many foreign branches, it may choose to train you at its United States branch before sending you to another overseas facility. Or you may be an international management consultant who wants to enhance your professional skills by participating in a management consulting training program at a major United States consulting firm with which your company has professional links. The bottom line, therefore, is that this program must not be a hoax designed to give you a means of entering the United States. This is what the INS will be considering in reviewing your petition.

Applying for an H-3 Visa or Status: You must submit your notice of approval of your Form I-129-H, together with the appropriate form and filing fee and other documentation required for either applying for a change in non-immigrant status or an application for a nonimmigrant visa, depending on whether you are applying from within the United States or abroad. If you are applying for a change in nonimmigrant status, you must also submit the documentation in support of your H-3 visa petition.

H-3 visas are normally granted for up to 18 months. If you need an extension of stay, you will have to prove that the training program is still underway and that you still meet all the requirements of eligibility for this program. In many cases, you will receive your visa for 18 months, but your Form I-94 will only admit you for a few months. At the end of this period, you may apply for an extension of stay that will be granted for one year, if the INS believes your training program is still ongoing for this time.

H-4

Purpose:

This visa is for the immediate family members of all H visa holders. Employment is not allowed.

Media Workers: I Visas

Purpose/Eligibility:

You are eligible for this visa if you are a newspaper, radio, or television journalist or technician, or any other kind of information media worker, employed by foreign media organizations.

Special Limitations and Conditions:

You are only permitted to work for the employer who obtained your I visa on your behalf. If you want to change your medium, for example, switch from television to newspaper reporting, or you want to change your foreign employer, you may only do so with permission from the INS. This category is for media workers who will be working only for the newspaper, radio, or television station by which they are employed, and their immediate families. Visas are issued on a reciprocal basis with other countries. Spouses and unmarried children under the age of twenty-one are included in this category. They are not allowed to work.

Exchange Visitors/Students Programs: J Visas

J-1

Purpose:

J-1 visas enable foreigners to come to the United States for study and/or research or to work in businesses or participate in training programs offered by United States companies.

Eligibility:

Your prospective employer must be recognized by the United States Information Agency (USIA), which is an agency of the State Department, as an exchange visitor program sponsor. In order to be eligible to participate in such a program, you must be a bona fide student, scholar, medical graduate, trainee, teacher, professor, research assistant, or leader in a field of specialized knowledge or skill coming to the United States on a temporary basis to teach, instruct, lecture, study, observe, conduct research, consult, demonstrate your skills, or receive training. Alternatively, you may be the employee of a multinational company coming to the United States to gain experience at your company's United States office. Many companies, such as oil companies and banks, regularly bring in foreign staff using "in-house exchange visitor programs." This means the companies are USIA-approved program sponsors who are offering a particular kind of training to their international staff. These business trainees have to be employed full-time and have to be paid the same wages as their United States peers. If you are coming to the United States to participate in an industrial training program, your employer, apart from guaranteeing a decent wage, will also have to undertake to provide you and your family with medical insurance from the time you leave home until the time you return. Small companies that do not have the resources to operate their own training programs, may subscribe to a J-1 "Umbrella Program." For a fee, they may hire foreigners with special skills from various organizations/companies that have been granted jurisdiction by the USIA to operate as private agencies in granting J-1 visas.

Special Limitations and Conditions:

You will have to show that you have enough money to cover your expenses in the United States or that your employer or host organization in the United States will be paying you a salary. In addition, you must demonstrate a proficiency in the English language in order to participate in any J-1 program. You will probably be asked to provide some form of proof that you intend returning to your home country once you have completed your program, because one of the conditions for obtaining a J-1 visa is your intention to return home. If you are a medical graduate, you will not get a J-1 visa unless you have passed the Foreign Medical Graduates Examination, or have graduated from a United States or Canadian medical school. In addition, you have to have a written guarantee from your government that a job will be available once you have completed your postgraduate studies in the United States. If you are participating in a government-sponsored program—either funded by the United States or your own government (even in the form of travel grants and scholarships), or if you have skills that are considered necessary in your own country, you will be subject to a two-year foreign residence clause on your J-1 visa. This means that you cannot change to another visa status or apply for adjustment of status to permanent residence without first living abroad for two years. It is possible to apply for a waiver against this rule unless you are a medical doctor. In this case, you have no option but to go home for two years before applying for immigrant or any other status. It is not easy to obtain a waiver and, generally, the following four conditions may increase your chances of doing so:

1. The United States government agency where you are working requests to employ you and the State Department supports this request.

2. You are able to show that leaving the country for two years would cause exceptional hardship to your family, including the possibility that certain members of your family are United States citizens or permanent residents.

3. You cannot return to your last country of residence or country of nationality because you fear persecution.

4. You obtain a "No Objection" letter from your government stating that it has "no objection" if you remain in the United States and the State Department, after reviewing this letter, makes a favorable recommendation to your United States employer.

Even in the unlikely event that a medical doctor gets a "no objection" letter, this will not change the INS's position on this rule. The Exchange Visitor Waiver Board was set up during the mid-1980s to review waiver applications if two or more government agencies disagree about whether a waiver should be granted. Waivers are not easily granted and, especially where there is reciprocity between the United States and other governments, there is little desire to antagonize foreign countries on the issue of depleting their skills pools.

Therefore, when applying for J-1 visas, you should realize that you may not qualify for a two-year foreign residence waiver in the future, and this could thwart, though not ruin, your long-term plans to immigrate.

If you are experiencing financial difficulties, it is possible to obtain permission to work in another job, provided you are able to meet the requirements of your J-1 program and continue to work in this program full-time. However, because you undertook to guarantee your financial security when you applied for your J-1 visa, you will have to have legitimate explanations for your plight.

Application Procedures:

Sponsors in the J-1 program all have designated officials within their organizations who take care of the immigration requirements of foreign participants. These people are known as Responsible Officers. When you apply at such an organization, the responsible officer will send you various forms to complete and you must submit these, with documentation to support your application, to your employer. Once they have ascertained that you are eligible to participate in their program, they will send you Form IAP-66, known as the Certificate of Eligibility. You must complete this form and submit it, together with your application for either a change in nonimmigrant status or nonimmigrant visa, depending on whether you apply in the United States or abroad, and you have relevant personal and travel documents.

Application for a Waiver of the Two-year Foreign Residence Requirement: You must submit Form I-612 to the INS together with one or more of the following: a "No Objection" letter from your government; a notarized affidavit explaining the hardship you will endure if you do not obtain this waiver plus documentation to support this claim; proof that your wife and/or child is a United States citizen or permanent resident; documents that would entitle you to political asylum because of the threat of persecution in your home country; letters of support from your United States government agency employer, requesting that you be granted a waiver on its behalf. The latest legislation, in its attempt at reducing the bureaucratic load on the INS, is planning to use a single form—Form I-724, the Application to Waive Exclusion Grounds. There is a filing fee of $90.

Automatic Waivers to Chinese Nationals: The nationals of mainland China who were in the United States on J-1 visas anytime between June 5, 1989 and April 11, 1990, have been granted Home Residency Waivers by an Executive Order of the President of the United States. There are no special forms to complete, but people eligible must write at the top of their immigration applications: "J-1 visa waiver granted by Presidential Executive Order of April 11, 1990."

J-1 visas are generally granted for the duration of the program as indicated by your employer on the Form IAP-66 that is sent to you in accepting you as a participant. Visas are granted from 12 months, in the case of cultural exchange visitors, to ten years, in the case of the USIA's own agency, the International Communications Agency. Cultural exchange visitors are also eligible for Q visas, which provide a viable alternative particularly in view of the fact that Q visa holders are not subject to any foreign residence requirements nor do their employers have to be recognized sponsors of exchange visitor programs. Business and industrial trainees are generally limited to 18 months, whereas foreign medical graduates can get J-1 visas for up to seven years. Most other participants in research and/or study programs are granted visas for three to five years.

Other Considerations:

If you are a student, you may be wondering if and why the J-1 visa is preferable to either the F-1 or M-1 visa. The M-1 is the most restrictive, because it is given for the shortest time period and also allows the least amount of additional time for practical training—only six months. The F-1 and J-1 both have their advantages, with the F-1 less restrictive in adjusting status later on and the J-1 more generous in allowing an additional 18 months for practical training, compared to 12 months available on an F-1. Even more attractive is the fact that your J-1 program sponsor can grant you the additional 18 months without having to go through the INS, which the F-1 visa requires. The J-1 is only valid for the specific educational program in which you are participating, whereas the F-1 will allow you to change schools and courses of study, provided you inform the INS of these changes. Therefore, if you are not randomly pursuing education in the United States and are coming to a specific institution to pursue a specific course of study, the J-1 is probably better—particularly if this institution is privately funded. If, on the other hand, you will be studying on a government-funded scholarship and you are contemplating immigrating to the United States at some stage after completing your studies, you could be stymied by the two-year foreign residence clause. Therefore, you might avoid the bureaucratic hassle (and additional financial expense) of having to apply for a visa waiver later by applying, rather, for an F-1 visa.

J-2

Purpose/Eligibility:

This visa is for immediate family members of J-1 visa holders.

Special Limitations and Conditions:

J-2 spouses and/or children can obtain permission to work from the INS if the family is experiencing financial difficulties. In order to get employment authorization they must submit Form I-765 together with their I-94 cards and a filing fee of $60. They must submit these applications in person at the INS Local Office. An Employment Authorization Card (EAC) will be issued within one to two months. If a decision has not been reached within 60 days, they may return to the INS local office and show the receipt for the application fee. They will then be given an Interim Work Authorization Card, which will enable them to be legally employed for 120 days.

At the time of publication, the United States Information Agency (USIA) was in the process of altering procedures involving J-1 visas. The main thrust of this rule is to tighten the USIA's control of the J-1 exchange visitor program. Sponsors will be designated for five years at a time and will have to submit annual reports about the workings of their J-1 programs. They also will have to show how many IAP-66 forms are sent out each year and how many are in use. Sponsors also will have a greater liability for insurance of their J-1 employees, trainees, or students.

Some of the main points of the proposed J-1 rule are:

- J-1 professors and researchers may work only in temporary, nontenure track positions for a maximum of six years.
- A "short-term scholar" category will be created.
- Training plans will have to be approved for all training programs and training will only be permitted for "specialty" and "nonspecialty" occupations.
- "Umbrella organizations" and all programs for which they supply J-1 employees will be closely monitored.
- J-1 foreign students must pursue a full-time course of study and be on some kind of scholarship or program in which a government or educational institution has an economic or academic interest. Personal or family funding will not be allowed.
- Primary and secondary school teachers will get J-1 visas to teach full-time.

The rules propose additional programs for specific business and government interest groups and clarify the requirements for foreign medical graduates (subject to United States Medical Licensing Examination) and foreign youth and student programs.

Fiancés/Fiancées of United States Citizens: K Visas

K-1

Purpose:

This visa is for the foreign, future spouses of United States citizens.

Eligibility:

You are eligible for a K-1 visa if you are coming to the United States to marry your United States citizen fiancé or fiancée and the wedding is going to take place within 90 days of arrival.

Special Limitations and Conditions:

Since 1986, when the Immigration Marriage Fraud Amendment Act was passed, the law states that you must have met your betrothed in person within two years of applying for your K-1 visa, unless, for religious or cultural reasons, you will only be meeting him/her on arrival in the United States in accordance with your custom. If such is the case, you must specify this to the State Department and the Attorney General of the United States will waive this requirement at his discretion. The other requirement in terms of this law is that your intention to marry is for "bona fide" purposes, and not to circumvent the immigration laws. If the latter is really your intention, and you get caught, you are subject to a fine of up to $250,000 or a prison sentence of up to five years, or both.

You may not change to any other nonimmigrant status.

K-2

Purpose/Eligibility:

This category is for the unmarried, minor children of K-1 visa holders.

Application Procedures:

Your United States future spouse must petition to the INS on your behalf and supply all the details of your relationship and proposed marriage. He/she must submit Form I-130 (this is an immigrant petition for a relative, fiancé, or orphan; prior to the new laws, Form I-129F had to be submitted), together with documentary evidence of your relationship and intended marriage, and a filing fee of $75. Once this visa is approved, you will receive notification from the United States consulate or embassy nearest your home and must submit an application for a nonimmigrant visa, together with the approval notice for your fiancé/fiancée petition.

Other Considerations:

Once you marry, you will be eligible to adjust your status to that of permanent resident, except you will be granted a two-year temporary green card. Only once the INS is satisfied that your marriage is, indeed, legitimate and not intended to help you around the immigration laws, will it grant you full permanent residence.

Intracompany Transferees: The L Visa

L-1

Purpose:

This visa allows foreign companies that have businesses in the United States to transfer staff from overseas offices to work in their United States offices. It also allows United States companies with offices overseas to bring in foreign nationals to work for them. L-1 nonimmigrant visas are also available for the foreign employees of international accounting firms who are coming to work for a United States branch or affiliate, regardless of the relationship between them.

Eligibility:

For everyone other than employees of international accounting firms, you are eligible if you are an executive, manager, or specialized employee of a foreign corporation that has branches, subsidiaries, affiliates, or joint ventures in the United States. The foreign company must be the parent company of the United States counterpart for which you will be working and both the foreign and United States companies must be actively involved in the trade of goods or services. Definitions of what constitutes control are as follows:

- The United States company must be the branch, subsidiary, affiliate, or joint venture partner of the foreign company.
- The foreign company must be the parent company having control over its U.S. counterpart.
- Control can be in the form of either direct or indirect ownership.

Ownership is defined as follows:

- more than 50 percent of the business operation;
- 50 percent of a joint-venture where both parties have equal say;
- less than 50 percent ownership but control through majority shareholding of the U.S. company.

If you are coming to work for an accounting firm in the United States that has international connections, the relationships of ownership and control described above do not apply to you.

You will only be eligible for an L-1 visa if you have worked continuously in the same position for one of three years preceding your application and you will be coming to the United States to fulfill executive or management duties or to use your specialized knowledge and skills.

A manager is defined as a person who:

- manages an organization, department, subdivision or function;

- supervises and controls the work of other supervisory, professional, or managerial employees, or manages an "essential function";
- has the authority to make personnel decisions or to function at a "senior level";
- has discretion over the day-to-day workings of the business or function for which he/she has authority.

Within this definition, supervisors are only included if they are supervising professionals. Unlike the previous law, this expanded definition means that managers can be in charge of a function of the business operation rather than of a professional staff.

An executive must:

- manage an organization or a major component/function of that organization;
- have the authority to establish goals and policies;
- have a wide latitude in discretionary decision-making;
- be supervised only by higher-ranking executives, the board of directors, or the stockholders of the company.

This allows senior managers to execute company projects in the United States as opposed to managing others, while retaining their executive positions.

Specialized knowledge includes any employee who has:

> *"a special knowledge of the company product and its application in international markets or has an advanced level of knowledge of processes and procedures of the company."*

The INS has expanded the definition of specialized knowledge to include those who have advanced levels of expertise—either technical or professional—and proprietary knowledge of the organization's services, products, technology, strategies, or any other corporate function that is essential to the United States company's successful operation.

Special Limitations and Conditions:

In order to maintain eligibility for an L-1 visa, the foreign company must remain in business, either itself or through another foreign subsidiary, throughout your stay in the United States. If, for example, your company is Dutch and has branches in the United States and Belgium, the Dutch company can close as long as the Belgian one remains open. If the United States company is less than one year old, it must be able to prove to the INS that it has operating premises and you will have to submit a lease or deed of sale with your visa application.

With an expanded definition of specialized knowledge, the L visa category is, theoretically, available to a broader range of foreign corporate personnel and it is advisable for anyone in this category to consult with an immigration lawyer.

In view of the complexities of the L visa, we extend this advice to everyone applying in this category, not only to those people with specialized knowledge.

L-2

Purpose:

This visa is for the immediate family of L-1 visa holders. Employment is not allowed.

Application Procedures:

Submitting your L-1 Petition: You or your United States employer will have to submit Form I-129 with an L visa supplement, together with extensive documentation to show both the eligibility of your company to employ an L-1 employee and your eligibility in terms of the definitions supplied above, and a filing fee of $70. The INS will approve your petition if you have supplied enough proof that you meet the requirements for this visa. You will have to submit extensive business and tax documentation, clearly showing terms of ownership and control, as well as proof of your position and an extensive job description, in order to prove L visa eligibility. If you are applying based on your specialized knowledge, you will probably have to supply copies of your professional degrees or certification, which must be evaluated by special organizations within the United States to show that your qualifications are equivalent to those of United States professionals with similar designations. (For a list of organizations that specialize in evaluating foreign degrees for immigration purposes, see Appendix 7, page 270.)

Applying for an L-1 Visa or Status: Once the INS has approved your petition, you must submit this notice of approval, Form I-797, together with either your application for a nonimmigrant visa—Form OF-156—or application for change in nonimmigrant status—Form I-506, depending on whether you are applying for an L-1 visa abroad or L-1 status within the United States, and all other necessary documentation. If you qualify as a manager or executive in the L-1 category, it will be very easy for you to obtain a green card, as you will read in Chapter 9, where employment-based immigration is discussed at length. L-1 visas are available to executives and managers for seven years, and to employees with specialized knowledge for five years, with a blanket sixth-year extension available.

Blanket L-1 Visas:

If a large foreign company, actively involved in the trade of goods or services, needs to transfer staff to its United States branch, subsidiary, or affiliate on a frequent basis, and its United States company has been operating for at least a year, it may qualify for a blanket L-1 visa. This will enable the company to transfer qualified staff members whenever necessary without having to petition for individual L-1 visas. Similarly, United States companies with operating foreign parent companies can also qualify to bring in staff from abroad on a regular basis. Qualified staff members, for blanket approval, need to be executives, managers, or specialized knowledge *professionals*. Professional status is only a requirement for *blanket* L-1 visas, because individual L-1 visa applicants are eligible if they have specialized technical or professional knowledge. Before a company can get a blanket L-1 visa for the transfer of its staff, it must have already obtained at least ten L-1 visas in the preceding 12 months. It will also qualify, however, if it employs at least 1,000 people in the United States or has annual sales (or combined sales, if it controls several United States businesses) of at least $25 million. The company must also have at least three branches, subsidiaries, or affiliates, even if they are not all in the United States. A joint-venture operation does not qualify for blanket visas.

Application Procedures:

Your company, either here or abroad, must submit Form I-129-L. When this petition is approved, your United States employer will obtain Form I-129-S, a Certificate of Eligibility. If you are applying for an L-1 visa and your company has an approved blanket petition, you will have to submit all the same forms as you would to obtain either a nonimmigrant visa or change of nonimmigrant status, together with Form I-797 and Form I-129-S. Where this is the case, you will not have to prove you are eligible for an L visa, because this has already been taken care of. You will simply have to prove your personal eligibility.

Nonacademic and Vocational Students: M Visas

M-1

Purpose:

This visa allows foreign nonacademic or vocational students to study in the United States.

Eligibility:

You are eligible for this visa if you will be a full-time student in a vocational or nonacademic field coming to the United States to study for up to one year.

Special Limitations and Conditions:

If you remain longer than a year, you will have to apply for an extension of stay. You are allowed to work part-time on campus and may only work off-campus if your job is part of the practical training required for your certificate or degree. In this case, you must get permission from the INS. You may not change your course of study and may only change schools in the first six months with permission from the INS. You may not change your status to F-1.

Application Procedures:

You may only apply for your M-1 visa once the school you will be attending has issued you with a Certificate of Eligibility. This is a two-part form, I-20 M–N and I-20 ID. The latter is your student identity copy. You must submit both parts of this form, together with your nonimmigrant visa application form, OF-156 (if you are applying from abroad), or change of nonimmigrant visa application form, I-539 (if you are applying directly to the INS from within the United States), plus a filing fee of $70 for your change of nonimmigrant status. You will also have to submit a letter guaranteeing financial support for your course of studies. This can be in the form of a letter from your parents, lawyer, or bank manager, or through the completion of an INS form, I-134, which is an Affidavit of Support. The INS will return your student identity card, Form I-20 ID, when your visa or change of status is approved.

Other Considerations:

If you are applying for a student visa while in the United States and you entered the country on a B-2 tourist visa, you must be able to argue your case that you had no intention of studying when you came here and that this was not a preconceived plan. You will only be eligible to change your status if you have not violated your tourist status. This means you must have entered the country legally and never have worked. Also, your I-94 entry card must be valid. Anyone who entered the United States in the visa waiver program may not apply for a student or any other visa while in the country, because they are not in possession of any underlying visa.

M-2

Purpose:

This is for the immediate families of M-1 visa holders. You may not work in the United States if you have this visa.

Family of G-4 Special Immigrants: N Visas

N-8—Purpose/Eligibility:

This visa is for the parents of G-4 visa holders who qualify for permanent residence in terms of the special immigrant provisions legislated in the Immigration Reform and Control Act of 1986.

N-9—Purpose/Eligibility:

This visa is for the unmarried children under the age of twenty-one of those who qualify for N-8 status. In other words, this is for the unmarried siblings under the age of twenty-one of G-4 special immigrants.

Application Procedures:

There are no special forms or procedures. You may apply at a United States consulate by completing an application for a nonimmigrant visa, or you may apply from within the United States by submitting a change in nonimmigrant status application (Form I-539) to the INS, together with a filing fee of $70 and personal documentary evidence to prove both the credentials of the G-4 permanent resident and your relationship to this person. This documentary proof must be provided when you apply for a visa outside the United States as well.

Other Considerations:

The N visa category was added in 1987 and visas are granted for an initial period of three years, with three-year renewals. You are permitted to work in this country if you enter on an N visa.

NATO Visas

NATO-1–5—Purpose/Eligibility:

These visas are for the staff of member countries coming to the United States under NATO-1–5 Treaty provisions, and their immediate families.

NATO-6—Purpose/Eligibility:

This visa is for the civilian staff of back-up organizations accompanying NATO military staff, and their immediate families.

NATO-7—Purpose/Eligibility:

This visa is for the personal employees and their immediate families of NATO-1 to NATO-6 visa holders.

Employees of Extraordinary Ability: The O Visa

0-1

Purpose:

This visa allows foreigners with "extraordinary ability" in the arts, sciences, education, business, or athletics to work in the United States. In science, foreigners must be coming to the United States to fill leading or critical positions in an organization/establishment that has a distinguished reputation or record of employing extraordinary people. In the case of business projects, they must be highly complex, thus necessitating the services of an extraordinary executive, manager, or technical person.

Eligibility:

You must have sustained national or international acclaim and be publicly recognized in your field. If you are a scientist, you must have received a major international award (such as the Nobel Prize) or must be able to demonstrate three areas of recognition and/or expertise, in the form of published papers, books, or other professional material, participation in professional organizations within your field, or evidence of employment by organizations/institutions that have wide recognition as employing people of distinguished reputation. If you are in the arts, specifically the motion picture or television industry, you must have been nominated for a major industrial national or international award (such as an Academy Award, Emmy, Grammy, or Director's Guild Award), or must have at least three forms of documentation showing participation in acclaimed productions (the proof being reviews, publicity releases, contracts, endorsements, publications). You must be able to document all your successes and show articles or books that have been written about you and any other forms of proof of your sustained fame. In all fields, being able to command a high salary or receiving substantial remuneration is also acceptable proof of your extraordinary ability.

Special Limitations and Conditions:

To qualify in this category, you must be among a small percentage of people who have risen to the top of your field in science, education, business, or athletics. If you are in the arts (fine, visual, or performing arts), you must have reached a level of distinction that is notably above the level of your peers. If you work in the motion picture or television industry, you are required to show a "demonstrated record of extraordinary achievement." These achievements must be widely recognized in your field and you must be recognized as an outstanding, leading, or well-known person in this field. The INS has developed certain criteria by which to judge this record, including consultations with unions, management organizations, or peer groups that have expertise in the field in which the visa is being sought. Your petitioner will have to consult with the appropriate trade union as well as with any producers who would be involved in your projects. Letters of recommendation will have to be obtained from both sources. These letters of recommendation must state whether or not a person of extraordinary ability is required for the job and must support its claim with a specific statement of facts. In the arts, entertainment, and athletics it is possible to expedite the consultation process. If the INS approves an expedited petition, consultations with advisory organizations will take place over the telephone and the peer group, labor union, or management organization will have 24 hours in which to respond with its written advisory opinion. If an opinion is *not* from a labor organization, a copy will be forwarded to the appropriate labor organization within five days and they, in turn, have 15 days in which to respond. The INS must make its decision within two weeks of this. For people employed in the motion picture or television industries, prospective employers must provide consultations from both management organizations and labor unions. Only once they have given clearance, will the INS approve your visa. This procedure is not as stringent for other fields, but is still required before the INS will approve an O-1 visa petition. The INS will only approve your O-1 visa if it believes your presence will "substantially benefit" the United States in the future.

O-2

Purpose:

This visa allows those employed in a support role by O-1 visa holders to work in the United States with their O-1 colleagues.

Eligibility:

The Immigration Act of 1990 notes that O-2 foreigners must be "entering for the sole purpose of assisting in the performance of an alien of extraordinary ability and are an integral part of that performance, by way of critical skills or a longstanding relationship with the former." These critical skills and experience should not be of a general nature and, therefore, should not be able to be easily replaced by United States workers. Therefore, an internationally-acclaimed theater director may choose to use his/her own technicians, if they have been integrally involved with the production abroad, or a famous athlete may chose to bring his/her personal trainer.

Special Limitations and Conditions:

Your petitioner must consult with a labor organization before submitting a petition on your behalf. If you will be working in a support role in the motion picture or television industry, your petitioner must consult with both a labor and a management organization. The written advisory opinion in O-2 visa petitions must discuss if and why the foreigner is essential to the O-1 artist or athlete and describe the working relationship between them. It must also say whether or not there are United States workers who could perform the support service that is required. For support workers in the motion picture and television industry, the opinion must discuss the foreign worker's skills and experience and whether or not this person has a long-standing relationship with the O-1 worker. If so, the opinion must also address the issue of continuity within the production. Within the application process, the petitioner must submit these advisory opinions, and, in addition, the O-1 foreigner in whose support the petition is being submitted, must also submit a statement addressing the need to have this support person accompany him/her to the United States. In the case of a specific film production, production executives should also submit a written statement addressing the pre- and post-production needs and the need for the continuing participation of the foreign O-2 worker.

O-3

Purpose:

This visa is for the immediate families of O-1 and O-2 visa holders. Employment is not permitted.

Application Procedures:

Submitting Your O Visa Petition: You must first submit Form I-129 with the O Visa supplement, together with documentary evidence to show you are eligible for the category for which you are petitioning, and a filing fee of $70 to the INS. It is important to have as much supporting documentation as possible to prove your eligibility. Your petitioner, agent, or whoever else is acting on your behalf, must also submit a written advisory opinion from the management organization and/or labor union and/or peer group organization discussing your credentials and eligibility.

Applying for Your O Visa or Status: Once the INS has approved your petition, you must submit notice of this approval together with either your application to change your nonimmigrant status or your application for a non-immigrant visa (depending on whether you are applying in the United States or from abroad), and the appropriate fees and personal and travel documents. The INS has stated that the O visa will be valid for as long as the "event or assignment" lasts. In the case of sports stars and performing artists, it might be possible to judge when an event or assignment ends. In the case of people in science, education, and business, this might be more difficult. O visas may only be approved for the time required to complete the specific event/performance/production or whatever the work assignment, if these events have distinct or identifiable time periods. An approved petition will not exceed three years, but annual extensions will be possible to continue or complete the same event/activity.

Other Considerations:

This is one of the new nonimmigrant visa categories created by the Immigration Act of 1990. Formerly, people qualifying in this category were eligible for H-1B visas. This is no longer the case. People applying for O visas will not be required to maintain foreign residences, nor will they be liable for visa fraud if they apply for immigrant status while working in the United States in O status, because the rule of dual intent, originally applicable to H-1B and L visa holders, has been extended to include O and P visa holders as well.

Athletes and Performing Artists: P Visas

P-1

Purpose:

This visa allows world-class athletes and entertainers to perform in the United States.

Eligibility:

You are eligible if you are an internationally-recognized athlete or entertainer, or part of an internationally-acclaimed team or group in which 75 percent of the members have been together for at least one year.

Special Limitations and Conditions:

The Attorney General of the United States may waive the requirement for international fame in the case of nationally-recognized entertainment groups who have been acclaimed as outstanding for a sustained and substantial period of time. He may also waive the one-year relationship requirement in situations where a group member had to be replaced at the last minute, or where the addition of a new member significantly enhances the group. Circus members are not subject to either the one-year sustained relationship rule or the international recognition requirement if they are coming to the United States to join a nationally-acclaimed circus or as part of such a circus.

P-2

Purpose:

This visa allows artists and entertainers to perform in the United States as part of reciprocal cultural exchange programs.

Eligibility:

You are eligible if you are an individual performer, or part of a group (this includes people who are an integral part of the performance of a group, such as a sign-language translator), participating in a reciprocal exchange program between a United States organization and similar organizations abroad.

P-3

Purpose:

This visa allows artists and entertainers to enter the United States to perform, teach, or coach others in culturally-unique programs, both commercial and noncommercial.

Eligibility:

You are eligible if you are an artist or entertainer (individual, part of a group, or integral to the performance of the group) who will be presenting a culturally-unique program in the United States. Traditional or ethnic music or dancing ensembles and other unique performers qualify in this category.

P-4

Purpose:

This visa is for the spouses and minor children of P1, P-2, and P-3 foreigners. They may not work in the United States.

Special Limitations and Conditions:

P-1, P-2, and P-3 visa petitions are subject to the approval of relevant labor unions whose members could be adversely affected by the entry of foreign workers into the United States. Petitioners for all three visa categories have to consult with labor organizations prior to submitting their petitions. They must then submit, with their petitions, written advisory opinions pertaining to the foreign worker they wish to bring into the United States.

Application Procedures:

Submitting Your P Visa Petition: Your petitioner in the United States must submit Form I-129 with the P visa supplement to the INS, together with documentary evidence to show your eligibility for the category for which you are applying, and a filing fee of $70. In the case of a P-1 athlete, the petition must be accompanied by a tendered contract with a major United States sports league or team, or in an individual sport at an internationally recognized level. Two forms of documentation proving your prior participation in a major United States sports league, or in a national team that competed internationally, or any other proof of your eligibility must also be submitted. In the case of P-1 entertainers or performers, your petitioner must submit the name of the group and a list of members, detailing when they joined. He/she must also provide three forms of documentary evidence proving the group's international acclaim. These documents can be copies of reviews, articles, and other published materials; contracts from other distinguished organizations; sales figures for CDs, cassettes, or videos; and similar information. As in the case of O visas, showing that you are able to command high fees for your work is usually proof of your success in your field and this is also the case for P visas.

In the case of P-2 reciprocal visitors, petitions must be submitted with copies of the formal reciprocal exchange agreements between the United States petitioning organization and the organization abroad that will host United States performers. The petitioner must also describe the program and provide evidence that the organization has consulted with the appropriate labor organization. Documentary proof must also show that you are experienced and have comparable skills to other artists and entertainers participating in this program, and that the terms and conditions of employment are similar.

P-3 petitions must be submitted with affidavits, testimonials, or letters from recognized experts noting the group's recognized authenticity in the presentation of their culturally-unique program. These experts will not only have to address the culturally-unique program of the foreign individual or group, but will also have to present their own credentials, outlining the basis for their expertise in the field.

Applying for a P Visa or Status: You must submit your notice of approval of your P visa petition, together with your application for a nonimmigrant visa or change of nonimmigrant status (depending on whether you are applying from abroad or within the United States) and additional fees and other personal documentation. P visas are generally available for the duration of the event, although the maximum period of initial admission is one year, with annual extensions available. Individual athletes are the exception to this rule, because they can obtain P-1 visas for initial periods of five years, with another five-year extension available.

Other Considerations:

If you have a P visa, you can be granted an extension of stay even if you have applied for a green card in the interim. Like the H-1B, L, and O visa categories, you will not be penalized for dual intent within the immigration process.

Cultural Exchange Workers: Q Visas

Q-1

Purpose:

This visa is for people coming to the United States to participate in international cultural exchange programs.

Eligibility:

You are eligible for this visa if the program in which you will be participating will advance the knowledge of the history, culture, and traditions of your country. For example, you may be coming to work at your country's pavilion at Epcot Center in Walt Disney World. The program itself must be a designated one that provides practical training, employment, and a sharing of culture. Employers will have to undertake that wages and working conditions will be the same as for United States workers.

Q-2

Purpose:

This visa is for the immediate family members of Q-1 visa holders.

Application Procedure:

Submitting Your Petition: You must submit Form I-129 and a Q visa supplement, together with documentation about the program in which you will be participating and proof of your eligibility, and a filing fee of $70, to the INS.

Applying for a Q Visa or Status: Once your petition has been approved, you must submit notice of this approval with either your application for nonimmigrant status or change of nonimmigrant status and whatever other fees and documentation are required.

Q visas are issued for 15 months.

Other Considerations:

The newly-created Q visa provides an alternative to the J visa for cultural exchange workers. Q visas are available for 15 months, whereas J visas for cultural exchange workers are only available for 12 months. Other advantages of the Q-visa category are that it does not impose a two-year, foreign-residence clause on its visa holders who wish to adjust to permanent resident status, and Q-1 cultural programs do not need the approval of the United States Information Agency (USIA), as do J-1 programs.

Religious Workers: R Visas

R-1

Purpose:

This visa allows ministers and religious workers employed by religious, non-profit organizations to work for affiliated organizations in the United States.

Eligibility:

You must be a minister of religion, a professional religious worker or one involved in a religious vocation or occupation, or a general employee working for your religious, nonprofit denomination in order to qualify for this visa. Your organization must show it is a nonprofit one by being tax exempt, or, if it has never applied for tax-exempt status, may submit all the documentation that would be required by the IRS to prove nonprofit status to the INS. You must have been employed by your religious organization for at least two years before applying for this visa. An official of your religious organization must provide written support for your application by confirming your membership and employment. This letter must accompany your application.

Application Procedures:

You must submit form I-129 and the R visa supplement, together with a filing fee of $70 and documentation to prove eligibility for this category—including a letter from an official of your religious organization. If you are applying for a change in nonimmigrant status within the United States, you must submit form I-129, which replaces Form I-506, together with the appropriate documentation and filing fee of an additional $70. R-1 visas are granted for up to five years.

R-2

Purpose:

These visas are for immediate family members of R-1 visa holders. You may study, but not be employed.

Other Considerations:

Unlike most of the nonimmigrant visas that permit employment in the United States, you will not need to obtain an approved petition before you apply for your R-1 visa. You may simply submit both your application for a nonimmigrant visa and your application for R visa classification simultaneously to the United States consulate in your area. If you are coming to the United States as a religious worker, but you will not be paid and will be working purely as a volunteer, you may enter the country on a B-1 visa.

CHAPTER 6

The Canada-United States Free Trade Agreement

On January 1, 1989, the Canada-United States Free Trade Agreement (FTA) came into effect. This agreement aims at fostering trade between the United States and its largest trading partner, Canada, and to make it easier for the citizens of both countries to cross the border for business, employment, or investment purposes.

In order to accomplish this, certain immigration rules had to be revised. For example, it was necessary to overcome delays in visa processing. The result is that Canadians do not have to go through the same procedures as other foreign nationals for obtaining visas that will enable them to do business or work in the United States. Canadians who can prove their citizenship and document their eligibility, can obtain visas to do business or work in America from INS border officials at border posts or airports at the time of their departure from Canada. The only exception is for those coming to the United States on E treaty trader or treaty investor visas, which the FTA made available to Canadians for the first time. They have to apply in advance to the United States consulate. Canadians are not exempt from paying visa fees, but may do so in cash or by check at the border, where they present their travel documents and credentials of business or employment eligibility. Once again, those entering on E visas have to pay visa fees with their application at the United States consulate.

Another immigration requirement of the FTA is that Canadians and Americans crossing each other's borders do not plan to forsake their country of residence and will maintain their permanent residence and nationality. The point is that, being so close geographically and from a business point of view, the interaction between the two countries is simply being consolidated by the FTA—not created by it. This is not a policy of immigration, but of interaction.

Although Canadian citizens entering the United States to do business or to work are, in most cases, eligible in the same nonimmigrant visa categories as other foreigners, and although these categories are described in detail in the previous chapter, they will be described again in this chapter with particular reference to how they apply to Canadians, because, in some cases, more than just the application procedures are different. In all cases, you must be able to prove you are a Canadian citizen by presenting your passport, birth certificate, citizenship certificate or identity card, or naturalization certificate to the INS border official who is processing your application to cross the border.

TC VISAS

A new nonimmigrant category, the TC visa, is a feature of the FTA and is only applicable to Canadian citizens. It is available to people whose professions have been singled out by immigration officials and who have at least a baccalaureate degree, or a master's degree where required, or who have some academic credits as well as extensive practical experience.

Many of those who qualify for TC visas would also qualify for H-1B visas, which are for those in specialty occupations who have university degrees.

INS officials have a list of professions that qualify for TC status, known as Schedule 2 (see Appendix 9, page 273), and, as long as you can present proof of your eligibility, you will be admitted across the border and receive an I-94 card with details of your immigration status and length of permitted stay in the United States. Proof of eligibility must include your educational evaluation, including degrees, diplomas, certificates, or professional licensing; proof of membership in professional organizations; references from employers or professional peers; a letter of appointment from a United States employer, stating the professional capacity in which you will be working; and other proof that you have the education and, if necessary, the experience needed for this visa.

The professional listing that determines who is eligible for TC status specifies, in certain cases, that a university degree as well as experience is needed. For example, if you are a journalist, you will need a bachelor's degree plus at least three years of experience in your field before coming to work in America. If you are a management consultant, you must have either a bachelor's degree or five years of professional experience in your field. Medical doctors can only be admitted in TC status if they are coming to teach or conduct research and may not be involved in practicing medicine. Canadian medical doctors wishing to practice medicine in the United States, will, therefore, need to enter on H-1B visas (see the following section).

You must have with you the proof of your eligibility for TC visa status and complete forms for this visa at the port of entry to the United States or at a United States preclearance/preflight station in Canada. You will have to pay $50 U.S. in cash or by check. Once the INS official has checked the list of TC qualifying professionals, and has checked that you qualify in terms of your profession and in terms of your documentary evidence of support, he/she will approve your application and issue you an I-94 card to enter the United States.

TC visas are issued for one year and must be renewed annually for the term of the job. There is no time limit. Entertainers and athletes are not eligible for TC status and must apply either for O or P visas, as discussed below.

Your spouse and minor children will get B-2 visitors visas at the point of entry when your TC visa is approved, provided they are also Canadian citizens. If they are not, they will have to apply for these visas at the United States consulate prior to your departure. Either way, they will not have to pay an application fee. They may not work in the United States.

H, O, P, Q, AND R VISAS

All these nonimmigrant visa categories have the same terms of eligibility for Canadian citizens as for other foreign nationals (see Chapter 5 under "terms of eligibility" in each of these categories, listed alphabetically). The only difference is that Canadians, because of the FTA, do not have to go through the visa petition process before getting entry visas into the United States. Their visa applications are made at the port of entry or at a preflight inspection a few days before traveling. If your profession does not appear on the list in Appendix 9 (see page 273), but you still qualify as an H-1B professional, or if your qualifications are better suited to the O, P, Q, or R nonimmigrant visa categories (see Chapter 5), you must find out from the INS office at the place where you intend to enter the United States whether or not they process the I-129 form, which you have to complete for all of these nonimmigrant visa applications. You should do this several weeks in advance of when you plan to come to the United States. If the INS officials at the border or preflight inspection station where you will be applying do *not* process this form, you will have to submit it, together with all the documentary evidence in support of your application, to the INS Regional Service Center in the United States that has jurisdiction over the area where you will be working. Instead of taking a few days, this could take up to two months, so either plan to enter the United States at a border crossing or from an airport where INS officials *do* process these forms, or organize your paperwork well before you are scheduled to begin your job in the United States. The filing fee for all these visas, payable in cash or by check at the time you apply, is $70.

Canadians are also eligible to get H-2 and H-3 visas. The eligibility for these visas is described in the previous chapter. However, for Canadians, the application procedure is somewhat different than for all other foreign nationals. Canadians applying for H-2 visas have to first obtain a temporary labor certification from the Department of Labor in the United States. Once they have this, they can apply for their visa at the border or preflight post, provided the INS officials at these points process I-129 forms. If they do not, they must submit their visa applications to the INS Regional Service Center that has jurisdiction over the place where they will be working.

Canadians wishing to participate in training programs in the United States can also get their H-3 visas approved at the border or preflight posts a few days before they wish to travel. As is the case for both H-1 and H-2 visas, if the INS officials at these points do not process I-129 forms, they must be submitted to the INS Regional Service Center that has jurisdiction over the area where the training program will take place. You should ascertain this well in advance of your proposed trip, because it could take up to two months to get your visa if it has to be submitted to an INS Regional Service Center in the United States.

The filing fee, in all cases, is also $70.

If you are entering the country in any of these visa statuses, you will be admitted for the same length of time as are other foreigners in these statuses. The advantage over TC status is that, in most cases (other than H-2 and H-3 visas), this will be several years and you will not need to go through the bureaucratic procedure of applying for extensions of stay every year.

Your spouse and minor children will receive H-4 visas. If they are not Canadian citizens, they cannot get these visas at the point of entry, but must apply in advance to the United States consulate.

In all cases, you will be restricted to working for the employer whose letter of appointment you showed to the INS official who granted you entry into the United States. If you change employers, you must notify the INS. You will be considered out of status if you enter based on a specific job with a specific employer and then change employers and will be deported if caught.

The same applies to your training program. If you enter on an H-3 visa, you are only allowed to participate in the program that you cited when applying for this visa. If you change programs, you will have to notify the INS, but your total time limit in the United States will not be extended.

B-1 VISAS

Like all other nationals, Canadians going to the United States on B-1 visas cannot receive a salary there. However, unlike other nationals, Canadians can get B-1 status simply by giving the INS official at the border or airport a letter from their employers stating the nature of their business visit to the United States and confirming that they will continue to be paid their salaries in Canada.

The list of who qualifies for B-1 status, in terms of the FTA, is more extensive than it is for most other nationalities, and is known as the Schedule 1 list (see Appendix 8, page 271). Included on this list are people involved in the following general types of occupations or professions:

- Research and design
- Growth, manufacture, and production
- Marketing
- Sales
- Distribution
- After-sales service
- General service

Even if you are not involved in any of the above, described in more detail in Appendix 8, you will still be allowed to enter the United States on B-1 status if you can prove that your visit is business related, or to attend a conference, or to investigate the market for a potential investment—anything to do with your professional or business life. You must also be able to show that you will not be paid in the United States and that your visit there will be temporary.

You can get a B-1 visa for up to one year. In most cases you will be given a six-month, multiple entry visa, which you can renew for another six months. If you are a missionary or have religious affiliations, you can get a longer extension of stay, but you must prove you will not be soliciting funds, selling, or accepting donations.

If you are going to the United States to perform after-sales service on equipment or machinery purchased in Canada, you can get a B-1 visa anytime during the duration of the service or warranty agreement. This is different for other foreign nationals entering the United States because they may only enter the country in this capacity for one year. However, if a United States company purchased this equipment or machinery in the United States, Canadians going there in an after-sales service capacity must get a visa that will enable them to work there—in this case, an H-2B visa.

L VISAS

Canadian intracompany transferees must fulfill the same requirements of eligibility as all other foreigners going to the United States in this capacity (see Chapter 5, L-1 visas, page 60).

An application for an L-1 visa can be made the day of travel or a few days before at the border or preflight post where you will be entering the United States. You will have to bring with you extensive documentation to prove your eligibility for the visa, as well as proof that the relationship that exists between the Canadian and United States business counterparts qualifies to employ an L-1 intracompany transferee. In addition, your application petition must be signed by the employer who is sponsoring you, although this employer does not have to be present.

You will receive a visa for one year in the case of a start-up business and for three years, if the business relationship has existed between the Canadian and American counterparts for a year or longer. If you are an executive or manager, you will be able to remain in the country for up to seven years, and can obtain extensions of stay on your visa. If you are a specialized knowledge employee, you will be able to stay for up to five years, and can renew your visa accordingly.

You must check to make sure that the INS officials at the point where you intend entering the United States processes I-129 forms. If they do not, you will have to submit your visa application to the INS Regional Service Center in the United States that has jurisdiction over the area where your United States employing company in located.

There is a filing fee of $70 U.S. for an L-1 visa.

Your spouse and minor children will get L-2 visas at the INS border or airport unless they are not Canadian citizens, in which case they will have to apply in advance to the United States consulate. They may not work in the United States.

E VISAS

You should refer to the section on E visas (both E-1 treaty trader visas and E-2 treaty investor visas) in the previous chapter, because all the conditions and terms of eligibility for this visa also apply to Canadian citizens.

Unlike the other nonimmigrant visa categories available to Canadians coming to work or do business in the United States, the E visa cannot be obtained at the point of entry, but must be obtained in advance from the United States consulate. This takes between one and two weeks. The United States consul will subject an E visa application to a great deal of scrutiny and it is necessary to provide extensive documentation proving eligibility. There is a filing fee of $70 U.S.

Usually, E visas are issued for an initial five-year period, but can be renewed indefinitely for up to two years at a time. In order to have an E visa renewed, you must continue to be eligible for this visa.

Your spouse and minor children will also be issued E visas and are not officially entitled to work in the United States. However, if they do work without authorization, they will not be deported, as will the spouses of B, TC, L, or H visa holders.

If you are coming from Canada to work in the United States in terms of any of the above visas (excluding B-1 visas), you may bring your servants, who will get B-1 visas. These visas can always be obtained at the point of entry into the country, provided you can vouch for your servants and confirm that you will be supporting them while they are there, but paying their salaries in Canada.

The next part of this book will discuss who is eligible for permanent United States residence and examine the different ways of reaching this goal. Remember, although the strategies for obtaining a nonimmigrant visa differ from those for obtaining an immigrant visa (green card) the two processes are closely intertwined for many who leave their countries as tourists to the United States and return as United States permanent residents. Keep in mind that the nonimmigrant process you read about in this section carries through to the next, as you continue along the road to immigration.

PART TWO

THE ROAD TO PERMANENT RESIDENCE

CHAPTER 7

An Overview of Immigration in the Nineties

Many of you, having read the previous chapters covering entry into the United States and nonimmigrant procedures, may think that, apart from a few new regulations and additional nonimmigrant visa categories, not much has changed in immigration law. This is not true. If you had a basic knowledge of how immigration worked in the past, forget what you knew! The old laws for getting a permanent residence visa, or *green card*, are no longer relevant. This chapter provides a brief summary of the immigrant visa categories and how they are allotted.

IMMIGRATION CATEGORIES

The Immigration Act of 1990 is the most thorough revision of United States immigration law in 66 years. This law affects everyone who wants to obtain permanent residence in the United States. Currently, 700,000 people may immigrate to the United States every year. At the beginning of the 1995 fiscal year, which starts on October 1, 1994, this number will decrease to 675,000. The maximum annual immigration includes family-sponsored immigrants, employment-sponsored immigrants, and a group known as diversity immigrants.

For the first time, immediate relatives of United States citizens are included in the family-sponsored category, which consists of family-preference visas. There are currently 465,000 visas available annually in this category. From the beginning of the 1995 fiscal year, this number will increase to 480,000. An unlimited number of visas is available to immediate family members of United States citizens. The remaining visas are distributed among the family-preference categories. Because there is no upper limit for immediate family visas, a flood of applicants in this category could seriously reduce the number of visas available in other family-preference categories. The law accommodates for this and notes that at least 226,000 family-preference visas must be available every year for people being sponsored in the preference categories by their United States relatives. If immediate family visas reduce this minimum, additional visas will be issued to make up the shortfall. Shortfalls will be made up by reducing the number of visas available to the spouses and children of amnesty beneficiaries. There are currently 55,000 visas available in this category each year, until the 1995 fiscal year.

The family-preference visas are divided into four categories:

- the **family first preference** is for the adult, unmarried children of United States citizens;
- the **second preference** is for the spouses and minor children of permanent residents (2-A) as well as unmarried adult children of permanent residents (2-B);
- the **third preference** is for the married sons and daughters of United States citizens;
- and **the fourth preference** is for the siblings of adult, United States citizens.

The numerical breakdowns and the application procedures for each of these family-preference visas, as well as for immediate family visas, will be discussed in detail in Chapter 8.

There are 140,000 visas available for employment-based immigration, which is divided into five preference categories. The first preference is for priority workers, which consists of people with "extraordinary ability," outstanding professors and researchers, and top executives and managers of multinational corporations. Many people who would qualify for O-1 nonimmigrant visas, are also likely to be eligible for priority worker immigrant visas. The second preference is for professionals with advanced degrees and those of "exceptional ability." The third preference consists of skilled workers, professionals who hold baccalaureate degrees, and unskilled workers, who are all grouped under the label of "other workers." The fourth preference is for "special immigrants"—including ministers of religion and religious workers, and the fifth preference is for investors. Employment-based immigration will be covered in detail in Chapter 9.

From the beginning of the 1995 fiscal year, 55,000 visas will be available annually for diversity immigrants. This group consists of people from countries—known as "low admission areas"—that have contributed relatively few immigrants to the United States during any five-year period this past decade. If you come from a low admission area, you will be eligible as a diversity immigrant.

These diversity visas are currently available each year until 1995 to the spouses and children of legalized aliens. This caters to the demand caused by the legalization program of the Immigration Reform and Control Act of 1986 (IRCA). Forty thousand "transitional" visas are also available each year until the end of the 1994 fiscal year (September 30, 1994) for the nationals of countries that were adversely affected by previous legislation, notably Ireland. This "transitional" visa program is part of the AA-1 Visa Lottery, which attracted a vast number of applicants during its first year when people were allowed to submit as many applications as they wished. During a one-week period from October 1, 1991, the State Department received 9.3 million applications in this visa lottery. The law was changed in December 1991 to reflect a fairer approach to this lottery. You may now only submit one application a year (no applications will be carried over to the following year if they are not selected in any current year) and these applications will be randomly selected—no longer in chronological order of being received. You will be disqualified if you submit more than one application. Citizens of Northern Ireland will be considered Irish for the purposes of this lottery and Canadians are also now eligible. If there is a shortfall in the number of lottery visas issued in any year, additional visas will be available the following year. With reference to Irish nationals, who are guaranteed a minimum of 16,000 visas a year, if fewer visas than this are issued, this shortfall will be made up to Irish nationals the following year. If any J-1 nonimmigrant visa holders qualify for permanent residence in this lottery, they will not have to meet the requirements of the two-year foreign residence clause, if it applies to them. At the time of going to print, lottery applications for the 1993 fiscal year were already being accepted, but you will still be able to apply for the 1994 fiscal year. Call the INS office nearest you or the United States consulate in your area to get further details. If you are too late for the AA-1 visa lottery, you may still qualify as a diversity immigrant.

Chapter 10 will examine the diversity program more closely and discuss other ways of getting permanent residence.

NUMERICAL "PER COUNTRY" LIMITS

There is a particularly high demand for visas from the nationals of certain countries. This demand and the fact that only a certain number of visas are available each year to the nationals of each country, means that they have to wait a long time—several years, in some cases—to get their green cards. Recent changes to the law are aimed at reducing the waiting time for some of these people by increasing the number of visas available. Each country will receive at least 25,620 visas a year, compared to 20,000 previously. No distinction is made for either family- or employment-related immigration within this per-country limit. In other words, it is acceptable for all the visas for one country to be issued to family members of United States citizens or residents if this is where the demand lies.

Immigrants from dependent areas and colonies will receive a minimum of 7,320 immigrant visas a year (compared to 5,000 previously). However, if these areas or colonies are considered "low admission areas" in terms of the diversity immigrant program, their nationals will be subject to the per-country limit of 25,620 (at least) visas a year.

Only one-quarter of the applicants in the 2-A family second-preference visa category, that applies to the spouses and minor children of United States permanent residents, will be counted within the numerical limitations. This should alleviate the backlog in the family second-preference category and help the nationals of those countries who have the longest wait.

There are currently 10,000 visas available annually for the citizens of Hong Kong. From October 1, 1993, Hong Kong will be treated as a foreign country with a minimum limit of 25,620 resident visas available each year.

PROCEDURES

There are two ways of getting a green card, based on the categories described above. One is to apply for a permanent residence visa from abroad. The other is to apply for an adjustment of status from within the United States. This term should not be confused with the term "changing status," which you do when you enter the United States as a nonimmigrant and change to another nonimmigrant category. Adjustment of status is a legal term applied only to applying for permanent residence when you have a nonimmigrant visa and are currently living in the United States. When you apply for a green card from abroad, you will have to wait outside the country until your visa is approved. When you apply for adjustment of status, you will have to remain in status in the United States at all times. If you are out of status, or have been in the past—which could be because you worked illegally, or your visa has expired—you will have to return to the country of your last permanent residence (not necessarily your country of birth) to apply for a green card from there.

Until now it has been mandatory to appear before the INS at an interview before adjustment of status is granted. However, as of November 1992, local INS offices will be able to waive the interview requirement for: employment-based applicants; children under the age of fourteen; parents of U.S. citizens; and Cubans applying under the Cuban Adjustment Act of 1966. An INS office may also waive the interview requirement if there is sufficient information on file to conclude that an adjustment of status application can be granted. By the same token, adjustment of status may be denied based on existing information. If the office is aware, for example, that the applicant worked in the United States illegally, adjustment of status may be denied.

PRIORITY DATES

When you submit your petition for an immigrant visa or for a labor certification (or labor certification waiver), the date on which this application is received becomes your priority date and determines your chronological "place in the line" behind those who have applied for a similar visa ahead of you. A priority date means that there are no visas currently available in the category for which you applied or that the "per country" limit for your country of nationality has been reached. You get a priority date when a category is not current for either of these reasons.

According to a recent Report of the Visa Office issued by the U.S. Department of State Bureau for Consular Affairs, the priority system operates as follows. At the beginning of every month the consulates from all over the world send reports to the Visa Office in Washington D.C., listing the total numbers of immigrant visa applicants in the different preference categories. Similarly, the INS submits its numbers of adjustment of status applicants. Cases are then grouped numerically according to country of birth (chargeability), preference, and priority date. No names are given in this report. During the first week of every month, all this information is documented and tabulated. The Visa Office subdivides the annual preference and country limitations into 12 monthly amounts. The total number of requested preference visas and the nationalities of those requesting them are then measured against the monthly availability and numbers are allocated according to priority dates, with the earliest applicants receiving visas first. If the numbers and country limits tally in any month, the preference category is considered current. If there are more applicants than available numbers, the preference is said to be oversubscribed and the Visa Office starts a cutoff date listing. This date indicates the priority dates of those who just missed the previous allotment and whose applications will be dealt with first in the following month. Only those people who have a priority date earlier than the cutoff date for any preference category are entitled to receive a visa in that month.

Immigration involves both numbers and waiting. Every aspect of the immigrant visa system is governed by numerical limitations. The waiting aspect refers to whether a visa category is current or whether you will, instead, receive a priority date and have to wait your turn. In some cases, you will be lucky and your wait will be a matter of months. In others, you will be subject to a much longer wait. The following chapters detail all the visa categories and give a numerical breakdown for each.

Next is a look at family-related immigration—who is eligible, how to apply, and the prospects for success.

CHAPTER 8

Family-Related Immigration

Family unification has always been a cornerstone of United States immigration policy. As more and more foreigners have come to this country and become permanent residents and naturalized United States citizens, these people, in turn, have provided the avenues to immigration for other members of their families. Thus, immigration law has always facilitated a continuous flow of family-linked immigrants. However, as the demand for visas has increased, there has been an oversubscription to the available family visas and a steady increase in the number of illegals crossing the borders. The Immigration Reform and Control Act of 1986 (IRCA), in attempting to deal with illegal immigration, offered amnesty to hundreds of thousands of people who had been living illegally in the United States for five continuous years preceding the legislation. It also offered amnesty to agricultural workers who had been working in the United States for a certain period of time. Each immigration law seems to sow the seeds from which subsequent laws germinate, and, in giving legal permanent residence to all those who qualified for amnesty, the INS has had to address the issue of the amnesty beneficiaries in its current legislation. This has been done in two ways: there are more visas available for family-sponsored immigration than there have been in the past, and, until the end of the 1994 fiscal year, 55,000 visas are available annually for the spouses and children of those who obtained amnesty in the IRCA program.

This chapter discusses all aspects of family-related immigration and describes the application process both from within the United States and from abroad.

FAMILY-SPONSORED IMMIGRATION CATEGORIES

For the first time in immigration law, immediate family members of United States citizens are grouped together with all other eligible family members in the family-related immigration category. Of the currently available 700,000 immigrant visas available each year, there is a 520,000 cap on the number of visas available for family-sponsored immigrants. This 520,000 cap includes immediate family members, those eligible for family-preference visas, and qualifying spouses and children of those who received amnesty in the IRCA program. There is a 226,000 "floor" in the number of family-preference visas that will be available in any given year. This will ensure that even if a high number of people apply for immediate family visas, on which there is no annual limit, there will always be a minimum number of visas available for other family categories. In determining the number of preference visas available in any fiscal year, the INS will deduct the total number of immediate family visas issued the previous year from the total number of available family visas. The 55,000 visas currently available in the amnesty beneficiaries program will not be included. If, at any stage, the answer to this equation is less than 226,000, additional visas will be taken from those allotted to the amnesty spouses and children to cover the shortfall. In the 1995 fiscal year, when the program for amnesty beneficiaries ends, these 55,000 visas will be re-allotted to the diversity program and family-sponsored immigrants will be eligible for 480,000 visas a year.

Now look at each subcategory within family-sponsored immigration, and consider who is eligible.

Immediate Family

If you are the child under age twenty-one, spouse, or parent of a United States citizen age twenty-one or above, you are eligible for a green card. You may also be eligible if you were married to a United States citizen for at least two years and were widowed after this period and have not remarried. In the latter case, it is slightly more complicated because, according to legislation, you must have applied for permanent residence by November 29, 1992. Because this involves recent changes to the law, loopholes may evolve but it is too early to tell. You should consult an immigration attorney if you have any questions.

There is no limit to the number of immediate relative immigrant visas issued each year. It is estimated that the demand for these visas increases by 6 percent a year and this reduces the number of family-preference visas available in the following year. However, estimates are that the demand for immediate family visas should not affect family-preference visas for several years. Therefore, until the time comes that the minimum number of family-preference visas is available or that additional visas have to be issued to make up any shortfalls in the family-preference categories, all family-preference visas above the designated minimum of 226,000 will go to the second family-preference category— for the spouses and children of United States permanent residents.

People whose green card petitions have been approved but who have not yet applied for their permanent resident visas are also included among immediate relatives for the purpose of calculating the availability of family-preference visas for the following year.

Family First Preference

You are eligible in this category if you are the unmarried, adult (age twenty-one or older) son or daughter of a United States citizen. There are 23,400 visas available annually—plus any unused family fourth-preference visas. This category is generally undersubscribed and, therefore, you have a good chance of getting your green card without waiting too long.

Family Second Preference

The Immigration Act of 1990 split the second preference into two, to alleviate the massive backlog in this category. Family 2-A preference visas are for the spouses and minor children of United States permanent residents, whereas family 2-B visas are for their adult, unmarried children.

This category will receive a combined number of 114,200 visas a year, plus any unused visas from the family first-preference category, as well as all visas above the "floor" level, described above. The majority of visas will go to those in the 2-A category, who are guaranteed at least 88,000 visas a year, and 75 percent of these visas will not be counted within the per country limits. Therefore, legislation will not prevent the nationals of one country from obtaining the majority of 2-A visas. This should particularly benefit the nationals of Mexico, the Philippines, and the Dominican Republic.

Family Third Preference

There are 23,400 visas available in this category each year. You are eligible if you are the married child of a United States citizen. Any unused visas from the previous two preference categories will also be available, but this is highly unlikely, given the high demand for family second-preference visas.

Because the number of applications in this category has, in recent years, been higher than the present availability, you should expect a backlog and anticipate waiting for your green card.

Family Fourth Preference

You are eligible in this category if you are the brother or sister of an adult, United States citizen. There are 65,000 visas available in this category each year, plus any unused visas in the previous three categories. Given that the backlog in this category exceeds one million, you should not build your hopes on getting a green card through your sibling, but should, if possible, consider another strategy.

Spouses and Children of Those Who Received Amnesty

You are eligible for a green card in this category if your spouse or either of your parents is an "eligible, legalized alien." In other words, you are eligible if he/she obtained amnesty in terms of IRCA's general legalization program, special agricultural worker program, or amnesty program for Cuban/Haitian nationals. There are 55,000 visas available annually in this category until the end of the 1994 fiscal year, unless any shortfalls have to be made up in the family preference "floor level," in which case this number will be reduced. You will only be eligible if you were the spouse or child of the legalized alien before he/she became legalized. If the marriage or birth (or adoption, stepparenting or any other qualifying child-parent relationship) took place after your spouse/parent became legalized, you will have to apply for a family second-preference visa.

FAMILY REUNIFICATION

The spouses and children of those who received amnesty, who have been in the United States since May 4, 1988 are, in most cases, legally entitled to live and work there. This was determined by the Family Fairness Program initiated by the INS in the late 1980s. In terms of this program, "children" are defined as being unmarried sons and daughters under the age of eighteen. In other areas of immigration legislation, children, or minors, are defined as being under the age of twenty-one.

Therefore, many of those who do not get their green cards in terms of the current amnesty beneficiaries program will be eligible to remain in the United States without the threat of deportation. The Family Fairness benefits are not available to people who have been convicted of a felony or three or more misdemeanors in the United States, or who are otherwise inadmissable.

THE APPLICATION PROCEDURE

In order to obtain a preference visa, your sponsoring family member must complete Form I-130 (Petition for Alien Relative) and submit it at the INS local office that is closest to the place of his/her residence in the United States. If your relative is temporarily living outside the United States, he/she must submit this petition to the nearest United States consulate abroad. The date on which a petition is submitted on your behalf becomes your priority date and determines your place in the line in your particular preference category. It is necessary to file one petition for each family unit, unless one of the beneficiaries is a stepchild, in which case a separate petition must be submitted for this child. You must be eligible in your preference category at the time a petition is filed on your behalf. If you are the widow or widower of a United States citizen, you must submit Form I-360 instead, plus a filing fee of $75.

Your family sponsor must supply all the necessary documentation to prove that you are either an immediate family member, or eligible for a family-preference visa. You will have to supply your marriage and/or birth certificate in order to confirm this.

There is a filing fee of $75. You may pay by check, money order, or cash (though, when mailing a petition, it is not advisable to send cash).

Once your petition has been approved, this does not entitle you to legal entry into the United States or automatic permanent residence. You will still have to apply for either your entry visa (if you are applying from abroad) or your adjustment of status from a nonimmigrant to an immigrant (if you are applying from within the United States).

APPLYING IN THE UNITED STATES VS. APPLYING ABROAD

The majority of relative-sponsored green card applications are made abroad involving visa processing at United States consulates, whereas most of the adjustment of status applications are for spouses, adjusting from K-1 nonimmigrant status to permanent—or more correctly, conditional permanent—residence. If you are the immediate relative of a United States citizen, you have a greater chance of being able to adjust your status, because there is no numerical quota, and, therefore, no priority date system. If you qualify for a family-preference visa, the chances are much more likely that you do not qualify to adjust your status, unless you are in the United States with a visa that authorizes you to work. This is because, in most cases, there is a waiting period for your priority date to become current and if you are in the United States on a tourist visa, it is possible that you will become out of status while you wait. A current priority date means that visa numbers are available in your category within your country's numerical limit. The problem of keeping in status arises, because you may not adjust your status if you have violated the terms of your nonimmigrant visa. But this does not affect your eligibility and you are free to apply for your permanent residence visa abroad, even if you have worked in the United States illegally, or you remained in the country beyond the date stamped on your I-94 card (or your blue approval notice indicating an extension of stay or change of nonimmigrant status). If you are legally employed and are legally authorized to work, in terms of your underlying nonimmigrant visa, there is no problem, as long as your priority date becomes current before your employment authorization expires. However, if you are not employed, the probability is that you are in the United States on a tourist visa, which, at most, can be renewed for a total stay in the United States of one year from the date your visa was originally issued. The lengthy wait that many people have to endure before their priority dates become current would have the effect of making most of them out of status or subject to the suspicion of dual intent. For those of you legally employed, there may be a greater chance of getting a green card through your employer than through your relative—or, at least, a shorter waiting period. If you have various options, you should choose the one that will result in getting your green card the quickest!

Adjustment of Status

If you are in the United States on a nonimmigrant visa and your relative is submitting an I-130 petition on your behalf, you may submit your application for adjustment of status at the same time only if your visa category is current.

In addition to the filing fee of $75 for the family-sponsored petition, you will have to pay an additional fee of $120 with your adjustment of status application, Form I-485 (Application for Status as Permanent Resident). A separate application has to be submitted for each family member and there is a separate fee of $120 for each family member age fourteen years and older. Children under the age of fourteen must pay $95. You and each family member will also have to complete Form ER-531, which gives the address to which your green card must be mailed, and Form G-325A, which contains your biographic information. In addition, you will have to submit a fingerprint chart (Form FD-258), two passport-size color photographs, a valid passport with your I-94 card, a report of your medical examination, and your personal documentation, such as birth, marriage, and (where relevant) divorce certificates. Children under the age of fourteen and adults over the age of seventy need not complete Form G-325A, neither do they have to submit a fingerprint chart. If your application for adjustment of status is based on your marriage to a United States citizen, both you and your spouse will have to submit Form G-325A. You are also required to submit (in duplicate) IRS Form 9003, which will provide a record of your tax payments. The INS will keep one copy of this form and information from the other will be forwarded to the IRS. If you do not submit this form, for whatever reason, you could be liable for a $500 fine but you will not be prevented from adjusting your status.

Employment Authorization

If you are in the United States and plan to apply for an adjustment of status at the same time that your petition is submitted, you may also apply for temporary employment authorization. This is not automatically conferred, therefore, you will have to make a separate application on Form I-765. It is best to submit this at the same time as your green card application, because your I-94 card is needed for both. There is a filing fee of $60. Because you may not mail Form I-765 to the INS, this will mean personally delivering your application. Usually, your employment authorization is issued while you wait, and you will receive a laminated Employment Authorization Card (EAC) or Document (EAD) with your picture on it. You may work as soon as you have this card. If you do not get authorization at the time of your application, and you have not heard from the INS within 60 days, you may return to the office where you submitted your application and obtain temporary employment authorization valid for 120 days. You will have to prove you submitted Form I-765 originally; therefore, keep your filing fee receipt. In fact, remember to make copies of all the forms you file and keep all your filing receipts. These will come in handy if the INS loses or mislays your file at any point in the proceedings.

Advance Parole

If you leave the United States for any reason, once your green card application has been submitted, the INS will consider this application to have been withdrawn. Therefore, you need to obtain special permission if an emergency arises while you are waiting for your green card and you have to leave. This permission is called Advance Parole. In order to obtain this, you must go to the INS office where your green card application is being processed and complete Form I-512. You must have three, passport-size photographs of yourself and proof that you really have to leave for an emergency.

Visa Processing Abroad

After Form I-130 has been approved on your behalf, you may apply for your visa to enter the United States as a permanent resident. However, if your application is for a family-preference visa, you may only submit your application for permanent residence when the priority date in your category is current. If you have been living in the United States and working there illegally, you have no choice but to file for your green card abroad at the United States consulate—unless you are the immediate relative of a United States citizen, in which case you are exempt from this rule.

Once the consulate nearest your home has received notice from the INS that your I-130 petition has been approved, it will notify you by mail. It will also send you forms to complete, usually in two packages, one when your approved petition is received (3A) and one when your priority date is current (3). (The State Department is in the process of changing the designation of these immigrant visa packages, so the numerical reference may change. However, the procedure remains the same.) You must complete Form OF-179 as soon as you receive it and send it back to the consulate. This will enable them to start checking your biographic information and conducting a security check on you. The sooner this is done, the sooner your green card application can be processed. You will also have to submit Form OF-169, which confirms that you have in your possession all the necessary forms needed to complete your application and that you will attend an interview at the consulate. You will have to submit the balance of your application forms at your interview. These forms consist of:

- your medical examination report;
- Form OF-230—an Application for an Immigrant Visa;
- Form I-134—an Affidavit of Support, that should be signed by your petitioning relative, or, that you will sign on behalf of other family members if you already have a job in the United States;
- a police certificate (you will need a police certificate for every country where you lived for one year or longer since you turned age sixteen). Some countries do not issue police certificates and others will send these certificates directly to the United States consulate. Consulate officials in the different countries are aware of the protocol in the area and will inform you of the procedure to follow in your own country;
- IRS Form 9003 giving your tax I.D. number (TIN), if you have one; your address; and information about your tax returns for the three most recent taxable years. This form will be particularly relevant if you worked illegally in the United States in recent years.

There is a fee of $170 for each visa application and an additional $30 visa issuance fee. These payments must be made at the time of your interview.

Therefore, be prepared for an expensive day when you go for your green card interview at the United States consulate—particularly if you have a large family that will be immigrating with you. Your other major expense in this procedure will be for your medical examination, but doctors' fees will vary from place to place.

Once you obtain your visa, you will legally be permitted to enter the United States. The INS officials at the port of entry will stamp your passport and at this time, permanent resident status is conferred and you are eligible to live and work in the United States. All members of your family immigrating with you must enter the United States at the same time as you do or afterwards.

DOCUMENTATION

Whether you are applying for adjustment of status, or whether you are applying for your green card through the United States consulate nearest your home, you will have to provide the same documentation to prove that you are eligible for the visa for which you are applying. In the case of family-related immigration, these documents will have to prove your relationship to your sponsor. Proving the parent/child/spouse/sibling relationship is straightforward, because it involves obtaining the birth and marriage certificates of the relevant parties—the petitioner and the beneficiary/ies. But there are also more complex cases that involve issues of legitimacy and natural parentage. In these cases, additional documentation may be required, as discussed below.

Stepparents and stepchildren can petition on behalf of each other as long as the marriage that created the relationship is still viable and this marriage was entered into before the stepchild turned age eighteen. Marriage and divorce certificates—or, in some cases, death certificates—must be provided indicating the legal termination of previous marriages (if relevant). The stepchild's birth certificate must also be provided, indicating the names of his/her natural parents.

Either you or your illegitimate child can petition on each other's behalf. If you are the mother, you need simply provide your child's birth certificate. If you are the father, however, additional proof of the relationship is required in the form of proof of paternity and either proof of legitimation or that a genuine parent-child relationship exists between you and this child. Proof of legitimation may be a declaration before a court or government body that you are the father of the child. If you legitimated your child before he/she turned age twenty-one, your child may petition on your behalf, or vice versa. The INS may require proof of paternity in the form of a blood test, or in the form of a sworn affidavit from the mother of the child. The INS has the liberty to request whatever form of proof it wishes. However, at the time of writing, a New Jersey federal judge decreed that it was unconstitutional for a child to be penalized based on the behavior of his/her parent and noted that the concept of "illegitimacy" was an archaic and discriminatory one. This judgment could have a liberalizing effect on this law in the future.

If United States citizens adopt a foreign child, this child is treated as an immediate relative and can get a green card without consideration of quotas and preferences. If United States permanent residents adopt a foreign child, the child becomes eligible for a family-second preference visa. Because adoptive children or parents are subject to more complicated criteria of eligibility, this will be dealt with in greater detail in Chapter 10, when other ways of getting a green card are discussed.

GREEN CARDS THROUGH MARRIAGE

Probably the most contentious issue in family-sponsored immigration relates to marriage. Traditionally, foreigners have always thought the easiest way to get their green cards is to come to the United States as tourists and find United States citizens willing to marry them—in some cases, for a fee.

The Immigration Marriage Fraud Amendment Act of 1986 (IMFA) ostensibly put an end to this by making it more difficult to obtain a green card based on a qualifying marriage. Your United States citizen spouse can petition on your behalf for an immediate relative visa, but this visa is subject to a two-year conditional clause. This means, you may legally live and work in the United States during this time, but you will only get full permanent residence status after two years, when you and your spouse have filed a joint petition to have the two-year conditional term removed. If you came into the United States on a K-1 visa (or intend doing so), your wedding must take place within 90 days. If it does not, you will be violating the terms of your underlying nonimmigrant visa but you will not, however, be prevented from adjusting your status after you marry. As described, adjustment of status is usually only possible if you have been in status at all times while in the United States. This rule is waived if you are the parent, spouse, or child under the age of twenty-one of a United States citizen who is petitioning on your behalf for an immediate-relative, immigrant visa. In this case, you will not be denied your visa simply for being out of status.

In order for you or your spouse to get an immigrant visa, the United States citizen partner must submit a visa petition along with your civil marriage certificate as legal proof of this marriage. If you married in a country that does not keep legal marriage records, you must contact the foreign embassy or consulate and ask them to help you obtain proof that your marriage took place. If you or your spouse were previously married, you must also provide the divorce or death certificates to prove that your present marriage is valid. In addition, you must submit photographs of both you and your spouse. If you married abroad and your American citizen or permanent resident spouse returns to the United States alone and sponsors you from there, the consulate in your area may want your spouse to be present at your green card interview. If this happens and your spouse cannot attend this interview, he/she should consult an immigration attorney in the United States to get advice on what to do.

Joint Petition to Remove Conditional Status

In order to maintain your status and be eligible for unconditional permanent residence in the United States, you have to file a petition to remove your conditional status within 90 days of its expiration. You must complete Form I-751 (Application to Remove Conditions of Residence), jointly signed by you and your spouse, and submit it with a $65 filing fee to the INS Regional Service Center that has jurisdiction over the area where you live. You will have to provide documentary evidence to prove that your marriage is still valid. This evidence can be in the form of joint bank accounts, home insurance policies, car payments, or whatever other documents that will indicate that you are sharing a life together. You may also have to attend an interview at the INS and, from several accounts, could be subjected to extremely personal questions. INS officials will be looking for consistency in answers from both you and your spouse. If your spouse has died in the interim, you must submit a copy of his/her death certificate with your application for a waiver on joint filing, discussed next.

Waivers of the Requirement to File a Joint Petition

If you married a United States citizen in good faith and, during the course of the first two years, your marriage did not work out, you may still be eligible to maintain permanent residence and have the conditional status removed.

Waivers are possible in situations where your marriage ended in divorce or annulment for good cause; the termination of your status and deportation from the United States would result in extreme hardship; your spouse battered you or subjected you to extreme cruelty; or you are the child of a foreigner who came to the United States to marry a United States citizen and cannot be included in their joint petition. If you are the parent, your child can be included in your petition for a waiver. If you were widowed by your United States spouse, there is no doubt that you will be able to remain in the country as a permanent resident, if you can show that you had a bona fide marriage.

If any of the above apply to you, you must also file Form I-751, together with documents to support your application plus pay a filing fee of $65. This application, too, must be filed within 90 days of the expiration of your conditional status, and mailed to the INS Regional Service Center that has jurisdiction over the area where you live.

If you are filing because of divorce, you must provide your divorce decree and legal pleadings, as well as whatever proof you have to indicate that your marriage was entered into in good faith. If you are claiming maltreatment, such as abuse, you must supply police reports, photographs, sworn affidavits from friends, doctors reports, or whatever other evidence you have to support your claim. In all cases, you must also provide a written statement stating your reasons for requesting a waiver. If you will experience extreme hardship by being deported, you must describe this in detail and, if possible, provide documentary evidence of this. These cases are not viewed favorably by the INS and it is advisable to seek the advice of an immigration attorney before applying for this waiver. It is highly likely that you will be called for an interview at the INS local office, in which case you will be notified by mail.

If you submit this form within the given time period, before the expiration of your conditional status, this status will be automatically extended for a further six months, by which time you should have your green card.

The next chapter discusses how to get a green card through your job.

CHAPTER 9

Employment-Related Immigration

Employment, or the hope of finding employment, is the biggest attraction for foreigners coming to the United States. Some may be motivated by the hope of wealth and an easy life. Others may be seeking opportunities simply to earn a living—in many cases, to support their families both in the United States and abroad. Whatever their reasons, as long as jobs are available, or perceived to be available, people are drawn to them.

As the end of this century approaches, the global picture has altered and the workplace is no longer the same as it was in the past. Sophisticated technology has become central to a highly-competitive international market and the need for highly-skilled workers is growing. United States immigration law, recognizing this, makes it easier for highly-skilled people to immigrate and more difficult for unskilled people. The bottom line is, if you are bringing your intellectual or technical skills to the United States, or coming to invest your money and boost the economy, the doors are open. If you are an un-skilled person, willing to do virtually any job to get a foothold in North America, you will have a long, long wait.

This chapter looks at the employment-linked categories of immigration and discusses the visa application procedures, labor certification, how to maximize your chances of success in obtaining a visa, what to do if you fail, and issues pertaining to your application site.

EMPLOYMENT-LINKED CATEGORIES

There are 140,000 visas available for foreigners who are immigrating to the United States because of their work-related skills. To be eligible, you need a specific job offer from a United States employer—with very few exceptions, as you will read later—and you must meet all the educational and/or job-related criteria necessary to fill the position that is being offered to you. With the exception of priority workers (discussed below), you must have DOL clearance that establishes that you are not taking the job away from a qualified

United States worker, or that the working conditions for others will not be adversely affected by giving you the job. This procedure is known as labor certification.

A preference system determines the numerical allocation of the visas and defines the limits of eligibility, in much the same way as in the relative-sponsored categories described in the previous chapter. A discussion of these categories, including eligibility in each, follows.

First Preference: Priority Workers

There are 40,000 visas available in this category, plus any unused visas from the investor and special immigrant categories, discussed in the following chapter. As the term priority workers suggests, this category is subject to preferential treatment in terms of the immigration process. If you qualify as a priority worker, you will not have to obtain labor certification from the DOL before you can apply for your permanent resident visa. This category is divided into three subcategories:

- persons of extraordinary ability;
- outstanding university professors and researchers;
- executives and managers of multinational companies.

Persons of Extraordinary Ability

You must have publicly-recognized, national or international acclaim as a person of extraordinary ability in science, the arts, education, business, or sports in order to qualify. You do not need an offer of employment, as long as you continue using your extraordinary ability in the field in which you gained this reputation and your presence will be substantially beneficial to the United States in the future. If you previously entered the United States on an O-1 nonimmigrant visa, it is likely that you will qualify as a priority worker.

Outstanding University Professors and Researchers

You must have an international reputation as being outstanding in your academic field, in which you have at least three years of teaching or research experience. You must have a job offer from a university or from industry, which will be utilizing the academic skills in which you gained your reputation. If you are coming to work at a university in the United States, your teaching or research position must be a tenured or tenure-track one. If you are coming to work in industrial research or for a research organization, this company or organization must be recognized as a leader in its field of research and must have significant achievements to its credit. In addition, it must employ at least three other full-time researchers.

Executives and Managers of Multinational Companies

You must have worked in an executive or managerial capacity for your company abroad for at least one of the three years preceding your application. You must be employed by the United States branch, subsidiary, or affiliate of this company in an executive or managerial position.

If your sponsoring company abroad is different from your employing company in the United States, they must both be branches of the same foreign company. Alternately, your sponsor must have the majority shareholding in your employer company, or, conversely, be its majority-controlled subsidiary, or both companies must be affiliated in such a way that they are both controlled by the same overseas entity.

In order to qualify as a manager, in this context, you must fulfill the following conditions:

- manage an organization, department, subdivision, or function;
- supervise and control the work of other supervisory, professional, or managerial employees, or manage an "essential function";
- have the authority to make personnel decisions or to function at a "senior level";
- have discretion over the day-to-day workings of the business or function for which you have authority.

If you are a supervisor, you will only qualify as a manager if the people you supervise are professionals, which, in this context, means they have university degrees.

In order to qualify as an executive, you must fulfill the following conditions:

- manage an organization or a major component/function of that organization;
- have the authority to establish goals and policies;
- have a wide latitude in discretionary decision-making;
- be supervised only by higher-ranking executives, the board of directors, or the stockholders of the company.

If you are already working in the United States as an executive or manager on an L nonimmigrant visa, the chances are excellent that you are eligible in this subcategory, because the criteria of eligibility are identical. The Attorney General will determine whether or not you are acting in a managerial or an executive capacity by taking an overall look at your business and considering its stage of development and size. You will not be penalized if your company is relatively small and you are supervising relatively few employees, provided both you and your company meet all the necessary criteria and the United States entity is viable.

Second Preference

There are 40,000 visas available in this category, in addition to any unused first-preference visas. You must have a specific job offer in the United States and must obtain labor certification from the DOL before you or your employer can submit your permanent resident visa petition.

Members of the Professions Holding Advanced Degrees

You must have a master's degree or Ph.D. in your profession or must have completed postgraduate education, such as medical or legal internship. Unlike H-1B nonimmigrants, who must be professionals in "specialty occupations," second preference immigrants in this subcategory will not qualify with only a bachelor's degree. Therefore, certain professionals, such as engineers, without advanced degrees and who do not require postgraduate education to practice in their field, will not be eligible. You also might be eligible if you have a bachelor's degree but can prove that you have progressed in your profession and have held increasingly responsible positions in your field for at least five years.

People of Exceptional Ability

You must be a person of exceptional ability in the sciences, arts, or business, whose presence in the United States will be of substantial benefit to the economic, cultural, educational, or scientific interests of the country. You must have a reputation in your country for being exceptional in your field and must be nationally recognized there. If you are in the arts or in business, you do not necessarily need a university degree in order to qualify.

Third Preference

There are 40,000 visas available in this category, plus any unused visas from the first and second preferences. You must have a specific job in the United States and must get labor certification from the DOL before a petition for your permanent residence visa can be submitted. Unlike the previous two categories, this category, which also has subcategories, has a specific visa allocation: in this case, a limit of 10,000 visas for unskilled workers.

Skilled Workers

You do not need a degree, but must work in a field that requires a minimum of two years of training or experience. If you have undergone training in your field, or have been apprenticed to an employer, you will probably qualify. The DOL will determine whether or not you have met the eligibility requirements in terms of the required training or experience in your specific field.

Professionals

You must have a minimum of a bachelor's degree in a profession, or on-the-job experience that is equivalent to the required minimum level of education needed for the job. You will need to have your degree from a foreign university evaluated by a professional organization to determine whether it is equivalent to a similar degree from an American university. (For a list of organizations in the United States that do professional evaluations of foreign university degrees, see Appendix 7, page 270.)

Unskilled Workers

Although you do not need any education or formal training, you must be able to meet the requirements of the job, or the DOL will not approve a labor certification. In other words, you must have a certain amount of experience in the field for which you are applying in order to understand the requirements of the job, however simple they may be.

The following two preferences are grouped with employment-linked immigration for the purposes of allocating visa numbers, and will be described here briefly. They will be discussed in greater detail in the following chapters.

Fourth Preference: Special Immigrants

There are 10,000 visas available in this category, which will only exist until October 1, 1994. Many subcategories fall under the fourth preference, among them, religious workers, who are eligible for 5,000 special immigrant visas annually. The other subcategories are:

- people seeking reacquisition of citizenship;
- returning United States residents;
- United States government employees who have worked abroad for at least 15 years;
- Panama Canal Treaty employees;
- certain foreign medical graduates;
- commuters from the border;
- former G-4 international organization employees and their spouses and children;
- court dependents.

The first two subcategories listed are not included in the numerical limitation for this category. Special immigrants will have to submit Form I-360 plus a filing fee of $75 before they can apply for a visa. If you are applying as a special immigrant, you do not need a United States employer. Chapter 10 looks at the special immigrant category in more detail.

Fifth Preference: Investors

There are 10,000 visas available in this category, which will also be discussed in detail in Chapter 11. This category will be of particular interest to many foreign business owners who are not professionals and do not qualify as either extraordinary or exceptional, but who have capital to invest in the United States in employment-creating ventures.

THE APPLICATION PROCEDURE

Unless you are a first preference priority worker of extraordinary ability, or an investor bringing in a large sum of money into the United States and creating jobs on the local market, your employer will have to petition on your behalf to obtain an employment-based immigrant visa.

Before submitting a petition, your employer will have to obtain labor certification on your behalf from the DOL. This is a crucial step in the procedure and one that, if not handled properly, can result in a denial of your green card. It is therefore necessary to devote special attention to this process (see The Labor Certification Process, page 102).

If you are a priority worker, applying for a first preference visa, you do not need labor certification. In addition, if you have a professional skill that the DOL has precertified as being in short supply in the United States, you will be exempt from the labor certification process. These skills are listed on what is known as Schedule A (see The Labor Certification Process, page 102).

When you apply for labor certification, the date on which your application was received by the DOL becomes your priority date. This indicates the date of your entry onto the waiting list for a visa within your preference category. If you are exempt from labor certification because you are applying for a first preference visa, or if you are applying for a Schedule A Labor Certification Waiver, your priority date will be the date on which your visa petition (with your request for a waiver, if applicable) was received by the INS.

In submitting Form I-140 (Petition for Prospective Immigrant Employee), which has a filing fee of $70, your employer (or prospective employer) will have to prove that he/she has the financial ability to pay the wage you are being offered. For a small company, this proof may be in the form of an audited financial statement. A large company, employing more than 100 workers, may submit a statement from its financial officer indicating its ability to pay the wage that it has offered you. In the case of both small and large companies, a tax return is also required. In addition, your employer will have to provide evidence that you have the minimum educational and/or practical requirements needed for the job. As with all I-140 petitions, which are solely based on your employment-related credentials, you will have to provide extensive information regarding your education, training, and experience in your field. In addition, your education must be suitable in the field in which you are being employed.

For example, it is no good providing proof of an extensive liberal arts education in philosophy and history if you are coming to the United States to work in early childhood education. Your foreign university degree or diploma must be evaluated by a United States organization qualified to do such evaluations, and you must submit these results with the petition. (For a list of these organizations, see Appendix 7, page 270.)

If you are a person of extraordinary ability in the arts, science, business, education, or sports, you do not need a United States employer, and, therefore, must submit the I-140 petition on your own behalf. In order to substantiate your sustained national or international acclaim, you must provide extensive documentation in the form of journal, magazine, or newspaper articles, books, awards, and whatever other information is relevant. For outstanding professors and researchers, documentary evidence must include references from former employers, plus articles and other evidence proving your international acclaim in at least two countries and evidence of international awards. If you will be working at a university in the United States, your employer must write a letter to the INS indicating that you are being employed in a tenured or tenure-track position. Your employer must also submit a copy of your employment contract. If you are an executive or manager of a multinational company, your sponsor will have to provide proof of your position as well as of the company's eligibility to employ you. If you have been working in the United States on an L-1 visa, your employer need only resubmit all the documents that had to be submitted in your nonimmigrant visa application.

In cases where you qualify for a Schedule A Labor Certification Waiver (see The Labor Certification Process, following), your employer will have to submit proof of your credentials along with your petition. Examples of these credentials will be given when these waivers are discussed.

When your employer completes Form I-140, he/she must specify which visa preference category and subcategory applies to you. Even though the DOL may grant your labor certification, this does not mean that the INS will automatically approve your visa petition. Your job eligibility, as well as the job itself, will have to withstand thorough examination by the INS and, not only must your job be legitimate, it must legitimately require your skills. If the INS determines, for example, that your job does not require a professional, whereas you provide extensive proof of your professional credentials, your petition could be denied. When you read about the labor certification process, you will understand why the application procedure for employment-based immigrant visas is so complex.

THE LABOR CERTIFICATION PROCESS

Labor certification has been referred to several times already, always in the context of employment-related visas, both immigrant and nonimmigrant. Before a foreign worker is admitted for any length of time into the United States, the DOL has to make sure that United States citizens or permanent residents who are legally entitled to work, are not being deprived of jobs because of this. If United States workers felt that their job security was threatened by the admission of foreigners into the country, this would have extremely negative political ramifications. Immigration law protects the rights of these workers by requiring that all foreign applicants for employment-related visas first obtain labor certification from the DOL. This is not required in the case of specialty occupation, nonimmigrant professionals, or in the case of priority worker, first preference immigrants. Their skills are of such a high caliber that the benefit they bring to the United States far outweighs the detrimental effects, if any. Apart from ensuring that United States workers are not being deprived of jobs, the DOL also uses the labor certification process to establish that employers are not jeopardizing the salaries and/or working conditions of their United States workers.

Before you even consider applying for labor certification, you should ensure three things:

1. that your employer can pay the salary he/she has offered you, while maintaining the viability of the business;

2. that you have enough training and experience required for the job;

3. that you do not present a fraudulent case to the DOL, e.g., if you are the beneficiary of the labor certification and it is your business, you must inform them of this, presenting reasons why the viability of your business depends on you being employed in that capacity.

It is common for the DOL to grant a labor certification, only to have the INS deny the visa petition based on this because of one of the above reasons. Another reason why petitions are often denied after labor certifications are approved, is that the INS discovers that the employer was applying on behalf of a relative, but that this was not made clear to the INS. If there are any doubts about the legitimacy of your employer's intentions with regard to his/her labor certification application and subsequent visa petition, the chances are that this visa will be denied. Therefore, to avoid delays in getting your green card, you should try to avoid pitfalls along the way. In cases where the beneficiary of a labor certification is a family member of the employer, or where the employer is him/herself the beneficiary, it is advisable to discuss the labor certification application with an immigration lawyer.

Forms and Procedures

Before your employer is permitted to file a permanent resident visa petition on your behalf, he/she has to submit an application for labor certification to the DOL. This application, on Form ETA-750, parts A and B, must be filled out in duplicate, with original signatures on each copy. Two of the forms may be photocopies of the original. Part A of the form requires a detailed description of the job you will be doing, or are presently doing (whichever the case may be), and a detailed description of the qualifications required to do this job. Part B requires a detailed description of your qualifications and experience. You should discuss with your employer in advance that it is extremely important that there be no inconsistency between parts A and B of this application. If you are already working for your employer, you are not permitted to count the experience gained on your current job towards the experience required for the position if you will be doing the same job. In other words, if you have been working for your employer for one year—either legally or illegally—in the same capacity as the job for which your labor certification is being requested, and have two years of previous experience, you will not qualify for the job if it requires a minimum of three years of experience.

However, if you have been working for your employer in another position, but the experience gained in that position is relevant to the job for which your labor certification is being requested, this experience is admissible.

As with every rule, there are exceptions to this one as well. If your employer can prove to the DOL that the company will experience "substantial disruption" if they have to train an inexperienced person to do your job, you may be able to use experience credits from your current job. However, do not rely on this. The DOL has not clearly defined what it means by "substantial disruption" and, therefore, there is no guarantee that it will accept your employer's definition.

It was noted earlier that your employer must be able to pay the wage being offered to you. In addition, this wage must be within a 5 percent range of the prevailing wage for the minimum requirements of the job you will be doing. It is necessary for your employer to obtain a wage survey from the State Employment Office or to obtain information from the DOL's Job Service Office to ascertain what people in your field are being paid in the geographical area where you will be employed. Your employer may not offer you a wage less than 5 percent lower than the average wage for your job, although, he/she may offer you a higher wage. If the wage is lower, this is seen as jeopardizing the prevailing wage rate for United States workers in your field, because it is obvious that employers can obtain foreign workers for lower wages. Therefore, your labor certification will be denied.

When your employer describes the job you will be doing and gives a detailed job description, this description should not be so perfectly matched to your qualifications as to purposely exclude United States applicants. This would be grounds for denial. However, it should be stated in such a way as to maximize your chances. In completing Form ETA-750, immigration lawyers often advise their clients to complete Part B first and then complete the job description section of Part A, taking care not to list a skill for which you are not suitably qualified. This is particularly relevant for jobs where there are already a large number of suitably-qualified United States workers. However, if your employer has been advertising for some time for a person to fill your position and has not been able to find anyone suitable, this strengthens your case considerably.

Recruitment Campaigns

The latter point raises the question of recruitment. The DOL will need proof that your employer has conducted a legitimate and extensive job search on the local market, before granting your labor certification.

If your employer has already advertised extensively and can document this, by submitting tear-sheets from the publications in which the advertisements for your job appeared (photocopies are not acceptable), it may be possible to obtain a waiver from further advertising. If not, the DOL's State Job Service will contact your employer once it receives your Form ETA-750 and advise him/her how to proceed with advertising.

The State Job Service will advertise your job throughout the state in its computer bank for 30 days. All those who apply will have the chance to submit a job application to your company. In addition, your employer will have to advertise your job in the classified section of the local newspapers and/or trade journals, and will be required to specify all the details that are contained in the job description on Form ETA-750. If the full job description is not contained in the public advertisements, your employer will not be able to reject a United States job applicant.

Applicants recruited through newspaper or journal advertisements must respond to the State Job Service, which will then direct them to your employer. This enables the DOL to keep track of all recruitment efforts. All advertisements in local newspapers must run for three consecutive days. Advertisements in national newspapers and journals need only run for one day.

Apart from public recruitment campaigns, your employer must display a job advertisement with the same job description as contained in your labor certification application at your proposed (or current, if you are already employed) place of employment. Existing employees of the company must have access to such a posting for ten days and must be able to apply for the job. They do not have to contact the State Employment Office, but must see a member of personnel within the company. The name of this personnel member must be provided in the advertisement.

Your employer has 45 days to meet all advertisement requirements from the day on which he/she receives recruitment procedures from the State Job Service. If he/she fails to meet this deadline, it will be necessary to resubmit all the labor certification forms and you will lose your priority date. If there are reasons why it will not be possible to meet the deadline, your employer must write to the DOL to request an extension.

The State Job Service will mail your employer all resumés it receives through its computer bank recruitment. All qualified applicants must be interviewed and your employer must provide written details of why they were not suitable for the job. Lack of qualifications, as determined from resumés, is an acceptable reason for denial. If a United States applicant has less experience than you do, this does not constitute grounds to grant your labor certification. The DOL looks at an applicant's ability to do the job that is advertised, not his/her level of experience. Your employer will have to provide a sound business reason for needing you, as opposed to a qualified United States worker, for the DOL to grant your labor certification. This is particularly important during periods of high unemployment in the United States.

Special Handling

If you are a college teacher or professor, a sheepherder, or a person with exceptional ability in the performing arts, the DOL will treat your labor certification application differently. In all other labor certification applications, as long as a United States applicant meets the minimum requirements for the job, the job has to be offered to that applicant. But, in these "special handling cases," as they are known, your application will be successful provided you have the same level of experience—or more experience—than a United States applicant for the job. Your employer must submit specific job-related reasons why you are more qualified than each United States applicant. It is not enough simply to document your superior qualifications.

Schedule A Waivers

The DOL has a list of occupations for which it has already established that there are not enough United States workers. This list is known as Schedule A and if a foreigner has the skills required by these Schedule A occupations, he/she can obtain precertification from the DOL by applying for a labor certification waiver. There are three groups on the Schedule A list.

Group I: Physical Therapists/Professional, Registered Nurses

Physical therapists do not need state licenses to obtain a waiver, but they must qualify for these licenses. Nurses, on the other hand, need to have their state licenses and must be foreign graduates of United States or Canadian nursing schools, or must have passed their CGFNS (Commission on Graduates of Foreign Nursing Schools) examinations.

Group II: People of Exceptional Ability in the Arts/Sciences

Performing artists are excluded from this category, which requires applicants to be famous in at least two countries. Proof of exceptional ability can be in the form of books, newspaper articles, awards, or any other evidence that highlights the applicant's international fame.

In applying for a labor certification waiver, your employer must submit Form ETA-750, on which he/she must state that your occupation is listed under Schedule A, Group I or II, and that no recruitment is necessary.

The DOL has also compiled a Schedule B list, consisting of occupations for which there is an oversupply of skills in the United States. These jobs are either unskilled or semiskilled. If your labor certification is for a job that appears on Schedule B, there is very little chance of getting it, unless your employer can provide an irrefutable reason why a United States worker is not able to do the job. Your fluency in a foreign language could be a determining factor here, if your employer deals mainly with foreigners of your nationality and requires his/her support staff to be able to speak to clients in their native tongue.

As with all steps in the immigration process, applications have to be backed up with extensive documentary evidence and support in order to increase the chances of success.

Once a labor certification or labor certification waiver has been approved, your employer can go ahead and submit Form I-140, as described above. What happens if your labor certification is not granted or, later, if the INS rejects your visa petition? Many people stumble at this point in the procedure.

HOW TO FIGHT A DENIAL

When Your Labor Certification is Denied

If the DOL intends to deny your labor certification, it will outline the reasons why in a Notice of Findings (NOF) to your employer. This NOF gives your employer a 35-day deadline in which to provide information that may alter the perspective and change the outcome. If your employer does not respond before the deadline expires, your labor certification is denied. Therefore, keep a watchful eye of proceedings for your green card, because you must know the various stages of progress and be able to inform your employer of the urgency of maintaining government-imposed deadlines within the application procedure.

If, after your employer has provided additional information, the DOL still rejects your labor certification, it will send written confirmation of this denial to your employer, who then has the right to appeal. Your employer will have 35 days to submit a Notice of Appeal to the DOL, which will hand it over to the Board of Alien Labor Certification Appeals (BALCA). Over the past few years, BALCA members have applied stringent standards in judging appeals and the probability of succeeding is low. It also becomes extremely costly. Theoretically, you can still go one step higher, to the United States District Court, to appeal the decision of BALCA, but the time and money involved in such a procedure makes this a nonviable alternative.

If your labor certification was denied, you may submit another one for the same job with the same employer after a six-month wait. The DOL will tell you what the problems were that led to the denial of your labor certification so, hopefully, you will be able to resolve them in your next application and avoid making the same mistakes again. If you apply for a new labor certification based on another job—either with the same or a different employer—you may do so immediately.

When Your Visa Petition is Denied

There is no guarantee that your visa will be approved just because your labor certification was approved. If you followed the three-step warning about your employer having enough money to pay your salary, your qualifications being suitable for the job, and making a nonfraudulent claim, it is unlikely that your visa will be denied. However, a large number of companies fail to prove they can pay a salary that is being offered to their foreign employee, or that their prospective employee has the right credentials for the job, and their petitions are denied. Even if you have excellent credentials and are well qualified for a job, the INS may decide that the job does not, in itself, require such a high level of expertise and may deny it on this ground.

Depending on your financial situation, your time frame, and—if you are already in the United States—your status, you have a number of options available.

If you have additional documentation that you did not originally submit that enhances your case by proving additional skills or a major accounting error in the company that reveals there was more cash available than previously claimed, you have a good case for a Motion to Reopen. There is a $110 filing fee for this procedure, which has the advantage of being handled at a regional level. If the Motion is unsuccessful, it is sent for appeal to the Administration Appeal Unit (AAU) of the INS. This is a lengthy and costly procedure with few chances of success. Alternately, you can file an appeal directly with the AAU, if you do so within 30 days of receiving the denial. There is also a $110 filing fee for this procedure. This is a choice very few people should make, because it involves time, money, and lengthy bureaucratic procedures. As in the case of a labor certification appeal being denied, in the case of a petition denial, your final recourse is also the District Court. If you have not had an immigration lawyer on your case until now, it is undoubtedly too late!

The alternative many immigration lawyers suggest to people whose visa petitions have been denied, is to resubmit them. This is often a successful strategy, because you have the advantage of correcting past errors and reducing the financial and emotional investment. This alternative is $40 cheaper than the previous two! Often, the INS denies visa petitions based on a first impression assessment of the case. Second time around, you have a better chance of success, knowing how the INS viewed your original petition.

APPLYING IN THE UNITED STATES VS. APPLYING ABROAD

Once you have an approved I-140, the application procedure for your green card is much the same as it is for an approved I-130—the permanent resident visa based on family-sponsored immigration.

Adjustment of Status

You may apply for an adjustment of status to permanent residence in the United States if one of the following applies to you:

- your labor certification has been approved;
- you are applying as a first preference, priority worker;
- you qualify for a Schedule A labor certification waiver.

In all three cases, the priority date in your preference category must be current, which means a permanent residence visa is available at the time you apply. Your I-94 card must be valid as well or you must have a current blue approval notice of an extension of stay or change in nonimmigrant status.

You may not apply for adjustment of status if you have lived and/or worked in the United States illegally, though this will not jeopardize your chances of getting a green card. You will simply have to apply at your local United States embassy or consulate.

In addition to the filing fee of $70 for your employer-sponsored petition, you will have to pay an additional fee of $120 with your adjustment of status application, Form I-485 (Application for Status as Permanent Resident). Separate applications have to be submitted for family members, who must each pay an application fee of $120. Children under the age of fourteen must pay $95. You and each family member will also have to complete Form ER-531 (this form varies in different geographical locations), which gives the address to which your green card must be mailed, and Form G-325A, which contains your biographic information. In addition, you will have to submit Form FD-258 (fingerprint chart), three passport-size color photographs, a valid passport with your I-94 card, a report of your medical examination, personal documentation, such as birth, marriage, and (where relevant) divorce certificates, and proof that the job on which your labor certification (or waiver) was based is still available. Children under the age of fourteen and adults over the age of seventy need not complete Form G-325A, neither do they have to submit a fingerprint chart.

You will also be required to submit (in duplicate) IRS Form 9003, giving information about your tax returns in the three most recent taxable years. If you choose not to do this, you will still be able to adjust your status, but you may have to pay a noncompliance fine of $500.

Advance Parole

If you leave the United States for any reason, once your green card application has been submitted, the INS will consider this application to have been withdrawn. Therefore, you need to obtain special permission if a family or business emergency arises while you are waiting for your green card and you have to leave the country for a short time. This permission is called Advance Parole. In order to obtain this, you must go to the INS office where your green card application is being processed and complete Form I-512. You must have three passport-size photographs of yourself and proof that you really have to leave for an emergency. There is an additional filing fee of $65 for advance parole.

Visa Processing Abroad

After your Form I-140 petition has been approved, you may apply for a permanent resident visa to enter the United States. You may only submit your application for permanent residence when the priority date in your employment-linked preference category is current. If you have been living in the

United States and working there illegally, you have to file for your green card at your United States consulate or embassy abroad.

Once the consulate nearest your home has received a Notice of Approval of your I-140 petition from the INS, it will notify you by mail. It will also send you forms to complete, usually in two packages, one when your approved petition is received (package 3A) and one when your priority date is current (package 3). (The State Department is in the process of changing the designation of these immigrant visa packages, so they may have different numerical references. However, the process remains the same.) You must complete Form OF-179 as soon as you receive it and send it back to the consulate. This will enable them to start checking this biographic information and conducting a security check on you. The sooner this is done, the sooner your green card application can be processed. You will also have to submit Form OF-169, which confirms that you have in your possession all the necessary forms needed to complete your application and that you will attend an interview at the consulate. You will have to submit the balance of your application forms at your interview. These forms consist of:

- your medical examination report;
- Form OF-230—an Application for an Immigrant Visa (see page 246);
- Form I-134—an Affidavit of Support that, based on your job in the United States, you will be able to sign on behalf of other family members (see page 209);
- a police certificate (You will need a police certificate for every country where you lived for one year or longer since you turned age sixteen.) Some countries do not issue police certificates and others will send these certificates directly to the United States consulate. Consulate officials in the different countries are aware of the protocol in the area and will inform you of the procedure to follow in your own country;
- IRS Form 9003, giving your tax I.D. number (TIN), if you have one; your address; and information about your tax returns in the three most recent taxable years.

You will have to pay $170 for each visa application and an additional $30 visa-issuance fee. These payments must be made at the time of your interview. Therefore, be prepared for an expensive day when you go for your green card interview at the United States consulate—particularly if you have a large family that will be immigrating with you. Your other major expense in this procedure will be for your medical examination, but doctors' fees will vary from place to place.

Once you obtain your visa, you will be legally able to enter the United States. The INS officials at the port of entry will stamp your passport and at this time, permanent resident status is conferred and you are eligible to live and work in the United States. All members of your family immigrating with you must enter the United States at the same time as you do or closely afterwards.

The United States consul may deny your green card application if he/she thinks you are excludable or if, at your interview, you indicate anything that contradicts the information in your petition and/or visa application forms. This highlights the importance of consistency in your answers and the need to keep photocopies of all your application forms along the way. By doing this, you will have cross references when filling in forms for each successive step in the immigration process and maximize your chances of success.

In the following chapter, other ways of getting a green card are discussed. Some of the groups referred to earlier, notably adopted children and special immigrants, are examined more closely. The AA-1 visa lottery applicants and certain groups not subject to numerical limitations—refugees, those qualifying for asylum, and people with temporary protected status (TPS)—are considered. Finally, the third immigrant group, the diversity immigrant, is examined.

Other Ways of Getting a Green Card

Within both family-sponsored and employment-sponsored immigration, there are categories of people who qualify for permanent residence visas based on criteria that do not strictly adhere to the typical patterns and procedures. These categories include adopted children and special immigrants, which themselves are divided into several subcategories, as you will read in this chapter.

In the first part of this book, it was mentioned that not everyone who enters the United States needs a visa to do so. This group includes refugees, and those given political asylum or temporary protected status (TPS). Some of these people are eligible to apply for permanent residence and this chapter also looks at the procedures for doing so.

Immigration law has, in the past decade, become associated with luck-of-the-draw lotteries and the Immigration Act of 1990 maintains this feature. The AA-1 visa program, which makes 40,000 visas available a year for three years until the end of the 1994 fiscal year, and the diversity immigration program are part of this lottery, as you will read at the end of this chapter. This diversity immigrant program, together with family- and employment-sponsored immigration, forms the basis of the Immigration Act of 1990. Included in the diversity program are procedures for granting additional visas to the nationals of Hong Kong and Tibet, and for expediting the visa applications of Lebanese nationals.

ADOPTION

United States citizens and permanent residents may sponsor their adopted children for a green card, either as immediate relatives or as family second-preference immigrants. The INS applies stringent rules to the definition of adoption with regard to the immigration process. It also stresses that an adopted child may not confer immigration rights on his/her natural parents, unless he/she did not gain permanent residence through the adoptive parents, or unless he/she marries to obtain a green card, and the adoptive parents are no longer alive. He/she may, however, petition for a green card on behalf of his/her natural siblings.

The INS makes a distinction between orphans and non-orphans and the rules governing their permanent residence visas are slightly different.

Non-orphans

Non-orphans are defined as those children who have already been adopted. You must have adopted your child when he/she was under the age of sixteen and this child must have been in your custody and must have lived with you for two years, either before or after the adoption. You may petition on behalf of your adopted child even if he/she is older than age sixteen. The custody and residency requirement can be fulfilled simultaneously and need only be with one adoptive parent. You have to have official proof of legal custody and adoption, particularly where you may have adopted a relative's child. If your adopted child and his/her natural parent live with you, you will have to prove that you exercise the parental authority over this child.

Orphans

To be defined as an orphan, a child's natural parents must be dead, or they must have legally given up custody of this child. Only United States citizens can obtain immigrant visas for adopted orphans, provided that these children are living outside the country and they are under the age of sixteen. You do not have to have already adopted the child, because many United States couples or individuals go abroad to adopt babies and complete all the INS paperwork before they leave.

If you are a single parent, you must be at least twenty-five years old before you will be permitted to petition on behalf of an adoptive, orphan child.

The petition to sponsor an adopted orphan is known as Form I-600 and each petition has an application fee of $140. If you do not know the child, you can still apply for a petition in advance by completing Form I-600A—an Advanced Processing application, which also has a filing fee of $140. You will not have to pay this fee again later, even though additional information will have to be supplied in Form I-600. You will receive a Notice of Approval for this petition and, when you go abroad to collect your child, you will have to obtain his/her visa to enter the United States from the United States embassy or consulate there. You will need to submit all the forms the INS sends you at the time of approving the visa petition at the time of your consulate interview. You will have to pay a fee of $170 for each visa application you make on behalf of an adoptive child, and an additional $30 for the visa to be issued.

For adopted children (non-orphans), the visa application procedure is the same as it is for any other relative, only the appropriate adoption papers must be submitted to prove the relationship. In other words, a petition must first be submitted on Form I-130, and, for a second preference visa, you may either apply within the United States on Form I-485, or at a United States embassy or consulate abroad, on Form OF-179. In all cases, the appropriate accompanying forms must be submitted as well. (See Chapter 7, page 80, for details of the application procedure.)

SPECIAL IMMIGRANTS

Special immigrants fall into the employment-related fourth preference visa category. This category has 10,000 visas available a year, of which a 50 percent maximum may be allocated to religious workers. If you are a former United States citizen seeking reinstatement, or a United States permanent resident returning to the country after an absence abroad, you are considered a special immigrant, but are not restricted by the numerical limitations of this category. Other groups that fall into the special immigrant category are foreign medical graduates, former employees of the United States government, former employees of the Panama Canal Zone, retired employees of international organizations (former G-4 nonimmigrants) and their immediate families, employees of the United States consulate in Hong Kong, and certain juveniles who have been declared dependent on United States juvenile courts and whose interests will be best served by allowing them to remain in the United States.

Religious Workers

In order to qualify as a religious worker, you must have been a member, for at least two years, of a religious organization that has a legitimate, nonprofit affiliate in the United States and be coming to work there. You are eligible if you are a member of the clergy, or were employed abroad in a professional or nonprofessional capacity, and will be coming to the United States to work in a similar capacity. Religious workers will only be considered special immigrants until the end of the 1993 fiscal year.

Foreign Medical Graduates

You are eligible to apply for special immigrant status if you graduated in medicine abroad and came to the United States on either a J or H visa before January 10, 1978. In addition, you must have had a state license, and been living in the United States and practicing medicine there before this date. If you came to the United States on a J visa, you must also have a two-year foreign residency waiver. A "no objection" letter from your government is not valid for medical doctors.

United States Government Employees

If you have worked for at least 15 years for the United States government abroad, you are eligible to apply for special immigrant status. A top official of the United States Foreign Office where you worked must recommend you for this status, which must then be approved by the Secretary of State.

Panama Canal Zone Employees

You are eligible for special immigrant status if you lived in the Panama Canal Zone on or before April 1, 1979 and had worked for the Canal Zone government or Panama Canal Company for at least one year by October 1, 1979. Panamanians who worked for the United States government in this zone for at least 15 years before October 1, 1979 are also eligible, and, unlike the previous subcategory, do not need the recommendation of their employer.

Former G-4 International Organization Employees and Their Families

If you are retired from a United States-based international organization, where you worked for at least 15 years on a G-4 visa (or you qualified for an N nonimmigrant visa), you may apply for special immigrant status. You must have been in the United States for at least three-and-a-half of the seven years immediately prior to your green card application and must apply within six months of retiring. For the unmarried children of former G-4 nonimmigrants, also on G-4 or N nonimmigrant visas, you are eligible for special immigrant status if you, too, were physically present in the United States for at least three-and-a-half years of the seven years preceding your application. In addition, you must apply for your green card before you turn age twenty-five, and must have lived in the United States for seven years between the ages of five and twenty-one. If your spouse, through whom you would also be eligible for special immigrant status, has died, you are still eligible if you lived in the United States on a G-4 or N nonimmigrant visa for at least 15 years prior to his/her death.

United States Consulate Employees in Hong Kong

Under normal circumstances, government employees abroad only qualify for special immigrant status after 15 years of employment. However, the Immigration Act of 1990 gives similarly employed workers in Hong Kong the opportunity to apply for special immigrant status after three years. You must have the recommendation of the United States Consulate General and you must be able to demonstrate that the welfare of you and your family would be threatened because of your job. This provision will end on January 1, 2002.

Juvenile Court Dependents

If you are a minor and have been declared by a United States juvenile court to be a dependent of that court, you are eligible for special immigrant status. Alternatively, the juvenile court may have recommended you for long-term foster care or determined that it is in your best interests to be allowed to remain in the United States. If you get a green card for any of these reasons, you are not permitted to sponsor your natural or adoptive parents for immigration.

Special immigrant status is also given to the spouses and minor, unmarried children of those in the above subcategories.

The application procedure is similar to that for all other employment-related immigration, because this category falls into the employment-linked preference system. The major difference is in the application form and the type of documentation needed to prove eligibility. You will have to submit Form I-360, together with a filing fee of $75, to the local INS office that has jurisdiction over the area in which you will be living. In addition, you must provide sufficient evidence to the INS that you meet the requirements—either of employment or residence, or in the case of juvenile court dependents, court records—before your special immigrant petition will be granted. Once you have an approved petition, you can either apply for an adjustment of status, or for consular filing abroad, whichever is appropriate. This procedure is described in detail in the previous chapter.

REFUGEES, ASYLUM, PAROLE, AND TEMPORARY PROTECTED STATUS (TPS)

As you read in Chapter 3, refugees or those seeking political asylum (asylees) can gain entry to the United States without a visa. After one year, they are eligible to apply for immigrant status. However, those people who have been granted Temporary Protected Status (TPS), on account of the political upheavals or natural disasters facing their countries, are not eligible to apply for permanent residence on the basis of this. They may only get green cards if they go through the channels described in the previous two chapters.

Anyone claiming refugee status has to prove persecution, the threat of persecution, or the pattern or practice of persecution, based on their race, religion, nationality, political opinions, or membership in a particular group. However, the INS does not examine whether or not these grounds still apply before granting permanent resident status to refugees. There is a limit placed on the number of refugees admitted to the United States annually. However, once they are in the country, there is no annual green card quota and all are eligible for permanent residence after one year. The INS will contact all refugees as their first anniversary in the United States approaches and give them an interview date for their green cards. At these interviews, the refugees are fingerprinted and their biographic information is recorded. They do not have to pay a filing fee.

The immigration picture is somewhat different for political asylees. They are subject to the same criteria of eligibility as refugees are, but, unlike refugees, asylees are judged according to these criteria when their immigrant visa petitions are being considered. There is no limit as to how many people are given asylum in the United States every year. However, they are subject to an annual quota of 5,000 green cards. This means that some people have to wait years for their numbers to come up. Asylees have to renew their status each year and this status is subject to change, according to conditions in their country. Therefore, there is a chance that, by the time some asylees are within view of their green cards, conditions in their countries will have changed so dramatically, that they will no longer have claim to asylee status. When this happens, they are deported from the United States.

Therefore, if you have been granted political asylum to live in the United States, your prospects for getting a green card are increased by pursuing all avenues open to you—not simply relying on your asylee status. Unlike refugees, asylees have to monitor their own immigration and must, themselves, contact the INS at the end of their first year to apply for permanent residence.

Some refugees enter the United States as parolees, if the annual refugee quota has already been filled and their cases are urgent. Parolees may live and work in the United States, but must have their status renewed annually. This status may be revoked at any time and parolees are not guaranteed permanent residence in the United States. However, parolees from the former Soviet Union, Laos, Cambodia and Vietnam have been made eligible for immigrant status and may apply, like political asylees, by submitting Form I-485 to the INS. The filing fee for each application is $120 for those age fourteen and over, and $95 for those under age fourteen. Each family member must submit a separate application form.

As with the applicants for all immigrant visas, those people who are generally excludable, will also be excluded from obtaining immigrant status based on their refugee, asylee, or parolee status. They can apply for a Waiver of Excludability and, where health matters are the grounds for exclusion, or where a family would suffer extreme hardship, these waivers are often granted.

DIVERSITY IMMIGRATION

The Immigration Act of 1990 introduced this concept in order to broaden the ethnic base of immigration and to extend the diversity of cultures within the United States. Its other motives were to give the nationals of countries from where United States immigration has been relatively low, the opportunity to join the country's melting pot, and to offer people who were promised visas in the previous NP-5 lottery but who did not receive them, the opportunity to do so.

Diversity Transition Program

Within the framework of diversity immigration are two distinct programs. The one that is currently in effect is the diversity transition program. For three years, until the end of the 1994 fiscal year, 40,000 visas a year are being given to the nationals of qualifying countries who were adversely affected when the NP-5 lottery program of the Immigration Reform and Control Act of 1986 (IRCA) came to an end. The Immigration Act of 1990 extended the NP-5 program for a year, into 1991, to alleviate the disappointment to a certain extent, but the transitional program will expand the opportunities to thousands more. Forty percent of these visas are earmarked for Irish nationals, which caused some cynics to refer to the Immigration Act of 1990 as the "Irish Immigration Act." For the purposes of this program, the nationals of Northern Ireland will be included in the Irish quota. The balance of these visas are for the nationals of Albania, Algeria, Argentina, Austria, Belgium, Bermuda, Czechoslovakia, Denmark, Estonia, Finland, France, Germany, Gibraltar, Great Britain and Northern Ireland, Guadeloupe, Hungary, Iceland, Indonesia, Italy, Japan, Latvia, Lichtenstein, Lithuania, Luxembourg, Monaco, New Caledonia, Netherlands, Norway, Poland, San Marino, Sweden, Switzerland, and Tunisia.

Multiple applications for these visas were permitted and those applications for the first year of this program had to arrive at the Department of State in Washington D.C. on October 1, 1991. Any applications that arrived before then were discarded, as were any that arrived after the cut-off date. According to INS reports, more than 18 million applications were received for the 40,000 visas available during the first year. Applications will not be carried over into the following year, although any unused visas will be carried over and added to the 40,000 available in the following year. From October 1, 1992 (the beginning of the 1993 fiscal year), Canadians may apply in this program and selection will be random, not chronological as in the preceding two years. Another major difference is that, from this date, only one application per person will be permitted. If the State Department finds more than one application from the same person, that person will be disqualified from the program for that year.

During fiscal years 1992 and 1993, if any Irish visas are not used up, they will be added to the general availability of visas for the following year.

In order to be eligible for this AA-1 visa lottery, as the transition program is called, you must have a firm commitment for at least one year's employment from the time you arrive in the United States. You must also be otherwise admissible.

The 120,000 visas available during the three-year period of this program include spouses and children. All those people living in the United States in nonimmigrant status who obtain AA-1 lottery visas have until the beginning of the following fiscal year in which to adjust their status. Similarly, those winners from abroad have the same length of time in which to obtain their immigrant visas. Because no visas may be carried over into the following year, anyone who does not comply with this cutoff date risks forfeiting their immigrant status.

Hong Kong Nationals

The Immigration Act of 1990, within its diversity program, doubled the number of visas available for Hong Kong nationals from 5,000 to 10,000 a year. This three-year offer ends on September 30, 1993. In addition to these 10,000 visas, a further 12,000 visas are available each year during the same time period for the Hong Kong employees of United States companies in Hong Kong, or their Hong Kong subsidiaries or affiliates. The staff of Hong Kong accounting firms that provide services to the Hong Kong offices of these companies are also eligible to apply. In order to be eligible for these, you must have worked for at least a year as an officer or supervisor, or in a managerial, executive, or specialized knowledge capacity and must be planning to work in the same capacity in the United States.

In addition, your United States sponsoring company must employ at least 100 people within the United States and at least 50 people outside the country, and have a gross annual income of $50,000,000.

To apply for an immigrant visa based on these criteria, you must submit Form I-140, Form ETA 750B (the second half of the labor certification application form in which your qualifications and educational credentials are listed), and a letter from your employer outlining the basis of your claim and confirming that you are, in fact, eligible.

The new legislation relaxed its regulations about taking up permanent residence in the United States within a set time period with regard to Hong Kong nationals. If you are from Hong Kong and have already had a green card application approved, you will only need to take up residence in the United States by January 1, 2002. If you chose to delay your departure from Hong Kong until then, you must inform the United States consulate at the time your visa application is approved, or within four months of receiving this approval. If your children are young at the time you obtain your green card, but are no longer minors by the time you leave Hong Kong, they will still be eligible, as long as they are not yet married. Those people who choose to defer their immigration must continue to work in the same capacity or they will no longer be eligible for immigrant status in the United States.

Tibetans

Three thousand visas have been earmarked for native Tibetans, or their children or grandchildren, who have lived continuously in India or Nepal since before November 29, 1991. One thousand of these visas will be granted annually until the end of the 1993 fiscal year.

Lebanese

The program to expedite the visas of Lebanese nationals who applied for second or fifth preference family-sponsored immigrant visas, in terms of the old system, is now over. However, this was part of the general diversity trend, motivated by political factors, as are the programs pertaining to Hong Kong nationals and Tibetans.

Diversity Immigrants

From the 1995 fiscal year, there will be 55,000 visas available each year for the nationals of countries that had low levels of United States immigration during the previous five years. This program will be based on a mathematical formula used by the Attorney General of the United States, who will determine the number of people from different countries that legally entered the country as permanent residents during the preceding five-year period. Once he has these numbers, he will divide these countries up according to whether they are in high-admission or low-admission regions or states. The regions are grouped as follows: Africa, Asia, Europe, North America (apart from Mexico), Oceania, and South/Central America, Mexico, and the Caribbean.

In this program, Northern Ireland will be treated as a separate foreign state, whereas colonies or dependent areas will be treated as part of the foreign state to which they are politically associated.

High-admission regions are defined as those that have more than one-sixth of all immigrant visas issued to its nationals. Other regions are defined as low-admission. High-admission states are defined as those that had more than 50,000 admissions during the five-year period under consideration, whereas low-admission states are all others.

Only low-admission states will receive these diversity immigrant visas, with some going to low-admission states within high-admission regions, and the majority going to low-admission states in low-admission regions.

In order to maintain a balanced program, no state will be able to obtain more than 7 percent of the total number of diversity visas in any given year. This means that each state will be eligible for 3,850 visas a year.

In order to qualify as a diversity immigrant, you must have at least a high school diploma, or its equivalent, and—during the five years immediately preceding your application—you must have worked for at least two years in an occupation or trade requiring a minimum of two years of training or experience. Unlike the diversity transition immigrants, you do not have to have a job offer from a United States employer in order to get a visa.

You may only file one petition for this diversity lottery, and visas will be granted by random selection. If you send in more than one petition, and this is detected, you will be disqualified from the lottery program for the year. Applications will not count towards the following year, and each year, you will have to submit a new application form by a certain deadline that will be announced.

The formula that determines which countries are considered low-state and how many people from each low-state are eligible for immigration will be applied every year to ensure that nationals of all underrepresented countries eventually get a chance to immigrate.

In the following chapter various immigrant subgroups are discussed, with special reference to investors, who fall within the employment-related immigrant visa category, though as employment creators.

CHAPTER
11

Special Immigration
Categories and Considerations

For years, the INS has been subject to the changing pressures of lobbying groups or government agencies, and has subjected certain immigrant groups to a great deal of bureaucratic difficulties. These are not nationality groups, rather special interest groups or professional groups whose United States counterparts have felt threatened by their presence in the country.

Investors have always been able to enter the United States as L or E nonimmigrants, but the rules governing their entry into the country have become more and more restrictive over the years and the INS and State Department abroad have applied more stringent standards as set out by legal regulations. Many Americans are suspicious of foreign investors in the United States and see their presence as a detrimental factor, rather than as a factor that boosts economic growth and creates employment opportunities. Current law provides a new immigration category specifically for investors. It incorporates few of the stringent regulations to which foreign investors are subjected when they apply for nonimmigrant investor visas, and opens an avenue of easy access into the United States to foreigners with large sums of money to invest.

Artists and performers are another group who have been subjected to the INS's union-inspired regulations. Successful lobbying by groups involved in the arts and entertainment industries have resulted in stringent requirements for foreign artists and performers who wish to work in the United States. These requirements have been discussed to some extent in the nonimmigrant visa categories affecting artists and performers, but will be discussed in greater detail in this chapter.

The American Medical Association (AMA) is one of the most powerful lobbying groups in the country and exerts a great deal of pressure on policymakers. It is a known fact that, of all professionals seeking to immigrate to the United States, medical doctors have the most difficult time and are subject to the most stringent requirements of eligibility. This is a direct result of AMA lobbying. Yet, within the medical arena, related professionals, such as nurses and physical therapists, are desperately needed and foreigners seeking to enter the United States in these professions are helped and even encouraged by the law.

It may seem strange to discuss illegals in the context of a book on legal immigration, but it is necessary to know that, every year, more people immigrate to the United States illegally than legally. This is an embarrassing reality for the INS, which, over the years, has passed complex laws aimed at reversing illegal immigration—or, to be more realistic, at changing the deluge to a trickle. This was the intention of the Immigration Reform and Control Act of 1986 (IRCA).

This chapter looks at the various special interest groups and discusses their immigration options. In addition, it looks at IRCA and discusses some of the salient features of this law that affect all people coming to live and work in the United States—legally or not.

INVESTORS

The Immigration Act of 1990 makes 10,000 visas a year available to foreigners who invest a minimum of $1 million in a new business venture that employs at least ten full-time United States workers. This number may not include the investor or his/her family members, nor may it include other foreigners working on nonimmigrant visas. Although this category constitutes the fifth preference, employment-based immigrant visa category, there will be no handing down of unused visas from the higher preference categories.

If you are prepared to set up a business in an outlying, rural area or in an area where the level of unemployment is at least one and a half times the national average, you may only need to invest $500,000. These rural or high unemployment areas have been identified by the INS as "target areas." The need for job creation in these areas is so high, that, as a further incentive to investors, 3,000 of the available 10,000 visas are reserved for target area investment.

If you plan on locating in an area with low unemployment, your investment may need to be as high as $3 million. These are metropolitan areas where employment levels are significantly higher than the national average and where the need to create jobs is not as crucial as it is in high unemployment areas. The INS will determine which are "target areas" of high unemployment and which are low unemployment areas and will, accordingly, determine how much you will have to invest in the area where you plan to start a business. Make sure you hire a lawyer with experience in the business realm before sinking millions of dollars into an investment. It would be a blow to pursue an investment and find that, for some technical reason, you do not qualify for a green card.

The application procedure for an investor to become an immigrant follows the general procedure pattern for all immigration, other than having a different petition form and different documentation needed to prove eligibility. If you are an investor applying to immigrate to the United States, you must submit Form I-526 to the INS regional office that has jurisdiction over the area where your investment will be made, together with a filing fee of $140 and extensive financial documentation proving the viability of this investment and the staffing strategies, as well as any other documentation that can prove your eligibility in this category. Once your petition has been approved, you must go through the application procedure as described in Chapter 9, page 96.

Because this method of obtaining an immigrant visa is open to abuse, the INS is implementing various procedures to deter people from using this category to circumvent the immigration process. If you obtained a green card through investment, you will be subject to two years of conditional permanent residence. After two years, you will have to apply to the INS to remove the conditional basis of your visa. If you do not submit Form I-752 (Application by Investor to Remove Conditions) plus a filing fee of $85, your permanent residence status will be revoked and you will be subject to deportation. Also, if the ten jobs created by your investment do not survive this two-year period, you will forfeit your green card.

During this two-year period, the INS will have the authority to terminate your status if it establishes that you created your business to evade immigration laws, did not establish your business as stated, failed to invest the amount of capital required, or only kept your business going briefly to ensure your green card.

Any activities that you engage in to make it appear as if your investment was bona fide, but was, in fact, designed to get a green card, will be treated as fraud and render you subject to deportation.

The law created this immigration category as part of a wider plan to boost the United States economy by encouraging new business development. It was not intended to help existing businesses expand. There are many unanswered questions with regard to investor-status immigration—particularly regarding new investments in existing businesses in which you were not previously involved. The INS is likely to be open to negotiation as far as legitimate claims in this category are concerned. It is, however, wise to employ the services of an immigration lawyer with experience in business before sinking millions of dollars into an investment.

PERFORMERS AND ARTISTS

International artistic and creative circles assume a kind of unconditional reciprocity in the name of their art—in the international arena, that is. However, when national boundaries—in this case, those of the United States—are threatened by foreign artists or performers or support workers in the entertainment industry wishing to live and work within the arena of their American counterparts, unconditional reciprocity no longer works, except in special circumstances.

Currently, there are various ways for foreign performers and artists to work in the United States on a temporary basis. Those people with "extraordinary ability" in the arts can enter the United States and work there on O-1 nonimmigrant visas. The standards are extremely rigid and, to prove extraordinary ability, you must have sustained national or international acclaim and be publicly recognized in your field. If you are in the motion picture or television industry, you will be subject to an exclusive test in which you must be able to show a "demonstrated record of extraordinary achievement." The INS will judge this record using many different criteria, including consultations with unions, management organizations, or peer groups. Without a go-ahead from these powerful industry organizations, which your United States sponsor will have to get before submitting an O visa petition on your behalf, the INS will not approve your petition. The INS will only approve your O-1 visa if it believes your presence will "substantially benefit" the United States in the future.

You can obtain an O-2 visa if you are employed in a support role by an O-1 visa holder and this person wants you to continue working for him/her in the United States. You must be coming to the United States to assist in your employer's performance and must be an integral part of that performance, by way of your critical skills or a longstanding work relationship. Therefore, for example, an internationally-acclaimed theater director coming to direct a Broadway performance may choose to use his/her own lighting technicians, if they have been integrally involved with the production abroad, or a world famous film director may choose to bring his/her first camera operator to the United States to film part of a current production.

If you do not have "extraordinary ability," yet are a world class performing artist/entertainer, you are eligible for a P-1 nonimmigrant visa to perform in the United States. You are eligible if you or your group have international recognition. If you are part of a group, 75 percent of the members must have been together for at least one year in order to qualify for P-1 visas. This rule does not apply if you are coming to join a circus of national or international repute, or are traveling with such a circus.

Performing artists and entertainers from countries that are involved in a reciprocal cultural exchange program with the United States can obtain P-2 visas to perform there. You are eligible if you are an individual performer, or part of a group (including integral people, such as sign-language translators), participating in a cultural exchange performance. Culturally-unique performance artists are eligible for P-3 visas that will enable them to enter the United States and perform there. Traditional or ethnic music or dancing ensembles and other unique performers qualify in this category.

As in the case of O visas, the INS will only approve your P visa if your United States petitioner has consulted with the relevant labor unions whose members could be adversely affected by your entry into the country.

If you want to get a green card, it will be relatively simple for those who have O-1 visas, because it is likely that you will qualify as a person of extraordinary ability in the arts. This entitles you to a first preference, employment-linked immigrant visa reserved for "priority workers." You do not need a job offer in the United States, but must continue to use your extraordinary artistic talents in such as way that these will benefit the United States in the future. You will not need to obtain a labor certification before applying for a first preference immigrant visa.

Nonperforming artists with exceptional ability may qualify for a labor certification waiver under Schedule A, Group II, reserved for people of exceptional ability in the arts or sciences. You must be famous in at least two countries and must be able to prove your exceptional ability in the form of books, newspaper articles, awards, or any other evidence that demonstrates your international fame. You will qualify for a second preference immigrant visa in the subcategory reserved for people of exceptional ability in the arts. Although second preference visa applicants need a labor certification before they can apply, you will probably be eligible for a waiver if you can prove your achievements. Performing artists who qualify for second preference visas will have to obtain labor certification first. However, if you qualify as a performing artist with exceptional ability you will be subject to special handling in the labor certification process. This means that your employer will be able to employ you if he/she can show that you have as much or more experience than a United States applicant. In almost all other cases, a foreigner cannot be considered for a job if an American applicant fulfills the minimum requirements for the job and is otherwise suitable.

All other people in the arts will have to apply for a third preference visa, reserved for those with bachelor's degrees as well as for skilled and unskilled workers. You will need to get labor certification before you can petition for this visa.

For details of the application procedure, refer to the appropriate sections alphabetically listed in Chapter 5 (nonimmigrant visas), and listed in preference order in Chapter 9 (employment-related immigration).

THE MEDICAL PROFESSIONS

Within the medical profession, certain skills are in critically high demand, whereas others, although they may be in demand, are subject to extremely rigid professional control. Both nurses and physical therapists are in high demand in the United States and the government is trying to attract foreigners in these professions to the country. This is borne out by immigration laws that make it extremely easy for qualified staff in these professions to gain access to their green cards.

Doctors, on the other hand, fall into a category unto themselves, because the AMA exercises tight control over the influx of foreign medical doctors into the United States. The entire medical system in the United States has increasingly been coming under fire, so the conditions affecting the entry of foreign doctors into the country could well change in the future. The Immigration Act of 1990 made one conciliatory measure towards foreign doctors by permitting them to obtain H-1B visas, previously not possible, if they fulfill certain requirements that you will read about further on.

Nurses

The Immigration Nursing Relief Act of 1989, which became effective in September 1990, created a special nonimmigrant visa category for foreign nurses. This H-1A category was aimed at making it easier for foreign nurses to obtain visas to work in the United States and to get their green cards.

H-1A visas are available to professional foreign nurses working in hospitals and other medical institutions or organizations. You or your employer may only file an H-1A visa petition after your employer organization has attested to the Department of Labor (DOL) that they will experience a "substantial disruption" if it does not employ foreign nurses; that neither the pay nor the working conditions of similarly employed American nurses will be affected by employing foreign nurses, and that it is taking "significant steps" to recruit and train nurses who are either United States citizens or legal permanent residents.

If you will be working for a nursing agency that will send you to various hospitals, both the agency and the hospitals that will be using your services or the services of other foreign nurses must make such attestations. If you have a job and are moving to another medical facility to relieve a shortage of staff, your new employer will most likely obtain a waiver from submitting another attestation on your behalf.

The Immigration Nursing Relief Act of 1989 also made it possible for licensed professional nurses who had been employed in the United States in H-1 status for three years, at the date of enactment, to adjust their status to permanent residence.

This adjustment of status was not extended to immediate family members who were not already in the United States.

Professional, licensed nurses, as well as physical therapists, are able to obtain their green cards without prior labor certification. Both these professions have been singled out by the DOL as being in short supply in the United States and have been put on what is called the Schedule A list, which precertifies these occupations and makes those with the appropriate skills eligible for labor certification waivers. There are three groups on the Schedule A list and Group I consists of these medical support professions.

If you are a nurse, you do need to have a state license and must either be a foreign graduate of a United States or Canadian nursing school, or must have passed your CGFNS (Commission on Graduates of Foreign Nursing Schools) examinations. This examination is given biannually in many countries around the world. You can get information about this by writing to the Commission on Graduates of Foreign Nursing Schools, 3600 Market Street, Suite 400, Philadelphia, PA 19104-2651, USA, or by calling (215) 349-8767.

Physical Therapists

If you are a physical therapist, you do not need a state license to obtain a waiver, but your professional training and skills must be at a level that would enable you to qualify for this license.

Doctors

If you are a foreign medical doctor, you have two nonimmigrant options open to you. You can either enter the United States on an H-1B visa or on a J-1 visa. You are eligible for an H-1B visa if you are coming to the country at the invitation of a public or private educational or research institute to conduct research, teach, or both. You will not be able to do clinical work, other than in the course of your research or teaching, however. You *will* be able to work in the United States on an H-1B visa if you have passed the Federation Licensing Examination (FLEX), administered by the Federation of State Medical Boards of the United States; Parts I, II, and III of the National Board of Medical Examiners (NBME), or Steps 1, 2, and 3 of the U.S. Medical Licensing Examination (USMLE). Regulations are in the process of changing, and by 1995 USMLE will be the only exam that will be available to foreign doctors (including Canadian doctors) wishing to work in the U.S. In addition, you must be proficient in oral and written English or a graduate of a medical school (in the United States or abroad) that is accredited by the Department of Education.

The Chief of Operations of the INS has noted that allowing foreign doctors to do clinical work on H-1B visas is a matter of dispute and the INS may take an adverse position on granting visa petitions for this purpose. He noted that the INS would see what happened on appeal. Therefore, foreign doctors coming to the United States other than at the invitations of accredited schools or institutions, should be prepared to hire immigration lawyers, and, possibly, be ready for litigation of their cases.

You will be eligible for a J-1 visa if you are a bona fide medical graduate coming to the United States on a temporary basis to teach, instruct, lecture, study, observe, conduct research, consult, demonstrate your skills, or receive training. You will not get a J-1 visa unless you have passed the Foreign Medical Graduates Visa Qualifying Examination, or graduated from a United States or Canadian medical school. In addition, you have to have a written guarantee from your government that a job will be available once you have completed your postgraduate studies in the United States. You will probably be subject to a two-year foreign residence requirement before you can change to another visa status, either immigrant or nonimmigrant, and it will be extremely difficult to obtain a waiver of this requirement. Even if your government has given you a "no objection" letter, stating that it is prepared to relinquish you from your responsibilities of working in the medical field in your own country, you will find it difficult to get a waiver against this rule. The only possibility that you may get such a waiver will be if the United States government agency where you are working wants to employ you and the State Department supports this request; you can show that leaving the country for two years would cause exceptional hardship to your family—including the possibility that certain members of your family are United States citizens or permanent residents; or you cannot return to your last country of residence or country of nationality because you fear persecution. It is highly unlikely, however, that you will get a "no objection" letter from your government if you are a doctor. Therefore, when applying for a J-1 visa, you must realize that you will have to leave the United States for two years once your visa expires before returning as a permanent resident.

If you are a foreign medical graduate and came to the United States on either a J or H visa before January 10, 1978, you may be eligible to apply for special immigrant status. You must have had a state license and been living and practicing medicine there before that date, in order to be eligible. If you came to the United States on a J visa, you must also have a two-year foreign residency waiver.

If you want additional information regarding your educational credits to practice medicine in the United States, you may call the office of the Educational Commission for Foreign Medical Graduates at (215) 386-5900, or write to them at 3624 Market Street, Philadelphia, PA 19104.

ILLEGAL IMMIGRANTS

Every month hundreds, sometimes thousands, of people enter the United States illegally and, in most cases, simply melt into the urban landscape. An article published in *The New York Times* on March, 18, 1992, claimed that Kennedy International Airport in New York had been flooded by foreigners entering the country with illegal passports bought on the black market, forged papers, or no documents at all. Many of these people, with no luggage other than the clothes they were wearing, knew no English other than two words: "political asylum." The immigration law states that all those claiming political asylum have to receive a court hearing. However, as this article points out, the backlog for these court cases in New York City is 14 months and there are only 190 beds in the INS detention center there. At the international airports at Los Angeles, Miami, Houston, and Washington D.C., the number of people entering the United States illegally may not be as high as in New York, but the picture is the same.

The scene across the country in San Diego is totally different, because, there, illegals do not fly in, they simply run across the border or try to slip through the border turnstiles, undetected. Green INS border patrol trucks park high up on the mountainside near San Ysidro, or near other border crossings, their powerful binoculars waiting to catch a glimpse of some of the hundreds of people who enter the United States illegally every day.

On the northern border, foreigners try to evade the INS by slipping through Canada with green cards that have not been used in years: many people got their green cards in the United States and then returned to their own countries, confident that they would be able to return to live and work whenever they chose. The law states that permanent residents may not be out of the country for longer than a year without obtaining a special reentry permit. Many people with green cards go to the United States once a year to keep their cards valid. Many have heard that this tactic does not always work and, instead, drive across the border from Canada.

No one knows for sure exactly how many people immigrate to the United States illegally every year. It is virtually impossible to gauge these figures. However, it has always been a political embarrassment to the United States that illegal immigration is vastly larger than legal immigration. It is obviously tempting for many foreigners to consider coming to the United States illegally and finding a job once they are there. This option is frequently exercised, as everyone is well aware.

The INS made an attempt to stem the flow of illegal immigration by introducing the Immigration Reform and Control Act of 1986 (IRCA), which tried to involve United States employers in indirectly policing the borders. It hoped to achieve this by making it a punishable offense for employers to employ, knowingly, anyone who was not legally authorized to work in the country. The rationale behind this was that if the demand for illegal workers dropped, the supply, too, would dwindle and people would rather stay home than illegally cross into the United States where their hopes of finding a job were slim.

The INS made it mandatory for all employers to complete an I-9 form for each employee hired on or after November 6, 1986. In order to complete this form, employers have to see two documentary forms of identity for each employee: one document to show identity and the other, to show work authorization. This means that if you immigrate to the United States, you will have to have a green card, an employment authorization card, or a social security card that does not say "employment prohibited," as well as a driver's license, passport, or other personal identity document with your photograph on it, in order to be employed legally.

This law is still in effect and, although the INS is unable to check every employer in the country, anyone who employs a person illegally is liable for large fines—particularly if they are caught more than once. However, not all employers know or care about employer sanctions, as this aspect of IRCA is known. Therefore, theoretically, it is possible that you will find a person willing to employ you in spite of not having a green card. The difficult part may come later, when you decide that you want to be legal and you need your employer to sponsor you.

The other aspects of IRCA include the antidiscrimination clause, which makes it an offense to discriminate against employees on the basis of their immigrant status or national origin. This is the flip side of employer sanctions, because many employers, in an attempt to uphold employer sanctions, simply refuse to consider anyone who looks or sounds foreign and who, they erroneously assume, is not authorized to work in the United States. Thus, employers are really the ones who bear the brunt of IRCA, although, as a prospective employee in the United States, you should know that you, too, will need to fulfill your part of the deal by proving to your employer that you are legally entitled to work there.

There is one important thing to remember. Once you enter the United States and start working there, you are liable to pay tax on your income. In some circumstances, you may even have to pay tax on your worldwide income. The issues of taxation and other checks and balances on your status as an immigrant will be discussed in the following chapter.

CHAPTER
12

Walking the Tightrope: Checks and Balances on Immigration

Once you have your green card and are legally entitled to permanent residence in the United States, you will be under the same obligations as all other Americans, and have the same civic rights, with the exception of the right to vote and the right to hold public office. This means, among other things, that you will have to pay taxes, like everyone else, and that, if you are a male age eighteen or older, you will have to register for the draft. Immigration lawyers often fail to tell their clients about the draft registration requirement. This has caused problems in the past for young adult male immigrants who apply for naturalization. The INS is likely to delay your naturalization procedure if you have not complied with all the requirements of the law and your United States citizenship may be put on hold until you have met all your civic obligations as a permanent resident.

There is, however, one very important distinction between your rights as a permanent resident and your rights as a United States citizen. If you are convicted of a serious crime, or even attempt to commit such a crime, or if you abandon your United States residence for a year or more, you may forfeit your right to permanent residence. Thus, your green card allows you unconditional permanent residence but only if you maintain the laws of the country and the requirements of your status. The freedom that the laws of the United States afford you, does not include the freedom to transgress these laws and remain in the country.

This chapter discusses the checks and balances on immigration and acts as a warning to prospective immigrants that exclusion and deportation procedures may be applied at any stage of immigration, even after you have obtained your green card.

TAXATION

Lawyers and accountants throughout the United States and in other parts of the world have been confused about the rules of immigration and tax that apply to foreigners who live in the United States for part of each year. Until recently, thousands of people from all over the world created a way of life based on their belief that, while living in the United States, they did not have to pay taxes on their foreign income.

However, the United States Tax Reform Act of 1984 put an end to this comfortable arrangement for many. The tax law, effective since 1985, stipulates that three categories of people are required to pay taxes on their worldwide income. These categories are:

- people with green cards, regardless of where they spend their time and how long they spend in the United States every year;
- people who fail the "substantial presence" test by living in the United States more than four months on average over a three-year period;
- people who live in the United States for more than six months in any given year.

The latter two categories apply to people who are in the United States on nonimmigrant visas and who, although nonresidents, are viewed by the IRS as residents for the purposes of taxation. According to recent discussions with State Department and Congressional sources in Washington D.C., it seems as if foreign investors will be able to make their investment in the United States before taking up permanent residence. This will enable wealthy investors to delay paying taxes on their worldwide income, thereby enticing more people to subscribe to this investor program. (According to these sources, very few people have applied for the 10,000 investor immigrant visas currently available each year.) This strategy is similar to allowing Hong Kong residents to apply for their green cards now but to take up residency in the United States in 2001.

The three-year "substantial presence" test is based on a mathematical formula that is calculated as follows. During the current—or third—year under consideration, every day that you live in the United States is counted as one full day. During the previous—or second—year, every day that you lived in the United States is counted as one-third of a day. During the year before that—or first year—every day you lived in the United States is counted as one-sixth of a day. If the total number of days calculated according to this formula adds up to 183 days or more, you have met the "substantial presence" test and will have to pay taxes on your worldwide income. For example, if you lived in the United States for six months two years ago, and you lived there for six months last year, you would—according to the "sub. antial presence" test—be considered to have lived there for a total of 90 days. Therefore, in order to avoid paying tax on your worldwide income during this fiscal year, you will have to leave the United States after three months. If, during the current fiscal year, you are in the United States for 30 days or less, you will not be subject to the substantial presence test, even if—in the current three-year period—you have been in the country for 183 days or longer.

Many wealthy foreigners used to live in the United States for up to six months a year and travel the rest of the time, to avoid paying taxes. However, because of the heavy tax burdens imposed by the 1985 law, they now have to curtail their visits and keep moving, in some cases, between three and four countries a year. These people are referred to as "tax gypsies." Some may consider their lives as glamorous; however, they have no choice, if they wish to avoid paying hefty taxes on even heftier incomes.

Certain people are exempt from this ruling. They are foreigners working in government-related projects, teachers or trainees, students, and professional athletes who are visiting the United States temporarily to compete in charitable sporting events.

If you spend a certain number of days in the United States, these days will not be counted in calculating the "substantial presence" test if you are exempt from this rule, in transit, medically unfit to travel, or en route from Canada or Mexico to a job. In addition, even if you meet the substantial presence test, you will not be taxed in the current year if you have been in the United States for less than 183 days and have maintained a home abroad during this period and you have a "closer connection" to your foreign home than you do to the United States. The IRS will be looking at things like your business interests, property investments, family connections, community involvement, and other factors that suggest you are closely connected to a place when determining whether or not you are, indeed, closer to your "tax home" abroad than your temporary home in the United States.

The technical rules relating to tax treaties between the United States and various foreign countries may alter the picture in certain cases, and you will have to get clarification from lawyers or other corporate advisers in these rule of thumb cases. The current situation is that if you maintain dual residency in the United States and another country, you can apply to the IRS for tax exemption if your foreign country of residence has a tax treaty with the United States that will allow such an exemption. You must, in this situation, submit Form 1040NR to the IRS. If you are a permanent resident of the United States, you may have problems from the INS if they decide to query the legitimacy of your status. For example, if you have a green card and live abroad, you might have problems one day if the INS questions you about your tax liabilities when you enter the country.

The IRS routinely contacts employers of temporary foreign workers in the United States in order to outline their tax liabilities. This is now common practice in almost every case, whereas in the past this was done on a random basis.

The IRS published a pamphlet entitled *Tax Obligations of Legalized Aliens* which explains the tax obligations of those who obtained amnesty under the legalization program of the Immigration Reform and Control Act of 1986 (IRCA). Legalized aliens are liable for tax returns for the years in which they lived and worked in the United States illegally—even if they filed under a different name each year.

This is not a tax guide and you should realize that each situation can be argued on its own merits if there are any doubts about your liability in terms of the above information. You would do well to consult an immigration lawyer who has experience in dealing with the IRS before committing yourself to a life-style that could prove more costly than it's worth.

SELECTIVE SERVICE AND OTHER REQUIREMENTS

If there is a war or national emergency in the country, you cannot claim to be exempt from consideration for the armed services because you are not a citizen. All immigrants are liable for draft selection and, if you are a male aged eighteen or older who does not register at the local Selective Service office where you live, you could expose yourself to legal penalties.

After the Vietnam War, there was a great deal of debate sparked by those who refused to bear arms for the United States in a war in which they did not believe. All those who evaded military service between August 4, 1961 and March 28, 1973 were granted unconditional presidential pardon. However, in 1980, a presidential proclamation reinstated Selective Service registration and this applies both to citizens as well as male immigrants.

Failing to register for Selective Service has greater bearing on your ability to become naturalized than on your eligibility to maintain permanent resident status. However, you should know that there are many obligations for United States permanent residents and this is one of them.

LOSING OR GIVING UP PERMANENT RESIDENCE

Your permanent residence—even if there are no conditional clauses imposed either by your marriage or investor status—does not guarantee your permanency in the United States. If you obtained your green card by managing to conceal details about yourself that would have rendered you excludable, and if these details are ever revealed, your green card will be revoked and you will be deported from the country.

If you marry a United States citizen and divorce your spouse before the two-year conditional period of your residency has expired, you will lose your permanent resident status, through your inability to file a joint petition to remove your conditional status. You may be able to obtain a waiver from filing a joint petition if you can show that you were the victim of violence or abuse by your spouse, or that you entered into your marriage in good faith but that it broke up because of irreconcilable differences. You will also lose your claim to permanent residence if the INS can show that you entered into the marriage for the purposes of circumventing the immigration system, either by paying your spouse or a third party, or by setting up a home and pretending to be living in conjugal bliss, when, in fact, this was simply a front to get a green card.

Even if your marriage is a bona fide one, your permanent residence will be revoked unless you and your spouse file a joint petition for the removal of your conditional status, or unless you file an application for a waiver against filing a joint petition.

Any fraudulent attempt to obtain immigration will result in your green card being revoked and possible deportation. This extends to the conditional permanent resident status also granted to investors. If, during the two-year period after entering the United States as a resident, your business venture is no longer viable, or if it is shown that you used your money to set up a sham investment in order to get a green card, the INS will revoke your status and begin deportation proceedings against you. You will have to petition for the removal of your two-year conditional status within the time frame allowed. Failure to do this could, also, lead to the loss of your permanent resident status.

If you have a green card but do not take up permanent residence in the United States, you are likely to lose your permanent resident status if you are caught. Many people with green cards live abroad and come to the United States once a year to maintain this status. The law states that a permanent resident may not be out of the United States for more than one year without obtaining permission from the INS. This was not meant to offer foreigners the chance to keep their green cards, while, in fact, living elsewhere. It was meant, rather, for foreigners living in the United States, who, because of their work or other personal commitments, spend a great deal of time out of the country. Although thousands of people get away with living abroad and keeping their green cards, if you are caught, you must not be surprised if an INS official confiscates your green card for good. Any fraudulent procedure will result in a loss of your permanent residence and will make it very difficult, if not impossible, for you to return to the United States. If you are readmitted into the country, it will be after an extremely long wait.

To sum up, there are two ways of losing your permanent residence: one is by letting your green card lapse through either your lack of commitment to living in the United States or through your failure to comply with bureaucratic requirements; the other is by committing a fraudulent or criminal act that renders you excludable.

DEPORTATION AND EXCLUSION

When you apply for a visa abroad, the United States consul will usually check your records to see if you are admissible into the country. Even if you do get a visa to enter the country, when you arrive at the port of entry, immigration officials will conduct another check. In both instances, they will be determining whether or not there are any grounds for excluding you from entering the United States. According to immigration law, there are nine areas of exclusion.

- **Health related:** If you have a communicable disease that is of public health significance, you can be found inadmissible. You can also be excluded on the grounds of a physical or mental disorder that would pose a threat to society, or if you are a drug abuser or addict.

- **Criminal and related grounds:** If you have been convicted of, or admit to, crimes involving moral turpitude or drugs, you are considered inadmissible into the United States. If you have been involved in prostitution, you will not be granted a visa within ten years of this involvement. You may not enter the country for this or any other unlawful commercial vice. If you have been convicted of two or more offenses and received a sentence of five years or longer, you will be excluded from the country.

- **Security and related grounds:** You will not be admitted into the country if the United States consul or the Attorney General knows or believes that your motivation is to engage in espionage, or sabotage, or to become involved in any other activities that would pose a threat to the safety and security of the United States. Neither will you be admitted if your entry into the country would pose foreign policy problems for the United States. If you are the member of any totalitarian or Communist party, you will not be granted an immigrant visa, though you will be able to enter as a nonimmigrant. Anyone who belonged to the Nazi party is excludable.

- **Public charge:** If you are likely to become a public charge, you will not be granted a visa to enter the United States.

- **Labor certification and qualifications:** You will be excludable from the country if you try to enter for the purpose of working in a skilled or unskilled job without having an approved labor certification.

- **Illegal entrants and immigration violators:** If you try to enter the country within a year of being previously excluded and deported, you will not succeed. You will also be excluded if you were deported from the country and try to re-enter within five years. If you are a convicted felon, you may not enter the United States for 20 years from the time you committed your crime. If you committed visa fraud or used fraudulent documents of any kind to try to enter the United States, you will be excludable for a ten-year-period after you were last caught. Stowaways are excluded, as are those people who try to smuggle illegal aliens across the border. If you are a legal permanent resident who tried to help your family members to join you in the United States, you will be eligible for a waiver against deportation on humanitarian grounds.

- **No valid documents:** If you do not have valid documents to enter the country and you are neither a refugee nor asylee, you will not be admitted. Your passport must be valid for at least six months beyond the date of expiration of your United States visa.

- **Those ineligible for citizenship/draft evaders:** You are excludable from the United States if you are permanently ineligible to become a citizen and also if you evaded the United States draft.

- **Miscellaneous:** Practicing polygamists, foreigners accompanying others who have been ordered to leave the country, and foreigners who transgress child custody laws are also excludable.

According to the law, you are entitled to know why your visa is denied. You are also entitled to have your name removed from a computerized list of inadmissible people if you can prove that the grounds of exclusion previously ascribed to you are no longer valid.

Recent changes to the law have made it easier to get a waiver of excludability, particularly if family unity is threatened and a family would suffer undue hardship by the deportation of one of its members. For example, if you smuggled members of your family into the country and you, yourself, have a green card, you will be able to obtain a waiver of excludability or a stay of deportation. Also, if you have a communicable disease, there is a strong likelihood that you will get a waiver of excludability if you are the spouse, parent, or unmarried minor child of a United States citizen or permanent resident. This is in the name of family unity.

If you have a drug conviction but this involved 30 grams or less of marijuana for personal use, you will be able to get a waiver if this crime took place more than 15 years before you enter the United States. You must also be able to show that you have been rehabilitated.

There are certain crimes for which no waivers are available. If you are a convicted murderer or if you are guilty of torturing others, you will never be admissible into the United States. Nazis are not admissible and will be deported if, after becoming permanent residents, they are discovered. Crimes against the country are also considered in an extremely serious light. If you are a permanent resident who evaded or avoided the draft during a time of national emergency or war by departing from the United States and remaining outside the country, you will not be able to return to live in the United States. Anyone who participates in politically subversive activities or in any activities that threaten the security of the country, will, also, have their green cards revoked.

In order to apply for a waiver of excludability, or to apply for permission to return to the United States after an absence of a year or more (in the case of a permanent resident who has not given up his/her home in the United States), you must submit Form I-724, plus a filing fee of $90 to the same office of the INS where you filed your application for a green card. You should also include as much evidence in support of your waiver application as possible. This should include personal references, medical and professional reports, personal affidavits, family details, and whatever other documents you can put together to counter the INS's argument for deportation.

If you are deported from the United States, you are prevented by law from returning for five years. If you wish to reenter the country, you must submit Form I-724 plus a filing fee of $90 to the INS, together with any information that could support your request. This "application for permission to reapply for admission into the United States after deportation or removal" is unlikely to be granted, because no one is deported or removed from the country without good cause. You should not attempt this procedure without consulting an immigration lawyer.

Generally, you will be at an advantage in exclusion and deportation proceedings if:

- you have close family ties within the United States who are citizens or permanent residents;
- you have lived in the United States for at least seven years;
- you have people who will vouch for your sound character and, if previously convicted of a crime, proven rehabilitation;
- you can show that your family will incur hardship if you are deported;
- you have worked in the United States and have property and/or business interests there.

Conversely, the following negative factors could prevent you from maintaining permanent residence in the United States, once exclusion and deportation proceedings against you have begun:

- the grounds of exclusion are those that are unlikely to be waived;
- you have violated the terms of your immigrant visa by making fraudulent representations;
- you have a criminal record;
- there is evidence against you of bad character or that you are generally undesirable.

All these factors are important if you plan to become a United States citizen, because the INS will not grant you naturalization unless you have upheld all the legal and civil requirements that are part of your obligation of being a permanent United States resident. The next part of this book tells you all about naturalization and how to become a citizen of the United States.

PART THREE

NATURALIZATION AND CITIZENSHIP

Basic Requirements for Citizenship

In Parts One and Two of this book, you read about excludability. This exists at all stages of the immigration process, because the INS uses it to sift out undesirable people. For many, the last stage on the road to permanent residence is becoming a naturalized United States citizen and this, too, is subject to strict controls. This chapter examines the basic requirements for citizenship and discusses ways of meeting these requirements. First, however, it outlines the benefits of citizenship.

Naturalization means that you acquire the nationality of the United States by a process other than birthright. Once naturalization has been conferred upon you, you receive United States citizenship and are eligible for the same rights as all other citizens (except the public office of president of the country!).

Once you are a United States citizen, you become eligible to sponsor your parents, spouse, and unmarried, minor children as immediate relative immigrants, provided that you, yourself, are older than age twenty-one. You can confer citizenship on your child, whether you are already a citizen and your child was born abroad, or you become naturalized and your child is either a permanent resident of the United States, or born after your naturalization. If you are a citizen and your child is born abroad, this child is said to get citizenship by "acquisition." If you are a naturalized American and your child is a legal permanent resident, you can apply for citizenship for this child by what is known as "derivation." There are various rules governing citizenship by derivation that are all determined by the date on which your child was born. Given that immigration laws have changed several times during the past 50 years, the law that was effective at the time your child was born governs the rules that apply, even now. (The INS chart with the various dates and requirements for naturalization appears in Appendix 4, page 254.) As the law currently stands, you can only obtain citizenship by derivation if both your parents are naturalized and you are a legal permanent resident of the United States. If, for example, your mother is a United States citizen and your father is a legal permanent resident, you can only obtain derivative citizenship status if your father becomes naturalized and you are under the age of eighteen and not married.

If you are a naturalized United States citizen and you adopt a child, you can apply for citizenship on behalf of your child if he/she is under the age of fourteen and is already in your custody at the time you apply.

It is playfully suggested that citizenship allows you to break the rules without the threat of deportation. However, as you will now read, the requirements for citizenship make it unlikely that people of "bad moral character" will be granted naturalization. The INS attempts to exclude those of dubious character from becoming citizens and, therefore, reduces the risk of this happening! But, as you will read in Chapter 17, even after you become naturalized, you face the risk of losing citizenship by denaturalization or expatriation if the INS finds that your application for naturalization was based on ineligible grounds.

The fundamental requirement for naturalization is that you are a legal, permanent resident of the United States. You must live there for at least five years preceding your application for naturalization and be physically present in the country for at least half of this time. If your permanent residence was based on marriage to a United States citizen, you need only live there for three years, and be physically present in the country for one-and-a-half years.

If you travel out of the United States for one year or longer, you will not be able to count this time abroad towards your time credit for naturalization and will have to start counting over when you return. If you are away for six months or less, this will not affect your accrued time, however. In some circumstances, it may be necessary for you to be out of the United States after obtaining your green card—for example, if you are transferred to work abroad for one year at a foreign branch of your United States company. If this is the case, you can submit Form I-131—an Application for a Travel Document— and a filing fee of $65 to the INS, explaining your need to be out of the country for a lengthy period. In this way, you will not interrupt your residency requirement for citizenship.

If you have been a permanent resident in the United States for at least one year, and you get a job abroad with an American company that is engaged in the development of foreign trade and commerce, you may also be able to get permission to count your years abroad towards your citizenship residency requirement. You will have to submit Form N-470—Application to Preserve Residence for Naturalization Purposes—plus a filing fee of $90 to the INS, and provide details of your circumstances and documentary evidence to support your claim. You can submit this form either before you leave the United States or after your employment begins, but it must be done before you have been away from the United States for one full year.

When you file your naturalization application, you must have been a resident in the same state for a minimum of three months. Consider, for example, the following scenario. You move to California and, after one month, apply for naturalization. You cannot find a job there, so decide to return East a month after that. You will not have fulfilled the minimum three-month requirement and will, therefore, have to reapply for naturalization—and make sure that you remain "in state status" for at least three months.

You must be able to prove that you have been living in the United States continuously from the date you apply for naturalization until the date that you receive United States citizenship and must indicate your intention to reside there permanently. Many people come to the United States with the intention of obtaining an American passport, and then, living wherever they please in the world. They view citizenship simply as a means of obtaining a travel document that will not restrict them—as some foreign passports might do or might have done in the past. If you choose to live abroad within a five-year period after you become a citizen, the INS may presume that your stated intention to live permanently in the United States was false. If you are ever questioned about this, you should be able to submit rebutting proof, or you may face the risk of having your naturalization revoked.

At some stage after you become an American citizen, you may well decide to live abroad, but the law states that you must have the intention of living permanently in the United States at the time you apply for naturalization.

You have to be what the INS terms "of good moral character" in order to obtain naturalization. The INS applies stringent rules to what it considers "good moral character." If you have been living in the United States legally, but earning a living from illegal gambling, for example, you can forget about your chances of citizenship. If you have spent an aggregate period of 188 days or more in any penal institution, or if you have ever been convicted of murder, your naturalization application will be denied. Any moral grounds of exclusion pertaining to your criminal activities or antisocial behaviors will also be grounds for denying citizenship. In addition, you must fulfill your civic duties to become a citizen. Draft evasion, tax evasion, failure to support your dependents, and similar civic/social offenses could bar you from being naturalized, as could your membership in subversive political groups.

The INS regards your behavior in the time period preceding your application for naturalization as critical. If it finds that you have failed in your civic, moral, or financial duties, it could withhold your citizenship. Information revealed in the naturalization process may even render you deportable. Therefore, it is essential for you to be consistent and truthful in your immigration applications along the way and to keep in mind that your INS records are on file. Therefore, any inconsistencies or misrepresentations could come back to haunt you later in the procedure and thwart your chances for obtaining your ultimate goal: United States citizenship.

Many people worry about the test that they have to take in order to be naturalized. The test itself will be discussed in Chapter 15, but the aim of this test, which is given orally by the INS official assigned to your case, is to ensure that you are literate and able to read, write, and speak English at the elementary level. You must also have a knowledge of United States history and government. If you are disabled and are unable to demonstrate this knowledge, you will be exempt from this test. You will also be exempt from the English requirement if you are above the age of fifty and have been a legal permanent resident of the United States for 20 years or more, or above the age of fifty-five and have been a legal permanent resident for 15 years or more. You will, however, have to take the history and government test, but may do so in your own language. If you already took a history and government test in the second stage of your amnesty application, you will not have to pass this test again.

The last requirement for citizenship is loyalty. If you have ever refused to bear arms for the United States, or been a deserter in wartime, or claimed you were exempt from service because you were not a citizen, you may be denied citizenship. You are not expected to renounce or give up your attachment to your country of birth, nor are you expected to say that you believe the United States is a perfect society. However, you must take the oath of allegiance to the United States, or a modified oath based on a deeply-held religious or moral belief regarding your willingness to bear arms, if this is the case.

If you ever served in the United States armed forces abroad, you may qualify for naturalization without first having to obtain permanent residence. There are detailed rules governing this benefit and if you fall into this category, you should contact the United States consulate in your city or nearest your home to investigate the possibility of becoming an American citizen.

If you are a Filipino and served in the United States armed forces in the Far East, the Philippine Army, the Philippine Scouts, or a recognized guerilla unit between September 1, 1939 and December 31, 1946, you are eligible for naturalization. It does not matter where you live now or whether or not you have a green card. You must apply for naturalization by April 30, 1993 in order to qualify for this benefit. If you do apply, you may be asked to sign a document renouncing your allegiance to all other countries. This could prove problematic if you have a business or other concerns in a country that requires your continued residence and/or citizenship in order for you to continue operating there.

If you are a United States citizen and join a Communist, anarchist, or subversive organization within five years of becoming naturalized, this constitutes proof of your disloyalty to the principles of the country and could lead to your citizenship being revoked.

In the next chapter, the application process is described in detail.

Procedures, Documents, and Forms

According to the law, the Attorney General of the United States has the exclusive authority to grant you naturalization and you may choose to take the oath of allegiance before the INS, the United States District Court, or any state court.

You may apply for naturalization up to three months before the end of your continuous residency requirement. In other words, if your permanent residence was based on marriage to a United States citizen, you may apply for naturalization two years and nine months after you obtained permanent residence. If your permanent residence was based on employment, family sponsorship, or any other method, you may apply four years and nine months after the date you obtained permanent residence.

You must submit Form N-400—Application for Naturalization—to the INS local office that has jurisdiction over your place of residence, together with a filing fee of $90. This form has been revised to include the G-325A biographic data sheet information. Therefore, the latter form is no longer required for the N-400 naturalization process, but it is used in other application procedures. If you served in the United States armed forces and are exempt from the permanent residence requirement, you can apply for naturalization at any INS office. It would make sense to apply at the office nearest the place you intend to live. If you are a Filipino veteran, you must send your application to the INS Regional Service Center in Lincoln, Nebraska.

Each INS office follows its own set of procedures and, in one area, you may have to hand in your application personally, whereas, in another, it may be acceptable to mail it. You should call your local INS office to make sure what its requirements are before submitting your forms. If you personally submit your application, you have the advantage of having an INS official review your application while you wait. If necessary, you can make any corrections or provide additional information before leaving. If you mail your application, the INS will mail it back to you if any changes or corrections need to be made. You will then have to resubmit it. This is a time-consuming procedure that will delay your naturalization. If the INS office nearest you has a backlog of cases, this could mean a delay of several months. If you submit your application personally, keep the application receipt and if you mail it, be sure it is by certified mail and request a return receipt. Proof of application could be very important in the future if your forms are mislaid.

When you submit Form N-400, you must also submit your fingerprints on Form FD-258. You can get this form from the INS local office where you are filing your application. The best place to have your fingerprints taken is at your local police station. You must fill in this form using black ink and it must be signed by you and by the person who takes your prints. You must answer all the questions, and, unlike in your visa application forms, you must leave all "not applicable" answers blank.

You must also submit three passport-size and passport-style photographs (in other words, not a three-quarter view, like the photographs you submitted for your green card).

Once you have applied for naturalization, you cannot withdraw this application, except with the consent of the Attorney General. If he does not agree, and if you do not follow through on your application—in other words, if you fail to appear at your interview and test—you will not be granted naturalization. However, there are other circumstances in which naturalization may be denied, such as if the INS discovers that the basis of your green card was fraudulent or if you have participated in subversive activities. If, for any reason, your naturalization application is denied, the INS will inform you of your legal options of appeal. In most cases, you will be able to request a review in a United States District Court. However, as with all appeals in the immigration process, the complex legal nature of this procedure makes it necessary to have the services of an experienced immigration lawyer. In the case of a naturalization denial, your green card could be at stake too, unless you are at fault because you failed your exam or did not live in the United States for the required period of time before applying.

If you fail your naturalization examination, you will have the opportunity to take it again. Once you do pass your examination, and your application is ultimately approved, you are still not a naturalized citizen. This involves taking an oath of allegiance and being sworn in by a judge or an INS official.

The next chapter discusses the test you are required to take as part of the naturalization procedure.

CHAPTER
15

The Test

After you submit your application for naturalization, you will have to wait several months until the INS processes this application and calls you for an interview. At this interview, you will be given a test on your knowledge of American history and government and you will be expected to answer approximately 20 questions. These questions will all be taken from a booklet that has been developed for immigrants by the INS. This booklet is called the *Guide to Naturalization Benefits* and you can obtain it from the INS office nearest you or by writing to the Superintendent of Documents, United States Government Printing Office, Washington, D.C. 20402.

About 100 possible questions and answers are given in this booklet and you must know all of them. The INS official who tests you will choose your test questions from this list. You will need to know details about the United States Congress—how it works, how representatives are chosen, who these representatives are in your state and/or area, how many delegates there are in the Senate and the House of Representatives, and other details about this. You will also need to know the names of various presidents of the United States, some details about the American Civil War, dates, names, and places—in other words, some basic historical facts about the country.

You do not have to write anything at this test. It is administered orally by the INS official who conducts your interview.

The INS official may also ask you questions to clarify your eligibility. When you submit your application for naturalization, the INS will conduct an investigation to ensure that you are eligible. If it uncovers any inconsistencies from the information you provided to obtain your green card, or if you have committed a crime or been involved in subversive behavior in the five (or three) years preceding your application, these will be discussed at your interview. The objective of this interview is to make sure that you are acceptable as a citizen of the United States! Some INS offices first give you the test, then investigate your background and biographic details. Where this is the case, you will be called for another interview if any problems are uncovered.

If your naturalization application is denied, you can appeal this decision in a judicial review. The INS will provide you with information pertaining to your legal rights of recourse if it denies your naturalization application.

The next chapter discusses dual citizenship and the swearing-in ceremony.

CHAPTER
16

Dual Citizenship and Swearing In

If you come from a country where you are permitted to hold dual citizenship, and you become a naturalized American, you may retain the passports of both countries. The United States government does not encourage this, because it could result in split loyalties, but it will not prevent you from holding dual citizenship if you are eligible. If, on the other hand, you come from a country where dual citizenship is not permitted, you will have to renounce your former passport, in accordance with the laws of your country of birth or previous residence. This renouncing of your previous citizenship takes place at your swearing-in ceremony. The ceremony takes place before a district court judge or at the INS offices. You are sworn-in as a citizen of the United States by taking an oath of allegiance to the United States Constitution and renouncing other citizenship. As discussed, this will not be necessary if your previous country permits dual citizenship.

The swearing-in ceremony usually takes place with a large group of people in an atmosphere of celebration. After this ceremony, you will receive your Naturalization Certificate, confirming your United States citizenship. If you are married and both you and your spouse become naturalized, your children age eighteen and under will automatically become citizens at the same time as you do. If you are married and only you or your spouse becomes naturalized, your children age eighteen and under will *not* receive automatic derivative citizenship. If your children are eligible for citizenship and you wish them to receive Certificates of Citizenship at the naturalization ceremony, you must request this on your naturalization application.

If you become naturalized abroad, which might be the case if you are a veteran of the United States armed services, and you meet all the requirements for naturalization, as discussed in Chapter 12, you may keep dual citizenship if your country of residence does not object to this.

The following chapter deals with the loss of United States citizenship, either by having it revoked or by voluntarily giving it up.

147

Losing or Giving Up
Citizenship

You may lose your United States citizenship in two ways. One is by *denaturalization*, which means you have your naturalization revoked. The other is by *expatriation*, which means that you do something with the intention of giving up your United States citizenship.

The basis of having your citizenship revoked is that you withheld certain information from the INS that would have made you excludable, you knowingly misrepresented your case when you applied for naturalization, or you obtained naturalization—or your green card before that—using illegal documents. If any of these factors apply to you and the INS discovers this, it will bring a case against you in either a state or federal court. The INS cannot revoke your naturalization without a court action. If the court upholds the INS's claim against you, you will be given 60 days to show cause why your denaturalization should not take place.

The kinds of behavior that could lead to denaturalization are refusing to testify before a Congressional committee about your alleged subversive activities, if these activities occur within ten years of your naturalization and you are convicted of contempt for this refusal. Other grounds would be membership in or affiliation with an organization that is considered to threaten the security of the United States, establishing your lack of attachment to the country, or leaving the United States within a year of naturalization to settle in another country.

If you used fraudulent papers to gain entry into the United States, or misrepresented yourself in any other way to obtain a green card and citizenship, you could be denaturalized if this is ever discovered. The INS uses a term it calls "material misrepresentation" to determine whether or not a person is subject to denaturalization. It establishes whether or not you have materially misrepresented yourself by determining whether or not your action influenced the decision of the INS. For example, if you withhold certain information in order not to jeopardize your chances of getting a green card, this will obviously influence the INS's decision. If this is ever discovered, you will be subject to denaturalization.

Unfortunately, your illegal entry into the United States or misrepresentation will affect all those who gained derivative citizenship through you. If you are denaturalized, your spouse and/or children will lose their citizenship as well, if they obtained their citizenship through you.

Denaturalization, therefore, could apply to former legal permanent residents of the United States who become naturalized citizens as well as to those former legal permanent residents who either entered the country illegally or who withheld information or misrepresented themselves in any other way in order to obtain legal residence.

Both naturalized Americans and American citizens by birth can have their citizenship removed by expatriation. According to the law, your citizenship will be removed by expatriation if you voluntarily do any of the following:

- become the citizen of another country when you are age eighteen or older;
- join the armed forces of a foreign country and serve as a commissioned or noncommissioned officer;
- fight against the United States in the service of an enemy country;
- work in any capacity for a foreign government;
- formally renounce your citizenship in a written statement on a Department of State form before a diplomatic or consular officer;
- make a formal, written renunciation of your citizenship when the United States is at war;
- engage in any behavior that constitutes treason, such as attempting an armed overthrow of the United States government.

The United States government must be able to prove its case against you in order to revoke your citizenship, and you will have the opportunity to rebut any accusations against you. In addition, the government must be able to prove that not only did you voluntarily engage in what it terms "expatriating acts," but that you also intended to give up your United States citizenship. If you are naturalized in a foreign country and continue to show allegiance to that country—and maintain dual citizenship—it could be presumed that you are engaging in expatriating behavior. But this is not the case, neither would it be the case if you accepted a nonpolicy level job with a foreign government.

However, if you formally renounced your citizenship before a State Department official and took a policy level job in a foreign government, this would constitute expatriating behavior and result in your loss of citizenship. Being convicted of treason and behaving in such a way that would make it clear that your actions were inconsistent with the retention of United States citizenship would have the same result.

If you are issued a certificate of loss of nationality, you have one year to appeal this decision. If your citizenship is revoked, restricted, or denied, or if your passport is invalidated, you have 60 days in which to appeal. In all cases, your appeal must be made to the Board of Appellate Review, a division of the Department of State.

In Part Four, Canadian immigration and the ways of qualifying for entry into Canada are discussed.

PART FOUR

CANADIAN IMMIGRATION

An Overview of Immigration Policies and Procedures

Many of you may have family members in Canada and may, therefore, be thinking of immigrating there instead of to the United States. United States immigration makes it relatively simple to enter as a nonimmigrant and decide if you like it there, then adjust your status to an immigrant. In most cases, you may only apply for Canadian immigration from outside Canada, but Canadian immigration law does permit adjustment of status from visitor to permanent residence if you are the spouse or other close relative of a Canadian citizen.

Because adjustment of status is limited to a relatively small segment of the immigrant population, this section of the book concentrates on getting an immigrant visa from outside Canada. All visitors must have a visa to enter Canada unless they are exempt from this requirement by special regulation. (For a list of countries whose nationals do *not* require visas to enter Canada as visitors, see Appendix 10, page 275.) If you need additional information on entering Canada as a visitor, you should contact your local Canadian consulate or embassy, or immigration office.

If you compare Canadian immigration to American immigration, the first thing you will notice is that there are hundreds of thousands more immigrant visas available for immigrants to the United States than for immigrants to Canada. Currently, about 700,000 visas are available a year for American immigrants, while, on average, under 200,000 visas are available for Canadian immigrants. This number has fluctuated significantly over the years and, unlike United States immigration, Canadian immigration does not increase proportionately to the demand by immigrants, but either increases or decreases according to Canada's demand. This relates to the relatively low population levels in Canada compared to the population levels in the United States. Because of Canada's relatively small population, it is essential to Canadians that they are not pushed out of jobs or replaced in the job market by foreigners. Therefore, recessionary conditions within the country have as much to do with immigration policy as any other immigration-related factors.

Apart from the immigration policy of the Canadian government, the Free Trade Agreement with the United States (see Chapter 6) resulted in a lot of opposition from Canadians who felt their jobs were being threatened and that America would have too much say in the economics of the country. Just as Canadian citizens are given easy access into the United States to conduct business and work there, in terms of the FTA, American citizens are given easy access into Canada for the same reasons. This will be discussed in detail in Chapter 23. You will see a similarity, however, in Canada's and America's immigration laws in that they both have special provisions for family members as well as for those without family connections who want to work and/or invest their money in North America. Each category of immigration will be discussed separately in the following chapters.

According to government policy, Canadian immigration depends on a person's ability to adapt to Canadian life and to settle successfully. Anyone is legally entitled to apply for immigration. In some cases, you will get a fairly good idea of your chances of success because you may be required to submit a preapplication questionnaire. However, this is not a necessary component of Canadian immigration and you are entitled to file an immigration application without first submitting a preapplication form. If the Canadian consulate requires you to fill out a preapplication, they will supply you with this questionnaire for no fee. Once Canadian foreign service officials have established that you are eligible to apply, they will send you a formal application and you must submit this with a processing fee. However, like American immigration, you have to be admissible into the country in order to get a Canadian immigration visa.

Many of you will have heard of the "point system" in Canadian immigration. This system, whereby you need a minimum number of 70 out of 100 points in order to be considered for immigration, is used by Canadian immigration officials to process your application. You score points for your age, your education, your ability to speak English and/or French (the two official languages of Canada), your family ties, your job, and your experience. If you are not a close family member of a Canadian citizen or permanent resident, it is possible but difficult to get an immigrant visa and you should, therefore, rely on work. But, even if you have a good education, can speak fluent English and French, and are in the desired age group, but have no experience in your field, you will not get a visa. The rationale behind this is: why allow you, a foreigner, to come to Canada to work in a field in which you have no experience, if an equally inexperienced Canadian can do the job instead?

There is also a list of between 700 and 1,000 occupations and/or professions that are in demand in Canada (these vary from relatively low demand to high demand). If your job is on this list, and your point score is the required 70 or above, you will probably be allowed to immigrate. If your job is not on the list, it does not matter if you have a firm job offer, you will not be allowed to immigrate. The only exception to this rule is if your offer of employment is validated by a Canada Employment Centre, which has a similar function to the U.S. Department of Labor in granting labor certifications. This occupation list constantly changes, according to the labor needs of the country, so it is necessary to find out from the Canadian consulate or embassy if your job is on the list at the time you apply for immigration.

Unlike the United States, where the latest immigration laws virtually eliminate unskilled workers from being able to immigrate, while they aid the most highly qualified workers into the country, Canadian immigration does not discriminate between jobs that require university education and those that require on-the-job training.

One fairly confusing aspect of Canadian immigration is that, because Canada is divided into several different provinces, in some cases the provincial governments have their own requirements for immigration, particularly where immigration is based on entrepreneurship or investment. These issues will be discussed as they arise in the context of the following chapters. Family immigration, work-related immigration (including investors), the point system, the application process, and the FTA will all be discussed in this part of the book.

A look at family-related immigration follows next.

CHAPTER
19

Family-Related Immigration

According to Canadian immigration law, family-related immigration is divided into two groups: "family-class" immigrants and "assisted-relative class" immigrants. Canadian law is more liberal than American law when it comes to defining who can sponsor or be sponsored or otherwise assisted to immigrate to Canada in the name of family unity. Even grandparents, cousins, uncles, and aunts are legally included in this definition, though, in practice, it is not that easy to immigrate unless you are part of the family class group. Further, no distinction is made between Canadian citizens and permanent residents when it comes to sponsoring relatives from abroad.

FAMILY CLASS

Any Canadian citizen or permanent resident who is at least eighteen years old and who lives in Canada can sponsor his/her foreign relatives for Canadian immigration and will be required to take financial responsibility for these relatives. Family class members include:

- spouses;
- fiancé/es;
- unmarried children (including children adopted before they turned thirteen);
- grandparents over age sixty;
- grandparents under age sixty if widowed or unable to work;
- parents of any age (If your child is a permanent resident, he/she must have been living in Canada in this status for at least three years in order to sponsor you.);
- parents over age sixty or under age sixty if widowed or unable to work (If this applies to you, your son/daughter can sponsor you even if he/she has been living in Canada as a permanent resident for less than three years.);
- Orphans under age eighteen who are unmarried and are the grandchildren, brothers, sisters, nephews, or nieces of their sponsor;

- Adoptive children under age thirteen;
- One other relative, if the person acting as sponsor has no other close family member either in or outside Canada who can be sponsored as a family-class member.

Financial Responsibility of Sponsors

If your relative sponsors you for Canadian immigration, he/she has to sign an Undertaking of Assistance, stating that he or she is willing to support you if you are unable to work and support yourself. This sponsor must undertake to provide you with accommodation and food and to pay for your health care and other needs and, generally, to prevent you from becoming a burden on Canadian taxpayers for a maximum of ten years. You will not be eligible for welfare or public assistance programs for up to ten years after immigrating to Canada, but you will be eligible for unemployment insurance, workers' compensation, and the Canada Pension Plan if you contribute to these through your job. Therefore, your sponsor must undertake to support you if necessary.

The Application Procedure

In order to sponsor you, your Canadian relative must obtain from the Canadian Immigration Centre a booklet providing details of what documentation will have to be filed by mail in order to prove that he or she is an eligible sponsor. This documentation includes proof of your relationship, passport or other proof of Canadian status, proof of income, and whatever else is required by the provincial government where this relative lives.

Because of the financial responsibility that your sponsor automatically has when he/she applies for an immigrant visa on your behalf, the Canadian Immigration Centre officials will check to see whether he/she is financially able to be a sponsor. Your relative's income has to be a fixed minimum level in order to be eligible to sponsor you, unless you are the spouse or child under the age of nineteen, without children of your own. This level obviously depends on the number of people being sponsored, the area where your sponsor lives (which is significant because the cost of living is higher in certain areas), and other factors that apply to his/her ability to meet all the expenses of supporting you and your family.

Once it is established that your relative qualifies to act as your sponsor, he/she must complete Form IMM 1344—Undertaking of Assistance for Family Class—on your behalf. This is a one-page form that must be filed in triplicate and signed by your sponsor and his/her spouse (if applicable). Your relative sponsor will also have to submit Form IMM 1283—an Evaluation of Guarantor's Financial Circumstances.

Once this has been done, the Canadian embassy or consulate where your immigrant application was filed will contact you for an interview. You will have to fill in Form IMM 8E, an application form to immigrate, and also pass both a medical and security check.

The Point System

Your acceptance as an immigrant *does not* depend on the point system and you will not be assessed according to this system.

Adjusting from Visitor to Immigrant Status

If you are the spouse of a Canadian citizen or permanent resident, you can enter Canada as a visitor (provided you have a visitor's visa if you need one), and apply for a family class immigrant visa from inside the country. However, this is only the case if you are generally admissible as an immigrant and a bona fide marriage has taken place.

This is the only group that will not have trouble adjusting their status in Canada. All other family class visitors will be judged on an individual basis if they apply for immigration from within Canada on compassionate or humanitarian grounds. Just as it is essential to keep in status in United States immigration law, it is also essential to keep in status in Canadian law, because, if you are not in status and apply for special consideration, it will probably be refused, unless the circumstances are extremely critical.

Appealing Denials

Unlike most other immigrant groups who have no recourse if their visas are denied, you, as a family class sponsored immigrant, do have access, through your sponsor, to the Immigration Appeal Division of the Immigration and Refugee Board (IRB).

Your sponsor can submit an appeal to this board after your immigrant visa has been denied by an immigration officer abroad on the grounds that you or your sponsor do not meet the criteria of eligibility. Usually, visas are denied to foreigners seeking to enter Canada as family class immigrants because not enough documentation was provided to prove their relationships with their sponsors or because their sponsors are found to be financially unable of supporting them.

Processing immigrant visa applications can take many months and some people have waited up to one year after their sponsors applied for them, only to be refused their visas by Canadian immigration officials. Once you have been refused your family class visa, your sponsor must submit a Notice of Appeal to the Immigration and Refugee Board, Appeal Division. After this appeal has been filed, your sponsor will be sent a summary of the reasons why his/her sponsorship was not granted and must prepare evidence to counter these reasons.

The IRB has the power to grant compassionate or humanitarian permission for you to enter Canada before your case comes up. It is possible, but unlikely, that your case will be reopened and reconsidered and your visa denied a second time for different reasons. And it is also possible that the Appeal Division of the IRB does not allow an appeal but, rather, upholds the decision of the

Canadian immigration official abroad who denied your visa originally. The more likely scenario is that your relative will have to consult a Canadian immigration lawyer who has dealt with similar cases and deal with the appeal using sound, professional guidance.

ASSISTED RELATIVES

The other group of people who are eligible to apply for family-related immigration consist of "assisted relatives." This group must be sponsored by their Canadian relatives and is comprised of the following:

• married children (including those who are now either divorced or widowed);

• siblings;

• parents or grandparents under the age of sixty who are not widowed and who are able to work (in order to be nominated in this category your child or grandchild in Canada must be a Canadian permanent resident who has lived in Canada in this status for less than three years);

• Nephews, nieces, uncles, aunts, or grandchildren.

These categories include spouses and children as well.

This group, also a legal part of Canadian immigration law, has a difficult time getting immigrant status and, in the opinion of certain Canadian immigration lawyers, has few, if any, advantages.

Financial Responsibility of Sponsors

As an assisted relative, you are entitled to the same government benefits as any other Canadian immigrant. Your sponsoring relative in Canada must still sign an Undertaking of Assistance agreeing to support you for up to five years if this is necessary.

Application Procedure

The application system for assisted relatives is similar to that for family class immigrants. The difference is that either you or your sponsor may initiate the application from outside or inside the country, respectively. You must go to the Canadian consulate or embassy nearest your home that has an immigration division and make an application as an independent immigrant (see Chapter 20). Simultaneously, if you like, your Canadian relative may sponsor you from inside Canada. But you must provide a list of all your close Canadian relatives at the time of applying as an independent immigrant if you are to be assessed as an assisted relative. If the Canadian immigration officer decides that you have a chance of adapting to the Canadian way of life and settling in with the help of your relative, you will get notification of this decision.

If your application is processed first, you must send this letter to your Canadian sponsor and ask him/her to go to the Canadian Immigration Centre nearest the place where he/she lives to submit the necessary application form on your behalf (if this has not been done already). This form, Form 1344 (the Declaration of Support), is also used to sponsor a family class relative. Your sponsor must take with him/her documentation to prove your relationship, plus financial statements that prove he/she is able to support you for five years. Taking as much documentation as possible is always advisable.

As is the case in sponsoring family class relatives, your sponsor as well as his/her spouse must sign all the forms submitted on your behalf.

You will have to submit Form IMM 8E, an immigration application form, and pass both a medical and security check before you will be able to get your visa.

The Point System

Your application as an assisted relative will be assessed according to the point system. However, because of your relationship with Canadian citizens or permanent residents, you will get bonus points. If you are the sibling or child of your sponsor, you will get a 15-point bonus and will therefore need only 55 additional points to bring this up to 70 out of a possible 100. If you are in any of the other assisted relative categories, you will get a bonus of 10 points and will, therefore, only need another 60 points.

The catch is that if your occupation is in low demand and you do not get any points for this you will not be able to immigrate. In order to have a chance at success, you must have at least one experience point and one point for occupational demand. However, as Chapter 21 on the point system will discuss, the immigration official at the Canadian consulate or embassy where you apply has the final say in whether or not your visa is granted, regardless of whether or not you accrue the necessary minimum of 70 points. If your sponsor has a family business and can prove he/she needs someone who can be completely trusted and/or possibly take over the business one day, your assisted relative visa has a greater chance of being approved.

Appealing Denials

You have no recourse if your visa is denied, other than to apply again. Unlike those in the family class group, assisted relatives cannot, through their sponsors, challenge the decision of the immigration officials at a court hearing. However, if there is a miscarriage of justice, a challenge to that miscarriage may be brought in the Federal Court.

In the next chapter, independent applicants, who encompass all those not eligible to apply for family-related immigration in either the family class or assisted relatives categories, are discussed.

Independent Immigrants

If you do not have any family members in Canada who can act as your sponsor for an immigrant visa, you can still apply on your own behalf to be an independent immigrant. You have to be at least eighteen years old and must be admissible into Canada, although this does not have to be established until your visa is ultimately approved. Therefore, literally anyone can apply to immigrate to Canada, whether you have family there or not.

You have to apply from outside Canada—either from your country of residence or another country where you are legally entitled to enter for your interview, should one be required.

For example, if you are from Hong Kong, you may apply for a Canadian visa from the Canadian consulate in New York, provided that you are legally entitled to be in the United States during this application period. The Canadian government official at the New York consulate will need to see proof of your legal status within the United States (or wherever else you are when you apply, if you are not applying from your country of birth or permanent residence.)

THE APPLICATION PROCEDURE

You must first pass the prescreening by the Canadian consulate, embassy, or immigration office abroad and they will then send you Form IMM 8E, the application form. The prescreening is very important because, if you do not provide enough information at this stage, you will never be given the chance to apply for immigration. The Canadian immigration officials must be able to judge, right from the start, that you have a case on which to base your application. Therefore, you must give as many details as possible in your preapplication form.

When you get your Form IMM 8E, you will have to complete it and submit it with supporting documentation. You will then be asked to come to an interview, where you will need to show your passport or other travel documents, birth certificate, police certificate, and other relevant documents requested by the immigration official dealing with your case.

After your interview, you will be notified whether or not your application is successful. If it is, you must follow the immigration official's instructions for obtaining medical and security checks. You can expect to wait about one year for the process to be completed. However, in certain countries this could be longer and, where your job is in high demand and you are otherwise admissible, it could be shorter.

If your application is denied, you will be able to apply again, but you will not be able to appeal the decision of the consular office. You should try to establish in which areas in the point system you scored low so that you can rectify it in future applications for Canadian immigration.

IMMIGRATION PRIORITY LIST

In making a priority list of who gets preference in the Canadian immigration system, family class relatives are right at the top, along with what is termed "convention" refugees. These are refugees who have been identified as qualifying for refugee status (as opposed to those who are claiming refugee status). Assisted relatives are not given any special priority other than as they fit into the independent categories at large.

These independent categories are:

- entrepreneurs, investors, and self-employed persons;
- those with designated occupations;
- those with approved employment;
- those who score 5 or more points from the occupational demand list in the point system;
- all other applicants.

It doesn't matter if you are a doctor or a bricklayer, a scientist or a domestic worker—the Canadian system does not categorize people according to their skills levels or educational status. However, skills and education do add points to the assessment of independent applicants. From analyzing the priority list above, it is clear that, unless you have a great deal of money that you are planning to invest in Canada, thereby creating jobs and growth in the country, the safest bet is to secure a job offer before you apply for immigration, unless, of course, your skills are in high demand in the country.

INDEPENDENT IMMIGRANT SUBCATEGORIES

Investors

This subcategory is relatively new and was only introduced into the independent category in 1986, in Canada's attempt to attract new foreign capital to the country. It is aimed at attracting wealthy foreigners who do not intend to be involved in the running of their Canadian businesses or business interests.

In order to qualify as an investor, you must have a proven track record in business or commerce and a personal net worth of at least $500,000, which must have been personally accrued through your own endeavors. Therefore, if you inherit this amount of money, or are given it as a gift, you will not be eligible to be an investor in Canada. When you apply as an investor, you must not only be able to prove your net worth, you must also be able to track how you acquired this money.

You must be prepared to make an investment ranging from $150,000 to $500,000 on an irrevocable basis for a minimum of five years. This investment must either be in a business, private syndicate, or government-run, capital-venture fund. Your investment must create or continue employment in Canada and you must have enough money to support yourself, without regard to possible profits from your investment.

The Canadian provinces have raised capital by encouraging foreign investment in this way. The wealthier provinces, including Ontario, Quebec, Alberta, and British Columbia, require a minimum investment of $350,000 before approving a foreign investment by a person wishing to immigrate on this basis, whereas the economically less-fortunate provinces, including Manitoba, Newfoundland, New Brunswick, Nova Scotia, Prince Edward Island, and Saskatchewan, require minimum investments of $250,000.

The provinces have significant say in the immigration system at this level, because they all have economic needs that either can or cannot be met by foreign immigration. Provincial approval can never, in itself, be enough to permit people to immigrate. Their visas are still issued by the federal immigration authorities and they have to fulfill all the criteria of eligibility first.

At the two investment levels just mentioned, there are no guarantees and a certain amount of risk is, therefore, involved.

However, at a third investment level of $500,000, people with a minimum net worth of $700,000 who are willing to sink their money into a project for at least five years, irrevocably, are eligible to receive a third-party guarantee on their money.

You will receive a Canadian immigrant visa without any conditions attached if you qualify as an investor.

Entrepreneurs

Entrepreneurs are defined by Canadian immigration law as those people who intend and have the ability to establish, purchase, or make a substantial investment in a business or commercial venture in Canada. This should make a significant contribution to the economy and create or continue employment opportunities in the country for at least one Canadian citizen or permanent resident, excluding family members.

If you come to Canada as an entrepreneur, you must intend and have the ability to be actively involved in the ongoing management of your business or commercial venture.

Although the law states that you must create or continue at least one job, this is not considered sufficient. Clearly, in practice, the more jobs being created or continued, the better the chances of getting an immigrant visa as an entrepreneur. Although it is not specified what constitutes a substantial investment, Canadian immigration experts have suggested that a minimum investment in excess of $100,000 that purchases at least a quarter of the stock in an existing business, would qualify.

Once again, you will have to have a proven track record in business, be financially able to meet your responsibilities, and intend to work in the business or venture that you start or finance in Canada.

You will have to show that the money you plan to invest in your Canadian endeavor is your own and was earned in a legitimate way. For example, if your money comes from gambling or any other source that is not considered appropriate, you will not qualify as an entrepreneur. Your financial statements will have to be carefully documented and prepared to show your earnings, tax returns, assets, investments, and all other details that affect your application.

Entrepreneurs are divided into two categories for the purposes of immigration, those who receive their immigrant visas with no conditions attached, and those who have to fulfill certain conditional criteria before they get unconditional immigrant status.

Unconditional Immigrants

If your investment or business venture is approved by the province where you plan to work and this business is already operating and the money has already been invested, you are likely to get an unconditional immigrant visa. However, before this is granted, the immigration visa official will first consult with the provincial authorities involved in this decision.

Conditional Immigrants

If you are generally admissible as an entrepreneur, but you have not yet decided what your business plans are, or if you are still negotiating about various possibilities, you will get conditional admission as a Canadian immigrant.

This means you will be able to enter Canada as a conditional immigrant on condition that you start your business or commercial venture within a two-year period after entering the country. This business or venture must employ Canadians, other than members of your family, and must be economically beneficial to the province where you settle. If you fail to achieve this within two years, you will be subject to deportation.

If you plan to settle in any other province, you will have to present your business proposal to the Canadian immigration authorities as well as to provincial authorities. Viability studies may be carried out by the provincial authorities and if you get a favorable response, the chances are high that the immigration official abroad will approve your visa.

Canadian experts in the field advise those applying for immigrant visas as entrepreneurs to consult lawyers familiar with the procedure of preparing business proposals in the different provinces.

If you come to Canada on a conditional immigrant visa, you will be closely watched by both provincial and immigration officials. If you do not satisfy the necessary criteria within two years, your visa may be revoked. However, you will have recourse to the courts and will be eligible to submit an appeal to the Immigration and Refugee Board, Appeals Division.

Because the provinces of Canada have specific requirements that entrepreneurs have to meet, it will be necessary for you to consult immigration lawyers from these provinces if you wish to pursue an application in this subcategory. The nature and scope of this book does not allow for a detailed description of each province's agenda with regard to immigration, other than to say that the underlying motivation in every case is the creation of economic growth and employment opportunities for local residents.

Self-employed

You are eligible to immigrate as a self-employed independent if you have the means, ability, and intention to establish your own business in Canada and to provide employment for yourself. This must make a significant contribution to the Canadian economy or to the cultural or artistic life of the country.

This category includes all those who plan to establish businesses, including family businesses, that do not qualify as entrepreneurs, as well as artists and professionals who intend to work in their creative or professional fields.

You will have to make a business proposal to both immigration and provincial authorities, though not in as much detail as entrepreneurs need to. Also, your capital investment in your business will not be expected to be as high as for entrepreneurs.

If you are a professional and intend setting up a business consultancy or practice in Canada, you will not get an immigrant visa unless you are licensed and have the necessary training to practice or work in your field at the time you apply.

The point system features prominently in this subcategory since you will automatically get a 30-point bonus from the immigration official dealing with your application if he/she believes you will be able to establish yourself successfully in Canada. Even if you have a requisite 1 point for experience in your field, and score well on the point system, if the immigration official does not believe you will be suitable, you will not get the bonus points and your application has no chance of being approved.

Family Business

If your relative in Canada has a family business and you fit into the category of either family class or assisted relative (see previous chapter), you are eligible to get a visa in this subcategory. If you are a family class member, there is no point choosing this option, since the family class category is not subject to the point system and gets first priority in immigration anyway. But if you are in the assisted relative group, this is an important subcategory, because it may be your only way of getting into Canada. Alternately, if you applied as an independent and were refused, and then applied as an assisted relative and were also refused, this could be the last option available to you.

Your Canadian relatives must have already established the business where you will be working and must be running it themselves. They will have to demonstrate to the immigration officials that it is in the interests of the business to employ a close relative. The issue in the case of family business immigrant applications is family unity, not whether or not Canadian workers are available to fill the position being offered. Therefore, provided you will be coming to Canada to work in a position of trust in your family's business, or to fill a position that would be unreasonable to most Canadian workers who had no deep interest in the long-term success of the business (for example working long hours in a 24-hour business operation), the chances are high that your visa will be approved.

Your relative in Canada will be interviewed by the Canadian Immigration Centre and you will be interviewed by Canadian immigration officials in your country to establish that you have a qualifying relationship and that the business is viable and had been operating for at least one year before you made the application. Your relative will also have to show that the wages and working conditions being offered to you are within the normal limits for the occupation in the area where the business is located. If you will be coming to Canada to open up a new branch of the business, the main branch must have been in business for at least a year. The Canadian immigration official within Canada is likely to check that the job being offered involves a position of trust, a close working relationship, and/or has long working hours or is subject to other unusual expectations. In other words, he/she will be checking that it is viable for a close relative, rather than a Canadian resident, to get the job.

Independent Workers

If you plan to come to Canada and work as someone's employee, no matter what your field, you must apply as an independent worker. Because this subcategory is so closely tied to Canada's employment situation, it is very important to realize that it isn't the level of your education that counts, but, more often, the level of your training, because both professionals with experience as well as artisans with experience are factors in your favor when your competition may be inexperienced Canadian workers. However, there are certain designated occupations that are in short supply in Canada and, therefore, even if you have little or no experience in these fields, you are still likely to be considered for immigration because of your essential skills.

Employment Approval

Unless your job is considered to be in short supply, all independent workers will have to obtain the approval of the employment division of the Employment and Immigration Commission (Employment Canada)—which has a similar function in immigration as the Department of Labor in the United States—before their immigrant visas will be approved. All employees whose jobs are not on the list of jobs in short supply have to have this approval.

Investors, entrepreneurs, self-employed people, and assisted relatives in family businesses do *not* have to have employment approval, neither do those in the family class category.

Employment Canada's main function is to help Canadian citizens and permanent residents find jobs with the right employers. It also has the job of granting or denying approval of job offers that Canadian employers make to foreigners. Therefore, before you can come to Canada to work for an employer (unless you are in the subcategory that does not need employment approval), Employment Canada will first try to find a qualified Canadian for the job. Canadian workers have to be available, willing, and qualified for the jobs being offered. Your prospective employer in Canada will have to submit a Confirmation of Offer of Employment, giving detailed information about the job being offered to you and everything the job entails.

As is the case with obtaining labor certification for a prospective foreign employee in the United States, the key to success lies in showing that you are uniquely qualified for the job being offered, while, at the same time, not making the job requirements so specific as to rule out all Canadian workers.

Your Canadian employer will have to apply to the Canada Employment offices for a foreign worker and this office must complete the application form for your work permission. It could take up to one year, possibly longer, to process this application. Therefore, your prospective employer must be able to assess his/her future employment needs and realize that you will not be granted your visa immediately.

As is the case for getting labor certification in the United States, your employer must show that he/she has tried to recruit Canadian workers (clippings from the classified jobs section will do) and has made an effort to promote and/or train existing workers within the company. This must all be specified on the application form.

Employment Canada will then use this information and try to find suitable Canadians to fill the positions being offered to foreign workers. The search for workers will be conducted locally and possibly, provincially and even nationally, if this initial search is unsuccessful. Your prospective employer will be told whether or not it is necessary to advertise the job again and, if so, this could mean fairly high costs. This is another disadvantage to you, because many employers will not want to go to so much trouble for a foreign worker. Also, it will be difficult to refuse to hire a Canadian who is sent to interview and who is suitable for the job.

This process is neither simple nor secure, since many factors are against you in your attempt to work in Canada. If you are granted employment approval, however, Employment Canada will notify the Canadian consulate or embassy where you applied for immigration and your visa application will then be processed. It is likely that your application will be approved, because independent workers with employment approval are fairly high up on the immigration priority list.

If you are denied employment approval, you have no recourse and will not be granted an immigrant visa. Although you will be assessed on the point system, without employment approval, your application will not be approved.

The Point System

Your application will be assessed by the point system and you need a minimum of 70 out of 100 points. This system, which will be explained fully in the following chapter, is not infallible, since it does not guarantee that you will get a visa if you get 70 or more points. Neither does it guarantee that you will be denied a visa if you get under 70 points. There is still a certain amount of subjectivity involved in the selection process by Canadian immigration officials and you will have to convince them that you will be able to fit into the Canadian way of life and adapt to the country. Even if you score well on the point system, you must realize that independent workers whose jobs are not in demand in Canada and who do not have employment approval are at the bottom of the Canadian immigration priority list. Therefore, do not be too encouraged when you apply in this category.

In the next chapter the mechanism by which the Canadian immigration system operates—the point system—is examined.

CHAPTER 21

The Point System

All people who apply to immigrate to Canada in the independent category or in the assisted relative category are assessed on the point system. The number of points you need to be eligible for immigration depends on the subcategory in which you are applying.

There are nine factors that are considered in the point system. These are:

- education;
- specific vocational preparation;
- experience;
- occupational demand;
- arranged employment;
- age;
- knowledge of English and French;
- personal suitability;
- levels control.

All independent immigrant applicants are assessed according to all these factors, unless they are investors, entrepreneurs, self-employed, or coming to work in a family business, in which case the 10-point allocation of occupational demand falls away and they are assessed on a possible maximum of 90, not 100, points. The minimum number of points needed by *all* applicants to be considered eligible as an independent immigrant is 70.

Each factor and its individual point allotment is discussed in turn.

EDUCATION—12 POINTS

You will get 1 point for each year of primary and secondary school you have successfully completed, up to a maximum of 12 points. The points will be given on the basis of the equivalency of the educational standards in your country and those in Canada. Therefore, if you come from a country where the standard of education is significantly lower than it is in Canada, you could find that, whereas you expected a high number of points for education, you do not get credited with as many as you'd hoped. However, in most cases, it is assumed that the grade levels are equivalent.

SPECIFIC VOCATIONAL PREPARATION—15 POINTS

There are a maximum of 15 points available on the basis of your training. The points are given for the equivalent length of time it would take you to train for the same level in Canada as you have already reached in your home country. The minimum number of points is given for training that required less than one month and the maximum number of points is given for training that required at least ten years. Therefore, a highly qualified doctor who has specialized in psychiatry or any other field where lengthy postgraduate training was required, will obviously score high, whereas a domestic worker, who may have taken one month to train, will score low.

A manual known as the Canadian Classification and Directory of Occupations is used to determine how much training is typically required for specific jobs.

Your trade, professional, or technical certificates will have to be accepted by the equivalent organization in Canada in the province where you plan to work. For example, a journeyman's certificate will have to be acceptable to the appropriate Canadian trade union, and an engineering license will have to be acceptable to the professional engineers organization in the area where you plan to work.

EXPERIENCE—8 POINTS

There are a maximum of 8 points available for experience in the occupation for which you are applying. If you are an investor or entrepreneur, these points will be awarded according to your experience in the field in which you will be working in Canada. There are more points awarded to people whose job descriptions require more training. This is seen as unfair since the system discriminates against unskilled manual workers and favors skilled professionals, although they both may have the same amount of experience in their specific fields.

If you needed vocational training of any sort in order to do your job, no matter what this job may be or how much training was required, you must get at least 1 point for experience, or you will not be able to immigrate, even if you get 70 points altogether.

OCCUPATIONAL DEMAND—10 POINTS

Various jobs have been allocated points ranging from 1 to 10 on a specially drawn-up list by a collaborative effort of the immigration and employment departments of the Canadian government. Those jobs with high ratings are ones that are considered in high demand in Canada and those with low ratings, are in lower demand. Those jobs not on this list are given a zero rating and, unless you have a job offer from a specific employer in a zero-rated job, you will not be able to immigrate to Canada.

This government-drawn-up list is subject to continuous change, depending on the job market in Canada and how many qualified Canadians there are to fill the available positions. At times of high unemployment, this list becomes considerably shorter and it is important for you to check with the Canadian consulate, embassy, or immigration office where you plan to apply for your immigrant visa if your job is on this list or not. If it is not, you stand very little chance of success, unless you have a contact in Canada who is prepared to offer you a job. But, even then, as you read in the previous chapter, this is a time-consuming and costly procedure and one that not too many Canadian employers will be willing to do. Even if they were willing, their chances of success are slim, unless you will be an exceptional asset to them.

Even if your occupation is on the government list, but is a low-demand one, in terms of its points rating, you will not be assured of getting a visa, unless you have a job offer. Your employer will have the advantage of not having to obtain an employment approval on your behalf. All jobs that appear on the government-issued list are exempt from having to have Employment Canada approval. However, if your occupation is on the list and your employer has employment approval on your behalf, you will be credited with a 10-point bonus.

You are entitled to list all the jobs that you are qualified to do and you will be given points for the job that has the highest rating and is, therefore, in greatest demand in Canada. This helps both you, in your attempt in getting a Canadian immigrant visa, and Canada, in its attempt in getting the skills it needs.

The Canadian immigration official will assess your application according to your possibility of finding employment in Canada. Therefore, even if your skills are in short supply in Canada, you will significantly improve your chances by submitting proof of a job offer as well.

Unless you are exempt from the occupational demand factor in assessing your immigration application (investors, entrepreneurs, self-employed, and those coming to work in family businesses are not assessed in terms of this factor), you will have to get at least 1 point in this category. If you do not, your application will be refused. Although you will not be excluded from consideration if you do not have a job offer, if you think about the immigration priority list, you will remember that those with job offers are given preference, even if you score higher on an individual points basis for occupational demand than a person who *does* have a job offer.

ARRANGED EMPLOYMENT—10 POINTS

Up to 10 points are available if you have a confirmed offer of employment that is validated by a Canada Employment Centre. If this job appears to be a permanent one and if your employment will not adversely affect the employment opportunities of Canadian workers, you will score higher. You will also score higher if you meet all the professional licensing requirements for your job in the province where you plan to live and work. Having a job offer, even in writing, will not make you eligible to obtain points if it has not undergone a Canadian government employment validation process.

Employment Canada must give employment approval to an employer who submits an application to hire a foreign worker. If this is done, the consulate where you submitted your immigrant visa application will be notified and this notification will contribute to your points.

AGE—10 POINTS

If you are between the ages of twenty-one and forty-four, you will get the maximum 10 points. If you are under the age of twenty-one or over the age of forty-four, two points will be deducted from the maximum of 10 for each year under or over. For example, if you are forty-six years old, you will receive 6 points, if you are age eighteen, you will receive 4 points, and if you are forty-nine years old or over, you will receive 0 points.

KNOWLEDGE OF ENGLISH AND FRENCH—15 POINTS

There is a maximum of 15 points available if you are able to speak, read, and write both English and French, Canada's two official languages. You must be fluent in both.

If you are fluent in only one of these languages, you will get 9 points. You will get an additional 6 points for fluency in your second language.

If, in your first language, you can only speak and write fluently, but read well, you will receive 3 points each for speaking and writing and 2 points for reading. You get 2 points for the areas in which you do well in your first language, and 1 point for those areas in which you have difficulty. If you speak and/or read and/or write well in your second language, but not fluently, you will receive 1 point for each area you do well and 0 points for those areas in which you have difficulty. Therefore, if, for example, you are fluent in reading, writing, and speaking English, and can also read in French, you will receive 10 points—9 points for English fluency and an extra point for reading well in your second language.

You must expect to be tested in your ability to read, write, and speak English and/or French when you go to your interview at the Canadian consulate, embassy, or immigration office abroad.

PERSONAL SUITABILITY—10 POINTS

When you go for your interview at the Canadian consulate, embassy, or visa office, the immigration official dealing with your case will assess your ability to adapt to the Canadian way of life. This person will judge whether or not he/she thinks you will be successful, and whether or not you seem to have the initiative and motivation needed to make the transition. This is a subjective decision but you probably have more control over its outcome than you realize. First appearances are often what count and could also influence your immigration officer in deciding whether or not you will be an asset to Canada. Therefore, it is important that you go to your interview looking neat and dressed well. If you project yourself positively, you are likely to score well for personal suitability. There are a maximum of 10 points available.

LEVELS CONTROL—10 POINTS

The Canadian government uses levels control as a means of regulating the number of immigrants entering the country in any given year. When there are too many people immigrating to Canada, 0 points are given for levels control. Currently, no one will score higher than 5 points. However, if the immigration levels drop too low, the level of points will be increased up to 10. This serves to favor those people with the ability to obtain a high score in other areas and acts as a form of natural selection from among the most desirable immigrant groups.

All these factors add up to a total of 100, although, given the currently available maximum of 5 points for levels control, this, effectively, means that immigrants can only obtain a maximum of 95 points. You need a minimum number of 70 points in order to be eligible as a Canadian immigrant.

Certain groups of immigrants are eligible for bonus points, which reduces the number of points they will need to obtain in the various point system subcategories described above. Approved investors and entrepreneurs will automatically get 45 bonus points, which means they only need another 25 points. If you are approved as a self-employed immigrant you will get a bonus of 30 points, leaving only another 40 to obtain through the point system. If your parent or sibling is helping you immigrate as an assisted relative, you will receive a bonus of 15 points, leaving 55 more points to obtain, whereas if your uncle, aunt, niece, or nephew is helping you as an assisted relative, you will receive 10 points, leaving you with 60 more points to obtain.

Now that you have the points breakdown, it should give you some idea of your chances of success in obtaining Canadian immigration. The confusion comes, however, from the fact that even those who get 70 points are not always admitted into the country and those who get below 70 are sometimes admitted.

If there is no occupational demand in your field and/or you have no experience, it is highly unlikely that you will be allowed to immigrate, whether you are an assisted relative or not. Therefore, having relatives nominating you for immigration is not enough. You have to be employable and you have to have a good chance of finding work, if you do not have a job offer at the time of applying.

If you plan to immigrate to the province of Quebec, you must get special details from the provincial government, since the point system is slightly different there and administered locally as well as nationally.

Generally, however, if you are not a family class immigrant, or do not have a substantial amount of money to invest in Canada or to start a business there, having a job offer in a field that is in demand in Canada gives you the greatest chance of getting an immigrant visa.

As is the case for United States immigration, if you are not admissible as an immigrant to Canada because of health, economic, ideological/political, or criminal reasons, you will not get a visa—no matter how many points you have. When you apply for your immigrant visa, you should request a list of who is inadmissable into Canada from the Canadian consulate, embassy, or immigration office where you apply.

The next chapter looks at special immigrants.

Special Immigrants

REFUGEES

In order to be granted refugee status in Canada, you must be eligible to make a claim of being a refugee (according to the United Nations definition of "convention refugee") and you must be found to have a credible basis for making this claim. You will be considered for refugee status if you come from a country where there is a high degree of persecution and a strong *probability* that you, personally, are threatened with jailing, torture, and similar acts of persecution or that you have already experienced these.

The process is a lengthy one and you can only apply for refugee status at a Canadian embassy or consulate abroad, at the point of entry into Canada, or from within Canada itself. If you came into Canada as a visitor, it is preferable for you to claim refugee status as soon as possible rather than wait for your visa to expire and for your presence in Canada to be illegal. If you are illegally in Canada and you apply for refugee status, your claim will be heard at your immigration hearing, after you have appeared at a credible basis hearing to determine whether or not you have grounds for claiming this status. However, if you are in Canada legally when you make this claim, your case will be considered by the Convention Refugee Determination Division (CRDD) of the Immigration and Refugee Board (IRB). The CRDD will decide whether you have a credible basis for your claim and whether you are eligible.

The procedure is lengthy and complex, but when you eventually have a hearing, preferably represented by an immigration lawyer with experience in dealing with refugee cases, your status will finally be decided. If you are granted refugee status, you will be known as a convention refugee and be given priority in getting an immigrant visa, along with family class immigrants. If your status is not upheld, you will be deported from Canada within days or weeks.

The nationals of certain designated countries who have left these countries because of persecution and who are temporarily in another country outside Canada will be admitted as refugees without having to go through the lengthy refugee hearings.

People who have been categorized as refugees by Canadian immigration officials abroad can be sponsored by groups of not fewer than five people within Canada. These people can belong to a corporation or be private individuals who have banded together to sponsor a friend, relative, or person from their home country, provided their combined income is enough to support the refugee and his/her family. Group sponsors will have to undertake to support any refugees they bring into Canada for at least one year.

There is a huge backlog in processing applications for refugee status and anyone planning to go to Canada as a refugee should know that it could take many years before your case is considered. This vastly complicates your position, because you may not be able to work there while you wait for your case to be heard and conditions in your country could change dramatically during this waiting period so that, even if you were eligible as a refugee at the time you came to Canada, you may not be eligible any longer at the time when your case is heard.

Next, we consider another special immigrant group that is completely unrelated to refugees, but also subject to special procedures that depart from the norm within the Canadian immigration system.

LIVE-IN CAREGIVERS PROGRAM

The only category of workers who are legally entitled to adjust their status from visitor to immigrant while still in Canada are foreign live-in caregivers (previously referred to by Canadian immigration law as domestic workers and nannies.) This is according to a special program adopted by the Minister of Immigration in Canada in 1981, amended in April 1992, which allows live-in caregivers who have been working in the country for at least two years to apply for permanent residence without having to leave Canada first. In recent months, the laws have tightened with regard to this provision and it is now necessary for an employer to provide substantial proof that he/she was unable to find a live-in caregiver from within the Canadian labor force before permanent residence will be granted to a foreign worker in this category. In addition, the criteria that a foreign person must meet in order to qualify as a live-in caregiver have been changed to reflect the higher standards of education the Canadian government is imposing on prospective immigrants.

If you wish to work in Canada as a live-in caregiver, which is defined as a person who provides child care, seniors home support care, or care of the disabled, without supervision, in a private household, you first have to receive employment authorization. There are three main criteria that you will have to meet in order to be eligible as a live-in caregiver:

1. you must have completed the equivalent of a Canadian 12th grade education;

2. you must have completed at least six months training in a field or occupation related to the job you will be doing in Canada;

3. you must be able to speak, read, and understand at least one of the official languages of Canada, i.e. either English or French.

Apart from these criteria, you and your employer must realize that you will only be eligible if you are, in fact, living-in at the home where you will be working. Canada has enough live-out caregivers and will only issue employment authorization if the foreign caregiver will be working on a live-in basis.

Your employer will have to submit an application to hire you at the Canada Employment Centre (CEC) nearest his/her place of residence in Canada. Once the CEC has ascertained that there are no willing or qualified workers who are already in Canada able to do the job, it will validate the application and forward it to the visa office abroad, in your country of residence. You will then be called in for an interview to ascertain whether you are eligible for this program. If your application is approved, you will be sent for a medical test. Once the visa office has established that you are medically fit, and have met all eligibility requirements, it will issue you an employment authorization. This does not replace a travel document, and you will still need a passport and, if necessary, a visitor's visa into Canada. (The nationals of some countries do not require visitors' visas. Check at your nearest Canadian consulate, embassy, or High Commissioner's Office.)

Your employment authorization will be valid for one year and you must renew it for the second year to which you are entitled before the expiration date. You may do this by mailing it to the Canada Immigration Centre serving the area where you are living in Canada. You may only work for the employer whose name appears on this employment authorization document, but you are entitled to change employers, in which case you need to apply for a new employment authorization. You will not be deported for changing employers as long as you do not work without an employment authorization document that has the name of your new employer. You can organize this through the Canada Immigration Centre office nearest you.

You will have to negotiate a contract of employment with your employer and you should be aware of your rights as a worker within the country. After working for two years, you will be eligible to apply for an adjustment of status to permanent residence. If you were out of Canada for any length of time during your two-year stay, this time will be deducted from the two-year minimum requirement and you will have to work to make up the additional time before you can apply for permanent residence. Your employment authorization must be valid at the time of applying for adjustment of status, so you should make sure you have it extended if necessary.

In order to apply for adjustment of status, you must be able to prove that you have worked as a full-time live-in caregiver for two years. To prove this you may show a statement of earnings from your employer or your tax-return form. If the Canada Immigration Centre approves your application, you may apply for an open employment authorization. This will enable you to work anywhere you wish while your application for permanent residence is being processed. Once you have received permanent residence, you will be eligible to sponsor your family members to join you in Canada.

CHAPTER
23

The Canada-United States Free Trade Agreement

In January 1989, Canada and the United States entered into an economic agreement that was designed to boost trade and business between the two countries. This is called the Free Trade Agreement or FTA. An immigration component had to be included to facilitate easy access for Canadians into the United States (see Chapter 6) and Americans into Canada.

The FTA immigration policies only apply to United States citizens wishing to enter Canada temporarily to conduct business or to work for a Canadian company. They must plan to retain their permanent residence in America and plan to return there once their work or business assignment is completed.

American citizens can enter Canada in one of four categories:

- business visitors;
- traders and/or investors;
- professionals;
- intracompany transferees.

BUSINESS VISITORS

People entering Canada on business will be granted temporary entry if they can prove the nature of their business. Many of the qualifying jobs for business visitors appear on a list known as Schedule 1 (which appears in Appendix 8, page 271). This list, however, represents a general guide, but those whose jobs are not on this list but who can prove they have legitimate business to conduct in Canada also will be granted entry visas. Proof can be in the form of an employer's letter, a contract to perform service, copies of correspondence between the American and Canadian companies involved, or other documentation.

TRADERS AND/OR INVESTORS

Traders and/or investors will be admitted into Canada after obtaining employment authorization. Traders should be involved at executive, managerial, or "essential skills" levels in a company that is involved in trade, at least 50 percent of which is with Canada. They can be trading in goods or services, provided there is substantial trade and this trade is primarily between the United States and Canada. The word "substantial" refers both to the value of trade as well as the amount of goods/services being traded. Services, in this context, refers to a wide range of economic activities including banking, finance, insurance, advertising, accounting, data processing, public relations, and other similar kinds of services.

Investors must subject their cash to potential risk, which means that they must be willing to invest in a project without any guarantee of return, if the project fails. You are only eligible to be an investor if your funds are subject to potential loss.

You must have a legally-binding commitment to your investment, which must be substantial in order to qualify in terms of the FTA. The cash amount of your investment must be at least half of the amount needed to purchase or establish a business. In other words, at least half the cash value of your investment must be put at risk in order for you to obtain investor status. You must be able to show that you have another source of income apart from any income that may be generated from this investment.

In the case of both traders and investors, the United States company making the investment or conducting trade must be owned and/or controlled by United States citizens. In other words, at least 50 percent of the shareholders must be United States citizens and so must the representative of this company coming to trade or invest in Canada.

You must apply for trader or investor status at a Canadian embassy or consulate and must pay a fee of $100 Canadian. You may pay by money order or bank draft. You will also have to complete Form IMM 1296 (Application for Temporary Entry to Canada).

Your spouse can work in the business in which you have an investment or in which you are conducting trade with Canada, but may not find employment elsewhere without applying for his/her own employment approval. Your children will be permitted to study in Canada and will be granted student authorization.

PROFESSIONALS

A list of professionals has been compiled on what is known as Schedule 2. If a profession is listed on Schedule 2, Americans qualifying in this profession can enter Canada and Canadians, similarly, can enter America. (A list of Schedule 2 professions is given in Appendix 9, page 273.)

American professionals coming to work in Canada must have the identical professional qualifications as Canadian professionals going to work in the United States.

All cases are adjudicated at the point of entry into Canada and, therefore, any American citizen going to work in Canada in a professional capacity must take as much documentation with him/her to be able to prove his/her qualifications and, if necessary, experience (in the case of journalists and management consultants—see Chapter 6, page 73).

Nowhere does the FTA specify that an American must have a job offer in Canada in order to enter Canada as a professional, or vice versa. However, if you are planning to work in Canada and have a letter of appointment from a Canadian company, the likelihood that you will experience any problems at the border is greatly reduced. Such a job offer from an organization requiring your professional services clearly demonstrates that you have both the qualifications and experience to do the job and, therefore, there can be no queries about your eligibility.

You should dress appropriately so that you make a good impression on the Canadian immigration official at the border.

INTRACOMPANY TRANSFEREES

A United States citizen who is an executive, manager, or employee with specialized knowledge of a company who is coming to Canada to work in the same capacity for a Canadian company that is either the branch, subsidiary, or parent of the American one, can gain entry into Canada at the border. He/she must provide documentary proof of both his/her own credentials and of the relationship between the American and Canadian companies.

This documentary proof is extremely important since the immigration official at the border will use his/her discretion as to whether or not to admit you into Canada based entirely on how you present your case. Proof can be in the form of company letters, tax returns, salary history and job description, and legal documents (showing the relationship between the companies).

You should read Chapter 6 on the FTA as it affects Canadians going to work in the United States. You will find that there are fewer restrictions placed on Americans entering Canada than the other way around. In spite of this fact, you must still be prepared to carry substantial documentation with you across the border to prove that you are eligible to enter Canada in terms of the FTA.

No matter where you fit into the immigration picture, now that you have reached the end of this book, you should have recognized those chapters that apply to you. Go back, read them again carefully, and try to figure out how to reach the particular goal that you have set for yourself. Whether you do it alone or with the help of an immigration lawyer, good luck in your endeavor.

There have been millions before you and there will be millions to follow, but each person's case is unique—with both its ups and downs. This book should make *your* road to immigration a smooth one.

APPENDICES

Table of Immigration Forms and Fees

FORM NUMBER	NAME OF FORM	FEE	APPENDIX PAGE
ETA-750	Application for Alien Employment Certification (Labor Certificate from DOL)	None	184
ETA-9035	Labor Condition Application for H-1B Nonimmigrants	None	186
G-325A	Biographic Information for Adjustment of Status	None	187
I-20 A/B	Certificate of Eligibility for Nonimmigrant (F-1) Student Status—Academic or Language	None	188
I-20 M/N	Certificate of Eligibility for Nonimmigrant (M-1) Student Status—Vocational	None	190
I-94	Nonimmigrant Arrival and Departure Form	None	192
I-94W	Nonimmigrant Visa Waiver Arrival and Departure Form	None	193
I-129	Nonimmigrant Worker Petition (Used with supplements for the E, H, L, O, P, Q, or R nonimmigrant visa categories. Also used when people in these visa categories want to obtain extensions of stay or change in status)	basic fee: $70	194
I-129S	Petition Based on blanket L Nonimmigrant Petition	None	203
I-130	Immigrant Petition for relative, fiancé, or orphan	$75–$140	205
I-131	Application for Travel Document (Used by green-card holders who will be out of the country for a year or more and need reentry permits, and by people applying for advance parole or refugee travel documents)	$65	207
I-134	Affidavit of Support (to accompany student applications)	None	209
I-140	Immigrant Petition for Foreign Workers	$70	211
I-290A	Appeals and Motion to Reopen or Reconsider	$110	213

FORM NUMBER	NAME OF FORM	FEE	APPENDIX PAGE
I-360	Petition for Amerasian, Widow/er, or Special Immigrant	$75	214
I-485	Application to Register Permanent Residence and to Adjust Status	$95–$120	218
I-526	Immigrant Petition by Alien Entrepreneur	$140	221
I-539	Application to Extend Status or Change Nonimmigrant Status (for nonimmigrant visas other than those for which I-29 forms were used in the application procedure)	$70 plus $10 for each extra person	223
I-601	Application for Waiver of Grounds of Excludability (under revision at press time)	$90	226
I-751	Application to Remove Conditions on Residence	$65	229
I-752	Application by Investor to Remove Conditions	$85	231
I-765	Application for Employment Authorization	$65	233
IAP-66	Certificate of Eligibility for Exchange Visitor (J-1) Status	None	235
N-400	Application for Naturalization	$90	238
OF-156	Nonimmigrant Visa Application	Reciprocal	242
OF-179	Biographic Data for Visa Purposes	None	244
230 I-II	Application for Immigrant Visa and Alien Registration	$170	246

OMB Approval No. 44-R1301

U.S. DEPARTMENT OF LABOR
Employment and Training Administration

APPLICATION
FOR
ALIEN EMPLOYMENT CERTIFICATION

IMPORTANT: READ CAREFULLY BEFORE COMPLETING THIS FORM

PRINT legibly in ink or use a typewriter. If you need more space to answer questions on this form, use a separate sheet. Identify each answer with the number of the corresponding question. SIGN AND DATE each sheet in original signature.

To knowingly furnish any false information in the preparation of this form and any supplement thereto or to aid, abet, or counsel another to do so is a felony punishable by $10,000 fine or 5 years in the penitentiary, or both (18 U.S.C. 1001).

PART A. OFFER OF EMPLOYMENT

1. **Name of Alien** *(Family name in capital letter, First, Middle, Maiden)*

2. **Present Address of Alien** *(Number, Street, City and Town, State ZIP Code or Province, Country)*

3. **Type of Visa** *(If in U.S.)*

The following information is submitted as evidence of an offer of employment.

4. **Name of Employer** *(Full name of organization)*

5. **Telephone** *(Area Code and Number)*

6. **Address** *(Number, Street, City or Town, Country, State, ZIP Code)*

7. **Address Where Alien Will Work** *(if different from item 6)*

8. Nature of Employer's Business Activity	9. Name of Job Title	10. Total Hours Per Week		11. Work Schedule (Hourly)	12. Rate of Pay	
		a. Basic	b. Overtime	a.m. p.m.	a. Basic $ per	b. Overtime $ per hour

13. **Describe Fully the Job to be Performed** *(Duties)*

14. State in detail the **MINIMUM** education, training, and experience for a worker to perform satisfactorily the job duties described in Item 13 above.

15. **Other Special Requirements**

EDU-CATION (Enter number of years)	Grade School	High School	College	College Degree Required *(specify)*
				Major Field of Study

TRAIN-ING	No. Yrs.	No. Mos.	Type of Training

EXPERI-ENCE	Job Offered		Related Occupation		Related Occupation *(specify)*
	Yrs.	Mos.	Yrs.	Mos.	

Number

16. **Occupational Title of Person Who Will Be Alien's Immediate Supervisor** ➤ ➤

17. **Number of Employees Alien will Supervise** ➤

◄ **ENDORSEMENTS** *(Make no entry in section - for government use only)*

Date Forms Received	
L.O.	S.O.
R.O.	N.O.
Ind. Code	Occ. Code
Occ. Title	

Replaces MA 7-50A, B and C (Apr. 1970 edition) which is obsolete.

ETA 750 (Oct. 1979)

18. COMPLETE ITEMS ONLY IF JOB IS TEMPORARY			19. IF JOB IS UNIONIZED *(Complete)*	
a. No. of Openings To Be Filled By Aliens Under Job Offer	b. Exact Dates You Expect To Employ Alien		a. Number of Local	b. Name of Local
	From	To		
				c. City and State

20. STATEMENT FOR LIVE-AT-WORK JOB OFFERS   *(Complete for Private Household Job ONLY)*

a. Description of Residence		b. No. Persons Residing at Place of Employment				c. Will free board and private room not shared with anyone be provided?	*("X" one)*
("X" one)	Number of Rooms	Adults		Children	Ages		☐ YES ☐ NO
☐ House		BOYS					
☐ Apartment		GIRLS					

21: DESCRIBE EFFORTS TO RECRUIT U.S. WORKERS AND THE RESULTS. *(Specify Sources of Recruitment by Name)*

22. Applications require various types of documentation. Please read PART II of the instructions to assure that appropriate supporting documentation is included with your application.

23. EMPLOYER CERTIFICATIONS

By virtue of my signature below, I HEREBY CERTIFY the following conditions of employment.

a. I have enough funds available to pay the wage or salary offered the alien.

b. The wage offered equals or exceeds the prevailing wage and I guarantee that, if a labor certification is granted, the wage paid to the alien when the alien begins work will equal or exceed the prevailing wage which is applicable at the time the alien begins work.

c. The wage offered is not based on commissions, bonuses, or other incentives, unless I guarantee a wage paid on a weekly, bi-weekly or monthly basis.

d. I will be able to place the alien on the payroll on or before the date of the alien's proposed entrance into the United States.

e. The job opportunity does not involve unlawful discrimination by race, creed, color, national origin, age, sex, religion, handicap, or citizenship.

f. The job opportunity is not:

   (1) Vacant because the former occupant is on strike or is being locked out in the course of a labor dispute involving a work stoppage.

   (2) At issue in a labor dispute involving a work stoppage.

g. The job opportunity's terms, conditions and occupational environment are not contrary to Federal, State or local law.

h. The job opportunity has been and is clearly open to any qualified U.S. worker.

24. DECLARATIONS

DECLARATION OF EMPLOYER ▶   *Pursuant to 28 U.S.C. 1746, I declare under penalty of perjury the foregoing is true and correct.*

SIGNATURE	DATE

NAME *(Type or Print)*	TITLE

AUTHORIZATION OF AGENT OF EMPLOYER ▶   *I HEREBY DESIGNATE the agent below to represent me for the purposes of labor certification and I TAKE FULL RESPONSIBILITY for accuracy of any representations made by my agent.*

SIGNATURE OF EMPLOYER	DATE

NAME OF AGENT *(Type or Print)*	ADDRESS OF AGENT *(Number, Street, City, State, ZIP Code)*

Labor Condition Application for H-1B Nonimmigrants

U.S. Department of Labor
Employment and Training Administration
U.S. Employment Service

OMB Approval No.: 1205-0310
Expiration Date: 10/31/92

1. Full Legal Name of Employer	5. Employer's Address (No., Street, City, State, and ZIP Code)
2. Federal Employer I.D. Number	
3. Telephone No. ( )	6. Address Where Documentation is Kept (If different than item 5)
4. FAX No. ( )	

7. OCCUPATIONAL INFORMATION (Use attachment if additional space is needed)

(a) Three -Digit Occupational Groups Code	(b) Job Title (Check box if position is part-time)	(c) No. of H-1B Nonimmigrants	(d) Rate of Pay	(e) Period of Employment From To	(f) Location(s) Where H-1B Nonimmigrants Will Work (see instructions)
	☐				
	☐				
	☐				
	☐				

8. EMPLOYER LABOR CONDITION STATEMENTS (Employers are required to develop and maintain documentation supporting labor condition statements 8(a) and 8(d). Employers are further required to make available for public examination a copy of the labor condition application and necessary supporting documentation within one (1) working day after the date on which the application is filed with DOL. Check **each** box to indicate that the employer will comply with **each** statement.)

☐ (a) H-1B nonimmigrants will be paid at least the actual wage level paid by the employer to all other individuals with similar experience and qualifications for the specific employment in question <u>or</u> the prevailing wage level for the occupation in the area of employment, <u>whichever is higher.</u>

☐ (b) The employment of H-1B nonimmigrants will not adversely affect the working conditions of workers similarly employed in the area of intended employment.

☐ (c) On the date this application is signed and submitted, there is not a strike, lockout or work stoppage in the course of a labor dispute in the occupation in which H-1B nonimmigrants will be employed at the place of employment.

☐ (d) As of this date, notice of this application has been provided to workers employed in the occupations in which H-1B nonimmigrants will be employed: (check appropriate box)

  ☐ (i) Notice of this filing has been provided to the bargaining representative of workers in the occupations in which H-1B nonimmigrants will be employed; or

  ☐ (ii) There is no such bargaining representative; therefore, a notice of this filing has been posted and was, or will remain, posted for 10 days in a conspicuous place where H-1B nonimmigrants will be employed.

9. DECLARATION OF EMPLOYER. Pursuant to 28 U.S.C. 1746, I declare under penalty of perjury that the information provided on this form is true and correct. In addition, I declare that I will comply with the Department of Labor regulations governing this program and, in particular, that I will make this application, supporting documentation, and other records, files and documents available to officials of the Department of Labor, upon such official's request, during any investigation under this application or the Immigration and Nationality Act.

Name and Title of Hiring or Other Designated Official   Signature   Date

AN APPLICATION CERTIFIED BY DOL MUST BE FILED IN SUPPORT OF AN H-1B VISA PETITION WITH THE INS.
FOR U.S. GOVERNMENT AGENCY USE ONLY: By virtue of my signature below, I acknowledge that this application is hereby certified and will be valid from _____ through _____.

Signature and Title of Authorized DOL Official   ETA Case No.

Subsequent DOL Action: Suspended _____ (date) Invalidated _____ (date) Withdrawn _____ (date)

The Department of Labor is not the guarantor of the accuracy, truthfulness or adequacy of a certified labor condition application.

Public reporting burden for this collection of information is estimated to average 1 hour per response, including the time for reviewing instructions, searching existing data sources, gathering and maintaining the data needed, and completing and reviewing the collection of information. Send comments regarding this burden estimate or any other aspect of this collection of information, including suggestions for reducing this burden, to the Office of IRM Policy, Department of Labor, Room N-1301, 200 Constitution Avenue, N.W., Washington, DC 20210; and to the Office of Management and Budget, Paperwork Reduction Project (1205-0310), Washington, DC 20503.
DO NOT SEND THE COMPLETED FORM TO EITHER OF THESE OFFICES

ETA 9035 (Jan. 1992)

U.S. Department of Justice

Immigration and Naturalization Service

FORM G-325A
BIOGRAPHIC INFORMATION

OMB No. 1115-0066

(Family name) (First name) (Middle name)	☐ MALE ☐ FEMALE	BIRTHDATE (Mo.-Day-Yr.)	NATIONALITY	FILE NUMBER A-
ALL OTHER NAMES USED (Including names by previous marriages)	CITY AND COUNTRY OF BIRTH			SOCIAL SECURITY NO. (If any)

	FAMILY NAME	FIRST NAME	DATE, CITY AND COUNTRY OF BIRTH (If known)	CITY AND COUNTRY OF RESIDENCE
FATHER				
MOTHER (Maiden name)				

HUSBAND (If none, so state) OR WIFE	FAMILY NAME (For wife, give maiden name)	FIRST NAME	BIRTHDATE	CITY & COUNTRY OF BIRTH	DATE OF MARRIAGE	PLACE OF MARRIAGE

FORMER HUSBANDS OR WIVES (If none, so state)

FAMILY NAME (For wife, give maiden name)	FIRST NAME	BIRTHDATE	DATE & PLACE OF MARRIAGE	DATE AND PLACE OF TERMINATION OF MARRIAGE

APPLICANT'S RESIDENCE LAST FIVE YEARS. LIST PRESENT ADDRESS FIRST.

STREET AND NUMBER	CITY	PROVINCE OR STATE	COUNTRY	FROM MONTH	FROM YEAR	TO MONTH	TO YEAR
						PRESENT TIME	

APPLICANT'S LAST ADDRESS OUTSIDE THE UNITED STATES OF MORE THAN ONE YEAR

STREET AND NUMBER	CITY	PROVINCE OR STATE	COUNTRY	FROM MONTH	FROM YEAR	TO MONTH	TO YEAR

APPLICANT'S EMPLOYMENT LAST FIVE YEARS. (IF NONE, SO STATE.) LIST PRESENT EMPLOYMENT FIRST

FULL NAME AND ADDRESS OF EMPLOYER	OCCUPATION (SPECIFY)	FROM MONTH	FROM YEAR	TO MONTH	TO YEAR
				PRESENT TIME	

Show below last occupation abroad if not shown above. (Include all information requested above.)

THIS FORM IS SUBMITTED IN CONNECTION WITH APPLICATION FOR: ☐ NATURALIZATION ☐ STATUS AS PERMANENT RESIDENT ☐ OTHER (SPECIFY):	SIGNATURE OF APPLICANT	DATE
Are all copies legible? ☐ Yes	IF YOUR NATIVE ALPHABET IS IN OTHER THAN ROMAN LETTERS, WRITE YOUR NAME IN YOUR NATIVE ALPHABET IN THIS SPACE:	

PENALTIES: SEVERE PENALTIES ARE PROVIDED BY LAW FOR KNOWINGLY AND WILLFULLY FALSIFYING OR CONCEALING A MATERIAL FACT.

APPLICANT: BE SURE TO PUT YOUR NAME AND ALIEN REGISTRATION NUMBER IN THE BOX OUTLINED BY HEAVY BORDER BELOW.

COMPLETE THIS BOX (Family name)	(Given name)	(Middle name)	(Ailen registration number)

Form G-325 A (Rev. 10-1-82)   (1) Ident.

U.S. Department of Justice
Immigration and Naturalization Service
Please Read Instructions on Page 2

Certificate of Eligibility for Nonimmigrant (F-1) Student Status - For Academic and Language Students

OMB No. 1115-0051

This page must be completed and signed in the U.S. by a designated school official.

1. Family Name (surname)

   First (given) name (do not enter middle name)

   Country of birth

   Date of birth (mo./day/year)

   Country of citizenship

   Admission number (Complete if known)

For Immigration Official Use

Visa issuing post | Date Visa issued

Reinstated, extension granted to:

2. School (school district) name

   School official to be notified of student's arrival in U.S. (Name and Title)

   School address (include zip code)

   School code (including 3-digit suffix, if any) and approval date
   _____ 214F _____ approved on _____

3. This certificate is issued to the student named above for:
   (Check and fill out as appropriate)
   a. ☐ Initial attendance at this school.
   b. ☐ Continued attendance at this school.
   c. ☐ School transfer.
      Transferred from _____.
   d. ☐ Use by dependents for entering the United States.
   e. ☐ Other _____.

4. Level of education the student is pursuing or will pursue in the United States:
   (check only one)
   a. ☐ Primary   e. ☐ Master's
   b. ☐ Secondary   f. ☐ Doctorate
   c. ☐ Associate   g. ☐ Language training
   d. ☐ Bachelor's   h. ☐ Other

5. The student named above has been accepted for a full course of study at
   this school, majoring in _____.
   The student is expected to report to the school not later than (date)
   _____ and complete studies not later than (date) _____
   The normal length of study is _____.

6. ☐ English proficiency is required:
   ☐ The student has the required English proficiency.
   ☐ The student is not yet proficient, English instructions will be given at
      the school.
   ☐ English proficiency is not required because _____
   _____

7. This school estimates the student's average costs for an academic term of
   _____ (up to 12) months to be:
   a. Tuition and fees $ _____
   b. Living expenses $ _____
   c. Expenses of dependents $ _____
   d. Other (specify): $ _____
   Total $ _____

8. This school has information showing the following as the student's means of
   support, estimated for an academic term of _____ months (Use the same
   number of months given in item 7).
   a. Student's personal funds $ _____
   b. Funds from this school $ _____
      (specify type)   _____
   c. Funds from another source $ _____
      (specify type and source)   _____
   d. On-campus employment (if any) $ _____
   Total $ _____

9. Remarks: _____
   _____
   _____
   _____
   _____
   _____

10. School Certification: I certify under penalty of perjury that all information provided above in items 1 through 8 was completed before I signed this form and is true and correct; I executed this form in the United States after review and evaluation in the United States by me or other officials of the school of the student's application, transcripts or other records of courses taken and proof of financial responsibility, which were received at the school prior to the execution of this form; the school has determined that the above named student's qualifications meet all standards for admission to the school; the student will be required to pursue a full course of study as defined by 8 CFR 214.2(f)(6); I am a designated official of the above named school and I am authorized to issue this form.

Signature of designated school official | Name of school official (print or type) | Title | Date issued | Place issued (city and state)

11. Student Certification: I have read and agreed to comply with the terms and conditions of my admission and those of any extension of stay as specified on page 2. I certify that all information provided on this form refers specifically to me and is true and correct to the best of my knowledge. I certify that I seek to enter or remain in the United States temporarily, and solely for the purpose of pursuing a full course of study at the school named on Page 1 of this form. I also authorize the named school to release any information from my records which is needed by the INS pursuant to 8 CFR 214.3(g) to determine my nonimmigrant status.

Signature of student | Name of student | Date

Signature of parent or guardian if student is under 18 | Name of parent/guardian (Print or type) | Address(city) | (State or province) | (Country) | (Date)

Form I-20 A-B/I-20ID (Rev 04-27-88)N

For official use only
Microfilm Index Number

I-20 SCHOOL

IF YOU NEED MORE INFORMATION CONCERNING YOUR F-1 NONIMMIGRANT STUDENT STATUS AND THE RELATING IMMIGRATION PROCEDURES, PLEASE CONTACT EITHER YOUR FOREIGN STUDENT ADVISOR ON CAMPUS OR A NEARBY IMMIGRATION AND NATURALIZATION SERVICE OFFICE.

THIS PAGE, WHEN PROPERLY ENDORSED, MAY BE USED FOR ENTRY OF THE SPOUSE AND CHILDREN OF AN F-1 STUDENT FOLLOWING TO JOIN THE STUDENT IN THE UNITED STATES OR FOR REENTRY OF THE STUDENT TO ATTEND THE SAME SCHOOL AFTER A TEMPORARY ABSENCE FROM THE UNITED STATES.

For reentry of the student and/or the F-2 dependents (EACH CERTIFICATION SIGNATURE IS VALID FOR ONLY ONE YEAR.)

Signature of Designated School Official	Name of School Official (print or type)	Title	Date
Signature of Designated School Official	Name of School Official (print or type)	Title	Date
Signature of Designated School Official	Name of School Official (print or type)	Title	Date
Signature of Designated School Official	Name of School Official (print or type)	Title	Date
Signature of Designated School Official	Name of School Official (print or type)	Title	Date
Signature of Designated School Official	Name of School Official (print or type)	Title	Date

Dependent spouse and children of the F-1 student who are seeking entry/reentry to the U.S.

Name family (caps) first	Date of birth	Country of birth	Relationship to the F-1 student

Student Employment Authorization and other Records

U.S. Department of Justice
Immigration and Naturalization Service

Certificate of Eligibility for Nonimmigrant (M-1) Student
Status -For Vocational Students   (OMB No. 1115-0051)

This page must be completed and signed in the U.S. by a designated school official.

1. Family name (surname):

   First (given) name (do not enter middle name):

   | Country of birth: | Date of birth (mo./day/year): |
   | Country of citizenship: | Admission number (complete if known): |

2. School (school district) name:

   School official to be notified of student's arrival in U.S. (Name and Title):

   School address (include zip code):

   School code (include 3-digit suffix, if any) and approval date:

   _____ 214F_____ Approved on _____

For Immigration Only Use

| Visa issuing post | Date visa issued |

Reinstated, extension granted to:

3. This certificate is issued to the student named above for:
   (check and fill out as appropriate)
   a. ☐ Initial attendance at this school.
   b. ☐ Continued attendance at this school.
   c. ☐ School transfer.
      Transferred from _____ .
   d. ☐ Use by dependents for entering the United States.
   e. ☐ Other _____ .

4. Level of education the student is pursuing or will pursue in the United States: (Check only one)
   a. ☐ High school   b. ☐ Other vocational school

5. The student named above has been accepted for a full course of study at this school, majoring in _____ .
   The student is expected to report to the school not later than
   (date) _____ and complete studies not later than
   (date) _____ the normal length of study is

6. ☐ English proficiency is required:
   ☐ The student has the required English proficiency.
   ☐ The student is not yet proficient, English instructions will be given at the school.
   ☐ English proficiency is not required because _____

7. This school estimates the student's average costs for an academic term of_____ (up to 12) months to be:
   a. Tuition and fees $ _____
   b. Living expenses $ _____
   c. Expenses of dependents $ _____
   d. Other (specify): $ _____
              Total $ _____

8. This school has information showing the following as the student's means of support, estimated for an academic term of _____ months (Use the same number of months given in item 7).
   a. Students personal funds $ _____
   b. Funds from this school
      (specify type): $ _____
   c. Funds from another source
      (specify type and source): $ _____
              Total $ _____

9. Remarks: _____
   _____
   _____
   _____
   _____

10. School Certification: I certify under penalty of perjury that all information provided above in items 1 through 8 was completed before I signed this form and is true and correct; I executed this form in the United States after review and evaluation in the United States by me or other officials of the school of the student's application, transcripts or other records of courses taken and proof of financial responsibility which were received at the school prior to the execution of this form; the school has determined that the above named student's qualifications meet all standards for admission to the school; the student will be required to pursue a full course of study as defined by 8 CFR 214.2(f)(6); I am a designated official of the above named school and I am authorized to issue this form.

| Signature of designated school official: | Name of designated school official & title (print or type) | Date and place issued (city and state) |

11. Student Certification: I have read and agreed to comply with the terms and conditions of my admission and those of any extension of stay as specified on page 2. I certify that all information provided on this form refers to me and is true and correct to the best of my knowledge. I certify that I seek to enter or remain in the United States temporarily, and solely for the purpose of pursuing a full course of study at the school named on item 2 of this form. I also authorized the named school to release any information from my records which is needed by the INS pursuant to 8 CFR 214.3(g).

Signature of student:	Name of student (print or type):	Date
Signature of parent or guardian (if student is under 18):	Name of parent or guardian (print or type):	Date
Address of parent or guardian: (street) (city)	(state or province)	(county)

Form I-20M-N/I-20ID Copy (Rev. 5-3-90)N

For official use only
Microfilm Index Number

I-20M-N (SCHOOL) COPY

IF YOU NEED MORE INFORMATION CONCERNING YOUR M-1 NONIMMIGRANT STUDENT STATUS AND THE RELATING IMMIGRATION PROCEDURES, PLEASE CONTACT EITHER YOUR FOREIGN STUDENT ADVISOR ON CAMPUS OR A NEARBY IMMIGRATION AND NATURALIZATION SERVICE OFFICE.

This page, when properly endorsed, may be used for entry of the spouse and children of an M-1 Student following to join the student in the United States, or reentry of the student to attend the same school after a temporary absence from the United States.

For reentry of the student and/or the M2 dependents *(Each Certification Signature is valid for six months.)*

Signature of Designated School Official	Name School Official & Title *(Print or Type)*	Date
Signature of Designated School Official	Name School Official & Title *(Print or Type)*	Date
Signature of Designated School Official	Name School Official & Title *(Print or Type)*	Date
Signature of Designated School Official	Name School Official & Title *(Print or Type)*	Date
Signature of Designated School Official	Name School Official & Title *(Print or Type)*	Date
Signature of Designated School Official	Name School Official & Title *(Print or Type)*	Date

Dependent spouse and children of the M-1 student who are seeking entry/reentry to the U.S.

Name Family *(Caps)* First:	Date of Birth:	Country of birth:	Relationship to the M-1 Student:

Other Student Records:

Authority for collecting: Authority for collecting the information on this and related student forms is contained in 8U.S.C. 1101 and 1184. The information solicited will be used by the Department of State and the Immigration and Naturalization Service to determine eligibility for the benefits requested . The law provides severe penalties for knowingly and willfully falsifying or concealing a material fact, or using any false document in the submission of this form.

Reporting Burden: Public reporting burden for this collection of information is estimated to average 30 minutes per response, including the time for reviewing instructions, searching existing data sources, gathering and maintaining the data needed, and completing and reviewing the collection of information. Send comments regarding this burden estimated or any other aspect of this collection of information, including suggestions for reducing this burden, to: U. S. Department of Justice, Immigration and Naturalization Service (Room 2011), Washington, D.C. 20536; and to the Office of Management and Budget, Paperwork Reduction Project, OMB No.1115-0051, Washington, D.C. 20503.

U.S. Department of Justice
Immigration and Naturalization Service

OMB 1115-0077

Admission Number

804531027 02

Welcome to the United States

I-94 Arrival/Departure Record - Instructions

This form must be completed by all persons except U.S. Citizens, returning resident aliens, aliens with immigrant visas, and Canadian Citizens visiting or in transit.

Type or print legibly with pen in ALL CAPITAL LETTERS. Use English. Do not write on the back of this form.

This form is in two parts. Please complete both the Arrival Record (Items 1 through 13) and the Departure Record (Items 14 through 17).

When all items are completed, present this form to the U.S. Immigration and Naturalization Service Inspector.

Item 7 - If you are entering the United States by land, enter **LAND** in this space. If you are entering the United States by ship, enter **SEA** in this space.

Form I-94 (04-15-86)Y

Admission Number

804531027 02

Immigration and Naturalization Service

I-94 Arrival Record

1. Family Name
2. First (Given) Name
3. Birth Date (Day/Mo/Yr)
4. Country of Citizenship
5. Sex (Male or Female)
6. Passport Number
7. Airline and Flight Number
8. Country Where You Live
9. City Where You Boarded
10. City Where Visa Was Issued
11. Date Issued (Day/Mo/Yr)
12. Address While in the United States (Number and Street)
13. City and State

Departure Number

804531027 02

Immigration and Naturalization Service

I-94 Departure Record

14. Family Name
15. First (Given) Name
16. Birth Date (Day/Mo/Yr)
17. Country of Citizenship

See Other Side   **STAPLE HERE**

This Side For Government Use Only

Primary Inspection

Applicant's Name
Date Referred _____ Time _____ Insp. # _____

Reason Referred
☐ 212A ☐ PP ☐ Visa ☐ Parole ☐ SLB ☐ TWOV
☐ Other

Secondary Inspection
End Secondary Time _____ Insp. # _____
Disposition _____

18. Occupation
19. Waivers
20. INS File   A -
21. INS FCO
22. Petition Number
23. Program Number
24. ☐ Bond
25. ☐ Prospective Student

26. Itinerary/Comments

27. TWOV Ticket Number

Warning - A nonimmigrant who accepts unauthorized employment is subject to deportation.
Important - Retain this permit in your possession; *you must surrender it when you leave the U.S.* Failure to do so may delay your entry into the U.S. in the future.
You are authorized to stay in the U.S. only until the date written on this form. To remain past this date, without permission from immigration authorities, is a violation of the law.
Surrender this permit when you leave the U.S.:
  - By sea or air, to the transportation line;
  - Across the Canadian border, to a Canadian Official;
  - Across the Mexican border, to a U.S. Official.
Students planning to reenter the U.S. within 30 days to return to the same school, see "Arrival-Departure" on page 2 of Form I-20 prior to surrendering this permit.
Record of Changes

Port:
Date:
Carrier:
Flight #/Ship Name:

Departure Record

U.S. Department of Justice
Immigration and Naturalization Service

OMB No. 1115-0148

Welcome to the United States

I-94W Nonimmigrant Visa Waiver Arrival/ Departure Form
Instructions

This form must be completed by every nonimmigrant visitor not in possession of a visitor's visa, who is a national of one of the countries enumerated in 8 CFR 217. The airline can provide you with the current list of eligible countries.

Type or print legibly with pen in ALL CAPITAL LETTERS. USE ENGLISH

This form is in two parts. Please complete both the Arrival Record, items 1 through 11 and the Departure Record, items 14 through 17. The reverse side of this form must be signed and dated. Children under the age of fourteen must have their form signed by a parent/guardian.

Item 7 - If you are entering the United States by land, enter **LAND** in this space. If you are entering the United States by ship, enter **SEA** in this space.

Admission Number

608794120 02

Immigration and Naturalization Service
Form I-94W (05-29-91) - **Arrival Record**
VISA WAIVER

1. Family Name
2. First (Given) Name
3. Birth Date *(day/mo/yr)*
4. Country of Citizenship
5. Sex *(male or female)*
6. Passport Number
7. Airline and Flight Number
8. Country where you live
9. City Where you boarded
10. Address While in the United States *(Number and Street)*
11. City and State

Government Use Only

12. 13.

Departure Number

608794120 02

Immigration and Naturalization Service
Form I-94W (05-29-91) - **Departure Record**
VISA WAIVER

14. Family Name
15. First (Given) Name
16. Birth Date *(day/mo/yr)*
17. Country of Citizenship

See Other Side   **Staple Here**

Do any of the following apply to you? *(Answer Yes or No)*

A. Do you have a communicable disease; physical or mental disorder; or are you a drug abuser or addict? ☐ Yes ☐ No

B. Have you ever been arrested or convicted for an offense or crime involving moral turpitude or a violation related to a controlled substance; or been arrested or convicted for two or more offenses for which the aggregate sentence to confinement was five years or more; or been a controlled substance trafficker; or are you seeking entry to engage in criminal or immoral activities? ☐ Yes ☐ No

C. Have you ever been or are you now involved in espionage or sabotage; or in terrorist activities; or genocide; or between 1933 and 1945 were you involved, in any way, in persecutions associated with Nazi Germany or its allies? ☐ Yes ☐ No

D. Are you seeking to work in the U.S.; or have you ever been excluded and deported; or been previously removed from the United States; or procured or attempted to procure a visa or entry into the U.S. by fraud or misrepresentation? ☐ Yes ☐ No

E. Have you ever detained, retained or withheld custody of a child from a U.S. citizen granted custody of the child? ☐ Yes ☐ No

F. Have you ever been denied a U.S. visa or entry into the U.S. or had a U.S. visa canceled? If yes, when?_____ where?_____ ☐ Yes ☐ No

G. Have you ever asserted immunity from prosecution? ☐ Yes ☐ No

IMPORTANT: If you answered "Yes" to any of the above, please contact the American Embassy **BEFORE** you travel to the U.S. since you may be refused admission into the United States.

Family Name *(Please Print)*   First Name

Country of Citizenship   Date of Birth

WAIVER OF RIGHTS: I hereby waive any rights to review or appeal of an immigration officer's determination as to my admissibility, or to contest, other than on the basis of an application for asylum, any action in deportation.

CERTIFICATION: I certify that I have read and understand all the questions and statements on this form. The answers I have furnished are true and correct to the best of my knowledge and belief.

Signature   Date

Public Reporting Burden - The burden for this collection is computed as follows: (1) Learning about the form 2 minutes; (2) completing the form 4 minutes for an estimated average of 6 minutes per response. If you have comments regarding the accuracy of this estimate, or suggestions for making this form simpler, you can write to INS, 425 I Street, N.W., Rm. 5304, Washington, D.C. 20536; and the Office of Management and Budget, Paperwork Reduction Project, OMB No. 1115-0148, Washington, D.C. 20503.

Departure Record

Important - Retain this permit in your possession; you must surrender it when you leave the U.S. Failure to do so may delay your entry into the U.S. in the future.
You are authorized to stay in the U.S. only until the date written on this form. To remain past this date, without permission from Immigration authorities, is a violation of the law.
Surrender this permit when you leave the U.S.:
- By sea or air, to the transportation line;
- Across the Canadian border, to a Canadian Official;
- Across the Mexican border, to a U.S. Official.

WARNING: You may not accept unauthorized employment; or attend school; or represent the foreign information media during your visit under this program. You are authorized to stay in the U.S. for 90 days or less. You may not apply for: 1) a change of nonimmigrant status; 2) adjustment of status to temporary or permanent resident, unless eligible under section 201(b) of the INA; or 3) an extension of stay. Violation of these terms will subject you to deportation.

Port:
Date:
Carrier:
Flight #/Ship Name:

U.S. Department of Justice
Immigration and Naturalization Service

For sale by the Superintendent of Documents
U.S. Government Printing Office
Washington, DC 20402

OMB #1115-0168
Petition for a Nonimmigrant Worker

START HERE - Please Type or Print

Part 1. Information about the employer filing this petition.
If the employer is an individual, use the top name line. Organizations should use the second line.

Family Name	Given Name	Middle Initial

Company or Organization Name

Address - Attn:

Street Number and Name		Apt. #
City	State or Province	
Country	ZIP/Postal Code	

IRS Tax #

Part 2. Information about this Petition.
(See instructions to determine the fee).

1. **Requested Nonimmigrant Classification:**
    (write classification symbol at right) _____

2. **Basis for Classification** (check one)
    a. ☐ New employment
    b. ☐ Continuation of previously approved employment without change
    c. ☐ Change in previously approved employment
    d. ☐ New concurrent employment

3. **Prior petition.** If you checked other than "New Employment" in item 2. (above) give the most recent prior petition number for the worker(s): _____

4. **Requested Action:** (check one)
    a. ☐ Notify the office in Part 4 so the person(s) can obtain a visa or be admitted (NOTE: a petition is not required for an E-1, E-2, or R visa).
    b. ☐ Change the person(s) status and extend their stay since they are all now in the U.S. in another status (see instructions for limitations). This is available only where you check "New Employment" in item 2, above.
    c. ☐ Extend or amend the stay of the person(s) since they now hold this status.

5. **Total number of workers in petition:** _____

    (See instructions for where more than one worker can be included.)

Part 3. Information about the person(s) you are filing for.
Complete the blocks below. Use the continuation sheet to name each person included in this petition.

If an entertainment group, give their group name.

Family Name	Given Name	Middle Initial
Date of Birth (Month/Day/Year)	Country of Birth	
Social Security #	A #	

If in the United States, complete the following:

Date of Arrival (Month/Day/Year)	I-94 #
Current Nonimmigrant Status	Expires (Month/Day/Year)

Form I-129 (Rev. 12/11/91) N   *Continued on back.*

FOR INS USE ONLY

Returned	Receipt
_____	
_____	

Resubmitted
_____
_____

Reloc Sent
_____
_____

Reloc Rec'd
_____
_____

Interviewed
☐ Petitioner
☐ Beneficiary

Class: _____
# of Workers: _____
Priority Number: _____
Validity Dates: From _____
To _____

☐ **Classification Approved**
☐ Consulate/POE/PFI Notified

At: _____
☐ Extension Granted
☐ COS/Extension Granted

Partial Approval (explain)

Action Block

To Be Completed by
Attorney or Representative, if any
☐ Fill in box if G-28 is attached to represent the applicant
VOLAG#

ATTY State License #

Part 4. Processing Information.

a. If the person named in Part 3 is outside the U.S. or a requested extension of stay or change of status cannot be granted, give the U.S. consulate or inspection facility you want notified if this petition is approved.

Type of Office (check one): ☐ Consulate   ☐ Pre-flight inspection   ☐ Port of Entry

Office Address (City)   U.S. State or Foreign Country

Person's Foreign Address

b. Does each person in this petition have a valid passport?   ☐ Not required to have passport   ☐ No - explain on separate paper   ☐ Yes

c. Are you filing any other petitions with this one?   ☐ No   ☐ Yes - How many? _____

d. Are applications for replacement/Initial I-94's being filed with this petition?   ☐ No   ☐ Yes - How many? _____

e. Are applications by dependents being filed with this petition?   ☐ No   ☐ Yes - How many? _____

f. Is any person in this petition in exclusion or deportation proceedings?   ☐ No   ☐ Yes - explain on separate paper

g. Have you ever filed an immigrant petition for any person in this petition?   ☐ No   ☐ Yes - explain on separate paper

h. If you indicated you were filing a new petition in Part 2, within the past 7 years has any person in this petition:

   1) ever been given the classification you are now requesting?   ☐ No   ☐ Yes - explain on separate paper

   2) ever been denied the classification you are now requesting?   ☐ No   ☐ Yes - explain on separate paper

i. If you are filing for an entertainment group, has any person in this petition not been with the group for at least 1 year?   ☐ No   ☐ Yes - explain on separate paper

Part 5. Basic Information about the proposed employment and employer.
Attach the supplement relating to the classification you are requesting.

Job Title   Nontechnical Description of Job

Address where the person(s) will work if different from the address in Part 1.

Is this a full-time position?   ☐ No - Hours per week   ☐ Yes   Wages per week or per year

Other Compensation (Explain)   Value per week or per year   Dates of Intended employment From: To:

Type of Petitioner - check one: ☐ U.S. citizen or permanent resident   ☐ Organization   ☐ Other - explain on separate paper

Type of business: Year established:

Current Number of Employees   Gross Annual Income   Net Annual Income

Part 6. Signature.
Read the information on penalties in the instructions before completing this section.

I certify, under penalty of perjury under the laws of the United States of America, that this petition, and the evidence submitted with it, is all true and correct. If filing this on behalf of an organization, I certify that I am empowered to do so by that organization. If this petition is to extend a prior petition, I certify that the proposed employment is under the same terms and conditions as in the prior approved petition. I authorize the release of any information from my records, or from the petitioning organization's records, which the Immigration and Naturalization Service needs to determine eligibility for the benefit being sought.

Signature and title   Print Name   Date

Please Note: If you do not completely fill out this form and the required supplement, or fail to submit required documents listed in the instructions, then the person(s) filed for may not be found eligible for the requested benefit, and this petition may be denied.

Part 7. Signature of person preparing form if other than above.

I declare that I prepared this petition at the request of the above person and it is based on all information of which I have any knowledge.

Signature   Print Name   Date

Firm Name and Address

Supplement-1

Attach to Form I-129 when more than one person is included in the petition. *(List each person separately. Do not include the person you named on the form).*

Family Name	Given Name	Middle Initial	Date of Birth (month/day/year)
Country of Birth	Social Security No.		A#

| IF IN THE U.S. | Date of Arrival (month/day/year) | | I-94# |
| | Current Nonimmigrant Status: | | Expires on (month/day/year) |

Country where passport issued	Expiration Date (month/day/year)	Date Started with group

Family Name	Given Name	Middle Initial	Date of Birth (month/day/year)
Country of Birth	Social Security No.		A#

| IF IN THE U.S. | Date of Arrival (month/day/year) | | I-94# |
| | Current Nonimmigrant Status: | | Expires on (month/day/year) |

Country where passport issued	Expiration Date (month/day/year)	Date Started with group

Family Name	Given Name	Middle Initial	Date of Birth (month/day/year)
Country of Birth	Social Security No.		A#

| IF IN THE U.S. | Date of Arrival (month/day/year) | | I-94# |
| | Current Nonimmigrant Status: | | Expires on (month/day/year) |

Country where passport issued	Expiration Date (month/day/year)	Date Started with group

Family Name	Given Name	Middle Initial	Date of Birth (month/day/year)
Country of Birth	Social Security No.		A#

| IF IN THE U.S. | Date of Arrival (month/day/year) | | I-94# |
| | Current Nonimmigrant Status: | | Expires on (month/day/year) |

Country where passport issued	Expiration Date (month/day/year)	Date Started with group

Family Name	Given Name	Middle Initial	Date of Birth (month/day/year)
Country of Birth	Social Security No.		A#

| IF IN THE U.S. | Date of Arrival (month/day/year) | | I-94# |
| | Current Nonimmigrant Status: | | Expires on (month/day/year) |

Country where passport issued	Expiration Date (month/day/year)	Date Started with group

OMB #1115-0168

U.S. Department of Justice
Immigration and Naturalization Service

E Classification
Supplement to Form I-129

Name of person or organization filing petition:	Name of person you are filing for:

Classification sought (check one):	Name of country signatory to treaty with U.S.
☐ E-1 Treaty trader ☐ E-2 Treaty investor	

Section 1.   Information about the Employer Outside the U.S. (If any)

Name

Address

Alien's Position - Title, duties and number of years employed

Principal Product, merchandise or service

Total Number of Employees

Section 2.   Additional Information about the U.S. Employer.

The U.S. company is, to the company outside the U.S. (check one):

☐ Parent   ☐ Branch   ☐ Subsidiary   ☐ Affiliate   ☐ Joint Venture

Date and Place of Incorporation or establishment in the U.S.

Nationality of Ownership (Individual or Corporate)

Name	Nationality	Immigration Status	% Ownership

Assets	Net Worth	Total Annual Income

Staff in the U.S.	Executive/Manager	Specialized Qualifications or Knowledge
Nationals of Treaty Country in E or L Status		
Total number of employees in the U.S.		

Total number of employees the alien would supervise; or describe the nature of the specialized skills essential to the U.S. company.

Section 3.   Complete if filing for an E-1 Treaty Trader

Total Annual Gross Trade/Business of the U.S. company   For Year Ending
$

Percent of total gross trade which is between the U.S. and the country of which the treaty trader organization is a national.

Section 4.   Complete if filing for an E-2 Treaty Investor

Total Investment:	Cash	Equipment	Other
	$	$	$
	Inventory	Premises	Total
	$	$	$

Form I-129 Supplement E/L (12/11/91) N

OMB #1115-0168

U.S. Department of Justice
Immigration and Naturalization Service

L Classification
Supplement to Form I-129

Name of person or organization filing petition:

Name of person you are filing for:

This petition is (check one):   ☐ An individual petition   ☐ A blanket petition

Section 1.   Complete this section if filing an individual petition.

Classification sought (check one):   ☐ L-1A manager or executive   ☐ L-1B specialized knowledge

List the alien's, and any dependent family members' prior periods of stay in an L classification in the U.S. for the last seven years. Be sure to list only those periods in which the alien and/or family members were actually in the U.S. in an L classification.

Name and address of employer abroad

Dates of alien's employment with this employer. Explain any interruptions in employment.

Description of the alien's duties for the past 3 years.

Description of alien's proposed duties in the U.S.

Summarize the alien's education and work experience.

The U.S. company is, to the company abroad: (check one)

☐ Parent   ☐ Branch   ☐ Subsidiary   ☐ Affiliate   ☐ Joint Venture

Describe the stock ownership and managerial control of each company.

Do the companies currently have the same qualifying relationship as they did during the one-year period of the alien's employment with the company abroad?   ☐ Yes   ☐ No (attach explanation)

Is the alien coming to the U.S. to open a new office?

☐ Yes (explain in detail on separate paper)   ☐ No

Section 2.   Complete this section if filing a Blanket Petition.

List all U.S. and foreign parent, branches, subsidiaries and affiliates included in this petition. (Attach a separate paper if additional space is needed.)

Name and Address   Relationship

Explain in detail on separate paper.

Form I-129 Supplement E/L (12/11/91) N

OMB #1115-0168

U.S. Department of Justice
Immigration and Naturalization Service

H Classification
Supplement to Form I-129

Name of person or organization filing petition:

Name of person or total number of workers or trainees you are filing for:

List the alien's and any dependent family members; prior periods of stay in H classification in the U.S. for the last six years. Be sure to list only those periods in which the alien and/or family members were actually in the U.S. in an H classification. If more space is needed, attach an additional sheet.

Classification sought (check one):
- [ ] H-1A Registered Professional nurse
- [ ] H-1B1 Specialty occupation
- [ ] H-1B2 Exceptional services relating to a cooperative research and development project administered by the U.S. Department of Defense
- [ ] H-1B3 Artist, entertainer or fashion model of national or international acclaim

- [ ] H-1B4 Artist or entertainer in unique or traditional art form
- [ ] H-1B5 Athlete
- [ ] H-1BS Essential Support Personnel for H-1B entertainer or athlete
- [ ] H-2A Agricultural worker
- [ ] H-2B Nonagricultural worker
- [ ] H-3 Trainee
- [ ] H-3 Special education exchange visitor program

Section 1. Complete this section if filing for H-1A or H-1B classification.

Describe the proposed duties

Alien's present occupation and summary of prior work experience

Statement for H-1B speciality occupations only:
By filing this petition, I agree to the terms of the labor condition application for the duration of the alien's authorized period of stay for H-1B employment.
Petitioner's Signature   Date

Statement for H-1B specialty occupations and DOD projects:
As an authorized official of the employer, I certify that the employer will be liable for the reasonable costs of return transportation of the alien abroad if the alien is dismissed from employment by the employer before the end of the period of authorized stay.
Signature of authorized official of employer   Date

Statement for H-1B DOD projects only:
I certify that the alien will be working on a cooperative research and development project or a coproduction project under a reciprocal Government-to-Government agreement administered by the Department of Defense.
DOD project manager's signature   Date

Section 2. Complete this section if filing for H-2A or H-2B classification.

Employment is:
(check one)
- [ ] Seasonal
- [ ] Peakload
- [ ] Intermittent
- [ ] One-time occurrence

Temporary need is:
(check one)
- [ ] Unpredictable
- [ ] Periodic
- [ ] Recurrent annually

Explain your temporary need for the alien's services (attach a separate paper if additional space is needed).

Form I-129 Supplement H (12/11/91) N   *Continued on back.*

Section 3. Complete this section if filing for H-2A classification.

The petitioner and each employer consent to allow government access to the site where the labor is being performed for the purpose of determining compliance with H-2A requirements. The petitioner further agrees to notify the Service in the manner and within the time frame specified if an H-2A worker absconds or if the authorized employment ends more than five days before the relating certification document expires, and pay liquidated damages of ten dollars for each instance where it cannot demonstrate compliance with this notification requirement. The petitioner also agrees to pay liquidated damages of two hundred dollars for each instance where it cannot be demonstrated that the H-2A worker either departed the United States or obtained authorized status during the period of admission or within five days of early termination, whichever comes first.

The petitioner must execute Part A. If the petitioner is the employer's agent, the employer must execute Part B. If there are joint employers, they must each execute Part. C.

Part A. Petitioner:

By filing this petition, I agree to the conditions of H-2A employment, and agree to the notice requirements and limited liabilities defined in 8 CFR 214.2 (h) (3) (vi).

Petitioner's signature   Date

Part B. Employer who is not petitioner:

I certify that I have authorized the party filing this petition to act as my agent in this regard. I assume full responsibility for all representations made by this agent on my behalf, and agree to the conditions of H-2A eligibility.

Employer's signature   Date

Part C. Joint Employers:

I agree to the conditions of H-2A eligibility.

Joint employer's signature(s)   Date

Joint employer's signature(s)   Date

Joint employer's signature(s)   Date

Joint employer's signature(s)   Date

Joint employer's signature(s)   Date

Section 4. Complete this section if filing for H-3 classification.

If you answer "yes" to any of the following questions, attach a full explanation.

		No	Yes
a.	Is the training you intend to provide, or similar training, available in the alien's country?	☐	☐
b.	Will the training benefit the alien in pursuing a career abroad?	☐	☐
c.	Does the training involve productive employment incidental to training?	☐	☐
d.	Does the alien already have skills related to the training?	☐	☐
e.	Is this training an effort to overcome a labor shortage?	☐	☐
f.	Do you intend to employ the alien abroad at the end of this training?	☐	☐

If you do not intend to employ this person abroad at the end of this training, explain why you wish to incur the cost of providing this training, and your expected return from this training.

OMB#1115-0168

U.S. Department of Justice
Immigration and Naturalization Service

O and P Classifications
Supplement to Form I-129

Name of person or organization filing petition:

Name of person or group or total number of workers you are filing for:

Classification sought (check one):

☐ O-1 Alien of extraordinary ability in sciences, art, education, or business.
☐ P-2 Artist or entertainer for reciprocal exchange program
☐ P-2S Essential Support Personnel for P-2

Explain the nature of the event

Describe the duties to be performed

If filing for O-2 or P support alien, dates of the alien's prior experience with the O-1 or P alien.

Have you obtained the required written consultations(s)?   ☐ Yes - attached   ☐ No - Copy of request attached

If not, give the following information about the organizations(s) to which you have sent a duplicate of this petition.

O-1 Extraordinary ability

Name of recognized peer group	Phone #
Address	Date sent

O-1 Extraordinary achievement in motion pictures or television

Name of labor organization	Phone #
Address	Date sent
Name of management organization	Phone #
Address	Date sent

O-2 or P alien

Name of labor organization	Phone #
Address	Date sent

Form I-129 Supplement O/P/Q/R (12/11/91) N

OMB #1115-0168

U.S. Department of Justice
Immigration and Naturalization Service

Q & R Classifications
Supplement to Form I-129

Name of person or organization filing petition:	Name of person you are filing for:

Section 1.   Complete this section if you are filing for a Q international cultural exchange alien.

I hereby certify that the participant(s) in this international cultural exchange program:
- is at least 18 years of age,
- has the ability to communicate effectively about the cultural attributes of his or her country of nationality to the American public, and
- has not previously been in the United States as a Q nonimmigrant unless he/she has resided and been physically present outside the U.S. for the immediate prior year.

I also certify that the same wages and working conditions are accorded the participants as are provided to similarly employed U.S. workers.

Petitioner's signature	Date

Section 2.   Complete this section if you are filing for an R religious worker.

List the alien's, and any dependent family members, prior periods of stay in R classification in the U.S. for the last six years, Be sure to list only those periods in which the alien and/or family members were actually in the U.S. in an R classification.

Describe the alien's proposed duties in the U.S.

Describe the alien's qualifications for the vocation or occupation

Description of the relationship between the U.S. religious organization and the organization abroad of which the alien was a member.

U.S. Department of Justice
Immigration and Naturalization Service

OMB #1115-0128
Nonimmigrant Petition based on Blanket L Petition

START HERE - Please Type or Print

Part 1. Information about employer.

Sponsoring Company or
Organization's Name

Address - ATTN:

Street Number and Name		Room #
City or Town	State or Province	
Country	ZIP/Postal Code	

Part 2. Information about employment.

This alien will be a:

a. ☐ manager/executive

b. ☐ specialized knowledge professional

Blanket petition approval number is: _____

Part 3. Information about employee.

Family Name	Given Name	Middle Initial
Foreign Address Street Number and Name		Apt. #
City	State or Province	
Country	ZIP/Postal Code	
Date of Birth (Month/Day/Year)	Country of Birth	

Part 4. Additional information about the employment.

Address

Street Number and Name		Room #
City or Town	State or Province	
Country	ZIP/Postal Code	

Dates of intended employment (Month/Day/Year)	From	To
Weekly Wage	Hours per Week	

Title and detailed description of duties to be performed.

_____
_____
_____
_____
_____
_____

Form I-129S (Rev. 12/20/91) N   *Continued on back.*

FOR INS USE ONLY

Returned	Receipt
_____	
_____	
Resubmitted	
_____	
_____	
Reloc Sent	
_____	
_____	
Reloc Rec'd	
_____	
_____	

☐ Petitioner Interviewed

☐ Beneficiary Interviewed

Approved as:
☐ manager/executive
☐ specialized knowledge professional

Validity dates
From: _____

To: _____

Denied (give reason)

Action Block

To Be Completed by
***Attorney or Representative,* If any**

☐ Fill in box if G-28 is attached to represent the petitioner

VOLAG#

ATTY State
License #

Part 4. (Continued).

Give the aliens dates of prior periods of stay in the U.S. in a worked authorized capacity and the type of visa.

_____
_____
_____
_____
_____
_____

Give the alien's dates of employment and job duties for the immediate prior three years.

_____
_____
_____
_____
_____
_____

Summarize the alien's education and other work experience.

_____
_____
_____
_____
_____
_____

Part 5. Signature. Read the information on penalties in the instructions before completing this section.

I certify, under penalty of perjury under the laws of the United States of America, that this petition, and the evidence submitted with it, is all true and correct.   If filing this on behalf of an organization, I certify that I am empowered to do so by that organization. If this petition is to extend a prior petition, I certify that the proposed employment is under the same terms and conditions as in the prior approved petition.   I authorize the release of any information from my records, or from the petitioning organization's records, which the Immigration and Naturalization Service needs to determine eligibility for the benefit being sought.

Signature   Print Name   Date

Please Note: If you do not completely fill out this form, or fail to submit required documents listed in the instructions, then the person(s) filed for cannot be found eligible for the requested benefit, and your petition may be denied.

Part 6.   Signature of person preparing form if other than above.

I declare that I prepared this application at the request of the above person and it is based on all information of which I have knowledge.

Signature   Print Name   Date

Firm Name
and Address

*U.S. Government Printing Office: 1992 — 312-328/51144

For sale by the U.S. Government Printing Office
Superintendent of Documents, Mail Stop: SSOP, Washington, DC 20402-9328

U.S. Department of Justice
Immigration and Naturalization Service (INS)

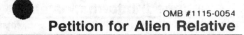

OMB #1115-0054

Petition for Alien Relative

DO NOT WRITE IN THIS BLOCK - FOR EXAMINING OFFICE ONLY

Case ID#	Action Stamp	Fee Stamp
A#		
G-28 or Volag #		

Section of Law:
- ☐ 201 (b) spouse ☐ 203 (a)(1)
- ☐ 201 (b) child   ☐ 203 (a)(2)
- ☐ 201 (b) parent ☐ 203 (a)(4)
-               ☐ 203 (a)(5)

AM CON: _____

Petition was filed on: _____ (priority date)
- ☐ Personal Interview   ☐ Previously Forwarded
- ☐ Pet ☐ Ben. "A" File Reviewed   ☐ Stateside Criteria
- ☐ Field Investigations   ☐ I-485 Simultaneously
- ☐ 204 (a)(2)(A) Resolved   ☐ 204 (h) Resolved

Remarks:

A. Relationship

1. **The alien relative is my**
   ☐ Husband/Wife ☐ Parent ☐ Brother/Sister ☐ Child ☐ Yes

2. Are you related by adoption?   ☐ No

3. Did you gain permanent residence through adoption?   ☐ Yes ☐ No

B. Information about you

1. **Name** (Family name in CAPS)   (First)   (Middle)

2. **Address** (Number and Street)   (Apartment Number)

   (Town or City)   (State/Country)   (ZIP/Postal Code)

3. **Place of Birth** (Town or City)   (State/Country)

4. **Date of Birth** (Mo/Day/Yr)   5. **Sex** ☐ Male ☐ Female   6. **Marital Status** ☐ Married ☐ Single ☐ Widowed ☐ Divorced

7. **Other Names Used** (including maiden name)

8. **Date and Place of Present Marriage** (if married)

9. **Social Security Number**   10. **Alien Registration Number** (if any)

11. **Names of Prior Husbands/Wives**   12. **Date(s) Marriages(s) Ended**

13. **If you are a U.S. citizen, complete the following:**

   My citizenship was acquired through (check one)
   - ☐ Birth in the U.S.
   - ☐ Naturalization (Give number of certificate, date and place it was issued)
   - ☐ Parents
     Have you obtained a certificate of citizenship in your own name?
     ☐ Yes ☐ No
     If "Yes", give number of certificate, date and place it was issued

14a. **If you are a lawful permanent resident alien, complete the following:**
   Date and place of admission for, or adjustment to, lawful permanent residence, and class of admission:

14b. **Did you gain permanent resident status through marriage to a United States citizen or lawful permanent resident?** ☐ Yes ☐ No

C. Information about your alien relative

1. **Name** (Family name in CAPS)   (First)   (Middle)

2. **Address** (Number and Street)   (Apartment Number)

   (Town or City)   (State/Country)   (ZIP/Postal Code)

3. **Place of Birth** (Town or City)   (State/Country)

4. **Date of Birth** (Mo/Day/Yr)   5. **Sex** ☐ Male ☐ Female   6. **Marital Status** ☐ Married ☐ Single ☐ Widowed ☐ Divorced

7. **Other Names Used** (including maiden name)

8. **Date and Place of Present Marriage** (if married)

9. **Social Security Number**   10. **Alien Registration Number** (if any)

11. **Names of Prior Husbands/Wives**   12. **Date(s) Marriages(s) Ended**

13. **Has your relative ever been in the U.S.?**
   ☐ Yes ☐ No

14. **If your relative is currently in the U.S., complete the following: He or she last arrived as a** (visitor, student, stowaway, without inspection, etc.)

   Arrival/Departure Record (I-94) Number   Date arrived (Month/Day/Year)

   Date authorized stay expired, or will expire, as shown on Form I-94 or I-95

15. **Name and address of present employer** (if any)

   Date this employment began (Month/Day/Year)

16. **Has you relative ever been under immigration proceedings?**
   ☐ Yes ☐ No Where _____ When _____
   ☐ Exclusion ☐ Deportation ☐ Recission ☐ Judicial Proceedings

---

INITIAL RECEIPT	RESUBMITTED	RELOCATED		COMPLETED		
		Rec'd	Sent	Approved	Denied	Returned

Form I-130 (Rev. 4/11/91) Y

C. (continued) Information about your alien relative

16. List husband/wife and all children of your relative (if your relative is your husband/wife, list only his or her children).

(Name)   (Relationship)   (Date of Birth)   (Country of Birth)

17. Address in the United States where your relative intends to live
(Number and Street)   (Town or City)   (State)

18. Your relative's address abroad
(Number and Street)   (Town or City)   (Province)   (Country)   (Phone Number)

19. If your relative's native alphabet is other than Roman letters, write his or her name and address abroad in the native alphabet:
(Name)   (Number and Street)   (Town or City)   (Province)   (Country)

20. If filing for your husband/wife, give last address at which you both lived together: From   To
(Name)   (Number and Street)   (Town or City)   (Province)   (Country)   (Month) (Year)   (Month) (Year)

21. Check the appropriate box below and give the information required for the box you checked:

☐ Your relative will apply for a visa abroad at the American Consulate in _____

(City)   (Country)

☐ Your relative is in the United States and will apply for adjustment of status to that of a lawful permanent resident in the office of the Immigration and Naturalization Service at _____. If your relative is not eligible for adjustment of status, he or she will

(City)   (State)

apply for a visa abroad at the American Consulate in _____ ,

(City)   (Country)

(Designation of a consulate outside the country of your relative's last residence does not guarantee acceptance for processing by that consulate. Acceptance is at the discretion of the designated consulate.)

D. Other Information

1. If separate petitions are also being submitted for other relatives, give names of each and relationship.

2. Have you ever filed a petition for this or any other alien before?   ☐ Yes   ☐ No
If "Yes," give name, place and date of filing, and result.

Warning: The INS investigates claimed relationships and verifies the validity of documents. The INS seeks criminal prosecutions when family relationships are falsified to obtain visas.

Penalties: You may, by law be imprisoned for not more than five years, or fined $250,000, or both, for entering into a marriage contract for the purpose of evading any provision of the immigration laws and you may be fined up to $10,000 or imprisoned up to five years or both, for knowingly and willfully falsifying or concealing a material fact or using any false document in submitting this petition.

Your Certification: I certify, under penalty of perjury under the laws of the United States of America, that the foregoing is true and correct. Furthermore, I authorize the release of any information from my records which the Immigration and Naturalization Service needs to determine eligibility for the benefit that I am seeking.

Signature _____ Date _____ Phone Number _____

Signature of Person Preparing Form if Other than Above

I declare that I prepared this document at the request of the person above and that it is based on all information of which I have any knowledge.

Print Name _____ (Address) _____ (Signature) _____ (Date) _____

G-28 ID Number _____

Volag Number _____

U.S. Department of Justice
Immigration and Naturalization Service

OMB #1115-0005
Application for Travel Document

START HERE - Please Type or Print

Part 1.   Information about you.

Family Name	Given Name	Middle Initial

Address - C/O

Street Number and Name		Apt. #
City	State or Province	
Country	ZIP/Postal Code	

Date of Birth (Month/Day/Year)	Country of Birth
Social Security #	A #

Part 2.   Application Type (check one).

a. ☐ I am a permanent resident or conditional resident of the United States and I am applying for a Reentry Permit.

b. ☐ I now hold U.S. refugee or asylee status and I am applying for a Refugee Travel Document.

c. ☐ I am a permanent resident as a direct result of refugee or asylee status, and am applying for a Refugee Travel Document.

d. ☐ I am applying for an Advance Parole to allow me to return to the U.S. after temporary foreign travel.

e. ☐ I am outside the U.S. and am applying for an Advance Parole.

f. ☐ I am applying for an Advance Parole for another person who is outside the U.S. *Give the following information about that person:*

Family Name	Given Name	Middle Initial
Date of Birth (Month/Day/Year)	Country of Birth	

Foreign Address - C/O

Street Number and Name		Apt. #
City	State or Province	
Country	ZIP/Postal Code	

Part 3.   Processing Information.

Date of Intended departure (Month/Day/Year)	Expected length of trip.

Are you, or any person included in this application, now in exclusion or deportation proceedings?

☐ No   ☐ Yes, at (give office name) _____

If applying for an Advance Parole Document, skip to Part 7.

Have you ever before been issued a Reentry Permit or Refugee Travel Document?

☐ No   ☐ Yes (give the following for the last document issued to you)

Date Issued	Disposition (attached, lost, etc.)

FOR INS USE ONLY

Returned	Receipt
Resubmitted	
Reloc Sent	
Reloc Rec'd	

☐ Applicant Interviewed on

Document Issued
☐ Reentry Permit
☐ Refugee Travel Document
☐ Single Advance Parole
☐ Multiple Advance Parole
Validity to _____

If Reentry Permit or Refugee Travel Document
☐ Mail to Address in Part 2
☐ Mail to American Consulate
☐ Mail to INS overseas office
AT

Remarks:
☐ Document Hand Delivered
On _____ By _____

Action Block

To Be Completed by Attorney or Representative, if any
☐ Fill in box if G-28 is attached to represent the applicant

VOLAG#

ATTY State License #

Form I-131 (Rev. 12/10/91) N   *Continued on back.*

Part 3. Processing Information. (continued)

Where do you want this travel document sent? (check one)

a. ☐ Address in Part 2, above

b. ☐ American Consulate at (give City and Country, below)

c. ☐ INS overseas office at (give City and Country, below)

City   Country

If you checked b. or c., above, give your overseas address:

Part 4. Information about the Proposed Travel.

Purpose of trip. *If you need more room, continue on a separate sheet of paper.*	List the countries you intend to visit.

Part 5. Complete only if applying for a Reentry Permit.

Since becoming a Permanent Resident (or during the past five years, whichever is less) how much total time have you spent outside the United States?	☐ less than 6 months ☐ 6 months to 1 year ☐ 1 to 2 years	☐ 2 to 3 years ☐ 3 to 4 years ☐ more than 4 years
Since you became a Permanent Resident, have you ever filed a federal income tax return as a nonresident, or failed to file a federal return because you considered yourself to be a nonresident? (if yes, give details on a separate sheet of paper).	☐ Yes	☐ No

Part 6. Complete only if applying for a Refugee Travel Document.

Country from which you are a refugee or asylee:

If you answer yes to any of the following questions, explain on a separate sheet of paper.

Do you plan to travel to the above-named country?	☐ Yes	☐ No
Since you were accorded Refugee/Asylee status, have you ever: returned to the above-named country; applied for an/or obtained a national passport, passport renewal, or entry permit into this country; or applied for an/or received any benefit from such country (for example, health insurance benefits)?	☐ Yes	☐ No
Since being accorded Refugee/Asylee status, have you, by any legal procedure or voluntary act, re-acquired the nationality of the above-named country, acquired a new nationality, or been granted refugee or asylee status in any other country?	☐ Yes	☐ No

Part 7. Complete only if applying for an Advance Parole.

On a separate sheet of paper, please explain how you qualify for an Advance Parole and what circumstances warrant issuance of Advance Parole. Include copies of any documents you wish considered. (See instructions.)

For how may trips do you intend to use this document?   ☐ 1 trip   ☐ More than 1 trip
If outside the U.S., at right give the U.S. Consulate or INS office you wish notified if this application is approved.

Part 8. Signature.   *Read the information on penalties in the instructions before completing this section. You must file this application while in the United States if filing for a reentry permit or refugee travel document.*

I certify under penalty of perjury under the laws of the United States of America that this petition, and the evidence submitted with it, is all true and correct. I authorize the release of any information from my records which the Immigration and Naturalization Service needs to determine eligibility for the benefit I am seeking.

Signature   Date   Daytime Telephone #

(   )

Please Note: *If you do not completely fill out this form, or fail to submit required documents listed in the instructions, you may not be found eligible for the requested document and this application will have to be denied.*

Part 9. Signature of person preparing form if other than above. (sign below)

I declare that I prepared this application at the request of the above person and it is based on all information of which I have knowledge.

Signature   Print Your Name   Date

Firm Name   Daytime Telephone #

and Address   (   )

OMB No. 1115-0062

U. S. Department of Justice
Immigration and Naturalization Service

Affidavit of Support

(ANSWER ALL ITEMS: FILL IN WITH TYPEWRITER OR PRINT IN BLOCK LETTERS IN INK.)

I, _____, *residing at* _____
           (Name)   (Street and Number)

_____   _____   _____   _____
           (City)   (State)   (ZIP Code if in U.S.)   (Country)

BEING DULY SWORN DEPOSE AND SAY:

1. I was born on_____at_____
                          (Date)   (City)   (Country)

   If you are **not** a native born United States citizen, answer the following as appropriate:

   a. If a United States citizen through naturalization, give certificate of naturalization number _____

   b. If a United States citizen through parent(s) or marriage, give citizenship certificate number _____

   c. If United States citizenship was derived by some other method, attach a statement of explanation.

   d. If a lawfully admitted permanent resident of the United States, give "A" number _____

2. That I am_____years of age and have resided in the United States since (date) _____

3. That this affidavit is executed in behalf of the following person:

Name	Sex	Age
Citizen of--(Country)	Marital Status	Relationship to Deponent
Presently resides at--(Street and Number)	(City)	(State)	(Country)

Name of spouse and children accompanying or following to join person:

Spouse	Sex	Age	Child	Sex	Age
Child	Sex	Age	Child	Sex	Age
Child	Sex	Age	Child	Sex	Age

4. That this affidavit is made by me for the purpose of assuring the United States Government that the person(s) named in item 3 will not become a public charge in the United States.

5. That I am willing and able to receive, maintain and support the person(s) named in item 3. That I am ready and willing to deposit a bond, if necessary, to guarantee that such person(s) will not become a public charge during his or her stay in the United States, or to guarantee that the above named will maintain his or her nonimmigrant status if admitted temporarily and will depart prior to the expiration of his or her authorized stay in the United States.

6. That I understand this affidavit will be binding upon me for a period of three (3) years after entry of the person(s) named in item 3 and that the information and documentation provided by me may be made available to the Secretary of Health and Human Services and the Secretary of Agriculture, who may make it available to a public assistance agency.

7. That I am employed as, or engaged in the business of _____with_____
                                                                    (Type of Business)   (Name of concern)

   at _____
            (Street and Number)   (City)   (State)   (Zip Code)

   I derive an annual income of *(if self-employed, I have attached a copy of my last income tax return or report of commercial rating concern which I certify to be true and correct to the best of my knowledge and belief. See instruction for nature of evidence of net worth to be submitted.)* $_____

   I have on deposit in savings banks in the United States $_____

   I have other personal property, the reasonable value of which is $_____

Form I-134 (Rev. 12-1-84) Y   **OVER**

I have stocks and bonds with the following market value, as indicated on the attached list which I certify to be true and correct to the best of my knowledge and belief. $ _____

I have life insurance in the sum of $ _____

With a cash surrender value of $ _____

I own real estate valued at $ _____

    With mortgages or other encumbrances thereon amounting to $ _____

    Which is located at_____

                     (Street and Number)   (City)   (State)   (Zip Code)

8. That the following persons are dependent upon me for support: *(Place an "X" in the appropriate column to indicate whether the person named is **wholly** or **partially** dependent upon you for support.)*

Name of Person	Wholly Dependent	Partially Dependent	Age	Relationship to Me

9. That I have previously submitted affidavit(s) of support for the following person(s). If none, state *"None"*

           Name   Date submitted

_____

_____

10. That I have submitted visa petition(s) to the Immigration and Naturalization Service on behalf of the following person(s). If none, state none.

           Name   Relationship   Date submitted

_____

_____

11.*(Complete this block only if the person named in item 3 will be in the United States temporarily.)*

    That I ☐ do intend   ☐ do not   intend, to make specific contributions to the support of the person named in item 3. (*If you check "do intend", indicate the exact nature and duration of the contributions. For example, if you intend to furnish room and board, state for how long and, if money, state the amount in United States dollars and state whether it is to be given in a lump sum, weekly, or monthly, or for how long.)*

_____

_____

_____

OATH OR AFFIRMATION OF DEPONENT

I acknowledge at that I have read Part III of the Instructions, Sponsor and Alien Liability, and am aware of my responsibilities as an immigrant sponsor under the Social Security Act, as amended, and the Food Stamp Act, as amended.

I swear (affirm) that I know the contents of this affidavit signed by me and the statements are true and correct.

Signature of deponent _____

Subscribed and sworn to (affirmed) before me this _____*day of* _____ ,19_____

at _____ .*My commission expires on* _____

Signature of Officer Administering Oath _____ *Title* _____

If affidavit prepared by other than deponent, please complete the following: I declare that this document was prepared by me at the request of the deponent and is based on all information of which I have knowledge.

_____

    (Signature)   *(Address)*   *(Date)*

U.S. Department of Justice
Immigration and Naturalization Service

OMB #1115-0061
Immigrant Petition for Alien Worker

START HERE - Please Type or Print

Part 1. Information about the person or organization filing this petition.

If an individual is filing, use the top Name line. Organizations should use the second line.

Family Name	Given Name	Middle Initial

Company or Organization

Address - Attn:

Street Number and Name		Room #
City	State or Province	
Country	ZIP/Postal Code	

IRS Tax #	Social Security #

Part 2. Petition Type. This petition is being filed for: (check one)

a. ☐ An alien of extraordinary ability
b. ☐ An outstanding professor or researcher
c. ☐ A multinational executive or manager
d. ☐ A member of the professions holding an advanced degree or an alien of exceptional ability
e. ☐ A skilled worker (requiring at least two years of specialized training or experience) or professional
f. ☐ An employee of a U.S. business operating in Hong Kong
g. ☐ Any other worker (requiring less than two years training or experience)

Part 3. Information about the person you are filing for.

Family Name	Given Name	Middle Initial

Address - C/O

Street # and Name		Apt. #
City	State or Province	
Country	Zip or Postal Code	

Date of Birth (month/day/year)	Country of Birth
Social Security # (if any)	A # (if any)

If in the U.S.	Date of Arrival (month/day/year)	I-94#
	Current Nonimmigrant Status	Expires on (month/day/year)

Part 4. Processing Information.

Below give the U.S. Consulate you want notified if this petition is approved and if any requested adjustment of status cannot be granted.

U.S Consulate: City   Country

Form I-140 (Rev. 12-2-91)   *Continued on back.*

FOR INS USE ONLY

Returned	Receipt
_____	
_____	
Resubmitted	
_____	
_____	
Reloc Sent	
_____	
_____	
Reloc Rec'd	
_____	
_____	

☐ Petitioner Interviewed
☐ Beneficiary Interviewed

Classification
☐ 203(b)(1)(A) Alien Of Extraordinary Ability
☐ 203(b)(1)(B) Outstanding Professor or Researcher
☐ 203(b)(1)(C) Multi-national executive or manager
☐ 203(b)(2) Member of professions w/adv. degree or of exceptional ability
☐ 203(b)(3) (A) (i) Skilled worker
☐ 203(b)(3) (A) (ii) Professional
☐ 203(b)(3) (A) (iii) Other worker
☐ Sec. 124 IMMACT-Employee of U.S. business in Hong Kong

Priority Date	Consulate

Remarks

Action Block

To Be Completed by Attorney or Representative, If any

☐ Fill in box if G-28 is attached to represent the petitioner

VOLAG#

ATTY State License #

Part 4.   Processing Information. *(continued)*

If you gave a U. S. address in Part 3, print the person's foreign address below. If his/her native alphabet does not use Roman letters, print his/her name and foreign address in the native alphabet.

Name   Address

Are you filing any other petitions or applications with this one?   ☐ No   ☐ yes attach an explanation
Is the person you are filing for in exclusion or deportation proceedings?   ☐ No   ☐ yes attach an explanation
Has an immigrant visa petition ever been filed by or in behalf of this person?   ☐ No   ☐ yes attach an explanation

Part 5.   Additional information about the employer.

Type of petitioner   ☐ Self   ☐ Individual U.S. Citizen   ☐ Company or organization
(check one)
               ☐ Permanent Resident   ☐ Other explain_____

If a company, give the following:
    Type of business

Date Established	Current # of employees	Gross Annual Income	Net Annual Income

If an individual, give the following: Annual Income
    Occupation

Part 6.   Basic information about the proposed employment.

Job Title	Nontechnical description of job

Address where the person will work
if different from address in Part 1.

Is this a full-time
position?   ☐ yes   ☐ No (hours per week _____)   Wages per
                                                              week

Is this a permanent position?:   ☐ yes   ☐ No   Is this a new position?   ☐ yes   ☐ No

Part 7.   Information on spouse and all children of the person you are filing for.

Provide an attachment listing the family members of the person you are filing for. Be sure to include their full name, relationship, date and country of birth, and present address.

Part 8.   Signature. *Read the information on penalties in the instructions before completing this section.*

I certify under penalty of perjury under the laws of the United States of America that this petition, and the evidence submitted with it, is all true and correct.   I authorize the release of any information from my records which the Immigration and Naturalization Service needs to determine eligibility for the benefit I am seeking.

Signature   Date

Please Note: *If you do not completely fill out this form, or fail to submit required documents listed in the instructions, you cannot be found eligible for the requested document and this application may to be denied.*

Part 9.   Signature of person preparing form if other than above. *(Sign below)*

I declare that I prepared this application at the request of the above person and it is based on all information of which I have knowledge.

Signature   Print Your Name   Date

Firm Name
and Address

★U.S. GPO:1992-312-328/51143

NOTICE OF APPEAL TO THE BOARD OF IMMIGRATION APPEALS

SUBMIT IN TRIPLICATE TO:

IMMIGRATION AND NATURALIZATION SERVICE

Fee Stamp

In the Matter of:

File No.

1. I hereby appeal to the Board of Immigration Appeals from the decision, dated _____, in the above entitled case.

2. Briefly, state reasons for this appeal.

3. I _____ desire oral argument before the Board of Immigration Appeals in
   (do)   *(do not)*
   Washington, D.C.

4. I _____ filing a separate written brief or statement.
   (am)   *(am not)*

_____
Signature of Appellant *(or attorney or representative)*

_____
(Print or type name)

_____
Date

_____
Address *(Number, Street, City, State, Zip Code)*

IMPORTANT: SEE INSTRUCTIONS ON REVERSE SIDE OF THIS NOTICE

Form I-290A
(Rev. 10-31-79)N

U.S. Department of Justice
Immigration and Naturalization Service

OMB #1115-0117
Petition for Amerasian, Widow or Special Immigrant

START HERE - Please Type or Print

Part 1. Information about person or organization filing this petition. (Individuals should use top name line; organizations should use the second line.) *If you are filing for yourself, skip to Part 2. A widow(er) must file for him/her self.*

Family Name	Given Name	Middle Initial

Company or Organization Name

Address - C/O

Street Number and Name		Apt. #
City	State or Province	
Country	ZIP/Postal Code	

U.S. Social Security #	A #	IRS Tax # (if any)

Part 2. Classification Requested (check one):

a. ☐ Amerasian

b. ☐ Widow(er) of a U.S. citizen who died within the past 2 years

c. ☐ Special Immigrant Juvenile

d. ☐ Special Immigrant Religious Worker

e. ☐ Special Immigrant based on employment with the Panama Canal Company, Canal Zone Government or U.S. Government in the Canal Zone

f. ☐ Special Immigrant Physician

g. ☐ Special Immigrant International Organization Employee or family member

Part 3. Information about the person this petition is for.

Family Name	Given Name	Middle Initial

Address - C/O

Street Number and Name		Apt. #
City	State or Province	
Country	ZIP/Postal Code	

Date of Birth (Month/Day/Year)	Country of Birth

U.S. Social Security # (if any)	A # (if any)

Complete the items below if this person is in the United States:

Date of Arrival (Month/Day/Year)	I-94 #

Current Nonimmigrant Status	Expires on (Month/Day/Year)

FOR INS USE ONLY

Returned	Receipt
————	
————	

Resubmitted
————
————

Reloc Sent
————
————

Reloc Rec'd
————
————

☐ Petitioner/ Applicant Interviewed

☐ Beneficiary Interviewed

☐ I-485 Filed Concurrently
☐ Bene "A" File Reviewed

Classification

Consulate

Priority Date

Remarks:

Action Block

To Be Completed by Attorney or Representative, if any
☐ Fill in box if G-28 is attached to represent the applicant

VOLAG#

ATTY State License #

Form I-360 (Rev. 09/19/91) N   *Continued on back.*

Part 4. Processing Information.

Below give the United States Consulate you want notified if this petition is approved and if any requested adjustment of status cannot be granted.

American Consulate: City	Country

If you gave a United States address in Part 3, print the person's foreign address below. If his/her native alphabet does not use Roman letters, print his/her name and foreign address in the native alphabet.

Name	Address

Sex of the person this petition is for.	☐ Male	☐ Female
Are you filing any other petitions or applications with this one?	☐ No	☐ Yes (How many? _____)
Is the person this petition is for in exclusion or deportation proceedings?	☐ No	☐ Yes (Explain on a separate sheet of paper)
Has the person this petition is for ever worked in the U.S. without permission?	☐ No	☐ Yes (Explain on a separate sheet of paper)
Is an application for adjustment of status attached to this petition?	☐ No	☐ Yes

Part 5. Complete only if filing for an Amerasian.

Section A. Information about the mother of the Amerasian

Family Name	Given Name	Middle Initial

Living? ☐ No (Give date of death _____) ☐ Yes (complete address line below) ☐ Unknown (attach a full explanation)

Address

Section B. Information about the father of the Amerasian: If possible, attach a notarized statement from the father regarding parentage. Explain on separate paper any question you cannot fully answer in the space provided on this form.

Family Name	Given Name	Middle Initial
Date of Birth (Month/Day/Year)	Country of Birth	

Living? ☐ No (give date of death _____) ☐ Yes (complete address line below) ☐ Unknown (attach a full explanation)

Home Address

Home Phone #	Work Phone #

At the time the Amerasian was conceived:

☐ The father was in the military (indicate branch of service below - and give service number here): _____

    ☐ Army   ☐ Air Force   ☐ Navy   ☐ Marine Corps   ☐ Coast Guard

☐ The father was a civilian employed abroad. Attach a list of names and addresses of organizations which employed him at that time.

☐ If the father was not in the military, and was not a civilian employed abroad. *(Attach a full explanation of the circumstances.)*

Part 6. Complete only if filing for a Juvenile.

Section A. Information about the Juvenile

List any other names used.

Marital Status:	☐ Single	☐ Married	☐ Divorced	☐ Widowed

Answer the following questions regarding the person this petition is for. If you answer "no" explain on a separate sheet of paper.

Is he/she still a juvenile under the laws of the state in which the juvenile court upon which the alien has been declared dependent is located?	☐ No	☐ Yes
Does he/she continue to be dependent upon the juvenile court?	☐ No	☐ Yes
Does he/she continue to be eligible for long term foster care?	☐ No	☐ Yes

Continued on next page.

Part 7. Complete only if filing for a Widow or Widower.

Section   A. Information about the U.S. citizen husband or wife who died.

Family Name	Given Name	Middle Initial

Date of Birth (Month/Day/Year)	Country of Birth	Date of Death (Month/Day/Year)

His/her U.S. citizenship was based on (check one)

☐ Birth in the U.S.   ☐ Birth abroad to U.S. citizen parent(s)   ☐ Naturalization

Section   B. Additional Information about you.

How many times have you been married?	How many times was the person in Section A married?

Give the date and place you and the person in Section A were married.

Did you live with this U.S. citizen spouse from the date you were married until he/she died?

☐ Yes   ☐ No (attach explanation)

Were you legally separated at the time of the United States citizen's death?

☐ Yes (attach explanation)   ☐ No

Give your address at the time of the United States citizen's death.

Part 8. Information about the children and spouse of the person this petition is for.
For a widow or widower, include any children of your deceased spouse.

	Family Name	Given Name	Middle Initial	Date of Birth (Month/Day/Year)
A.				
	Country of Birth	Relationship ☐ Spouse ☐ Child		A #
B.	Family Name	Given Name	Middle Initial	Date of Birth (Month/Day/Year)
	Country of Birth	Relationship ☐ Spouse ☐ Child		A #
C.	Family Name	Given Name	Middle Initial	Date of Birth (Month/Day/Year)
	Country of Birth	Relationship ☐ Spouse ☐ Child		A #
D.	Family Name	Given Name	Middle Initial	Date of Birth (Month/Day/Year)
	Country of Birth	Relationship ☐ Spouse ☐ Child		A #
E.	Family Name	Given Name	Middle Initial	Date of Birth (Month/Day/Year)
	Country of Birth	Relationship ☐ Spouse ☐ Child		A #
F.	Family Name	Given Name	Middle Initial	Date of Birth (Month/Day/Year)
	Country of Birth	Relationship ☐ Spouse ☐ Child		A #
G.	Family Name	Given Name	Middle Initial	Date of Birth (Month/Day/Year)
	Country of Birth	Relationship ☐ Spouse ☐ Child		A #
H.	Family Name	Given Name	Middle Initial	Date of Birth (Month/Day/Year)
	Country of Birth	Relationship ☐ Spouse ☐ Child		A #

Continued on back.

Part 9. Signature.

Read the information on penalties in the instructions before completing this part. If you are going to file this petition at an INS office in the United States, sign below. If you are going to file it at a U.S. consulate or INS office overseas, sign in front of a U.S. INS or consular official.

I certify, or, if outside the United States, I swear or affirm, under penalty of perjury under the laws of the United States of America, that this petition, and the evidence submitted with it, is all true and correct. If filing this on behalf of an organization, I certify that I am empowered to do so by that organization. I authorize the release of any information from my records, or from the petitioning organization's records, which the Immigration and Naturalization Service needs to determine eligibility for the benefit being sought.

Signature	Date

Signature of INS or Consular Official	Print Name	Date

Please Note: *If you do not completely fill out this form, or fail to submit required documents listed in the instructions, then the person(s) filed for may not be found eligible for a requested benefit, and it may have to be denied.*

Part 10. Signature of person preparing form if other than above. (sign below)

I declare that I prepared this application at the request of the above person and it is based on all information of which I have knowledge.

Signature	Print Your Name	Date

Firm Name
and Address

*U.S. Government Printing Office: 1991 — 303-532

U.S. Department of Justice
Immigration and Naturalization Service (INS)

Application for Permanent Residence

OMB # 1115-0053

DO NOT WRITE IN THIS BLOCK

Case ID#	Action Stamp	Fee Stamp
A#		
G-28 or Volag#		

Section of Law
- ☐ Sec. 209(b), INA
- ☐ Sec. 214(d), INA
- ☐ Sec. 13, Act of 9/11/57
- ☐ Sec. 245, INA
- ☐ Sec. 249, INA

Country Chargeable _____

Eligibility Under Sec. 245
- ☐ Approved Visa Petition
- ☐ Dependent of Principal Alien
- ☐ Special Immigrant
- ☐ Other _____

Preference _____

A. Reason for this application

I am applying for lawful permanent residence for the following reason: (check the box that applies)

1. ☐ **An immigrant visa number is immediately available to me because**
   - ☐ A visa petition has already been approved for me (approval notice is attached)
   - ☐ A visa petition is being filed with this application
2. ☐ I entered as the fiance(e) of a U.S. citizen and married within 90 days (approval notice and marriage certificate are attached)
3. ☐ I am an asylee eligible for adjustment
4. ☐ Other: _____

B. Information about you

1. **Name** (Family name in CAPS)   (First)   (Middle)

2. **Address** (Number and Street)   (Apartment Number)

   (Town or City)   (State/Country)   (ZIP/Postal Code)

3. **Place of Birth** (Town or City)   (State/Country)

4. **Date of Birth** (Mo/Day/Yr)

5. **Sex**
   - ☐ Male
   - ☐ Female

6. **Marital Status**
   - ☐ Married
   - ☐ Single
   - ☐ Widowed
   - ☐ Divorced

7. **Social Security Number**

8. **Alien Registration Number** (if any)

9. **Country of Citizenship**

10. **Have you ever applied for permanent resident status in the U.S.?**
    - ☐ Yes ☐ No
    (If Yes, give the date and place of filing and final disposition)

11. **On what date did you last enter the U.S.?**

12. **Where did you last enter the U.S.?** (City and State)

13. **What means of travel did you use?** (Plane, car, etc.)

14. **Were you inspected by a U.S. immigration officer?**
    - ☐ Yes ☐ No

15. **In what status did you last enter the U.S.?**
    (Visitor, student, exchange alien, crewman, temporary worker, without inspection, etc.)

16. **Give your name EXACTLY as it appears on your Arrival/Departure Record (Form I-94).**

17. **Arrival/Departure Record (I-94) Number**

18. **Visa Number**

19. **At what Consulate was your nonimmigrant visa issued?**   Date (Mo/Day/Yr)

20. **Have you ever been married before?**   ☐ Yes ☐ No
    If Yes,   (Names of prior husbands/wives)   (Country of citizenship)   (Date marriage ended)

21. **Has your husband/wife ever been married before?**   ☐ Yes ☐ No
    If Yes,   (Names of prior husbands/wives)   (Country of citizenship)   (Date marriage ended)

INITIAL RECEIPT	RESUBMITTED	RELOCATED		COMPLETED		
		Rec'd	Sent	Approved	Denied	Returned

FORM I-485 (REV. 2-27-87)N

22. List your present husband/wife, all of your sons and daughters, all of your brothers and sisters (If you have none, write "N/A")

Name	Relationship	Place of Birth	Date of Birth	Country of Residence	Applying With You?
					☐ Yes ☐ No
					☐ Yes ☐ No
					☐ Yes ☐ No
					☐ Yes ☐ No
					☐ Yes ☐ No
					☐ Yes ☐ No
					☐ Yes ☐ No
					☐ Yes ☐ No
					☐ Yes ☐ No
					☐ Yes ☐ No

23. List your present and past membership in or affiliation with every organization, association, fund, foundation, party, club, society or similar group in the United States or in any other country or place, and your foreign military service (If this does not apply, write "N/A")

A _____ 19 ____ to 19 ____
B _____ 19 ____ to 19 ____
C _____ 19 ____ to 19 ____
D _____ 19 ____ to 19 ____
E _____ 19 ____ to 19 ____
F _____ 19 ____ to 19 ____
G _____ 19 ____ to 19 ____

24. Have you ever, in or outside the United States:

a) knowingly committed any crime for which you have not been arrested? ☐ Yes ☐ No

b) been arrested, cited, charged, indicted, convicted, fined, or imprisoned for breaking or violating any law or ordinance, including traffic regulations? ☐ Yes ☐ No

c) been the beneficiary of a pardon, amnesty, rehabilitation decree, other act of clemency or similar action? ☐ Yes ☐ No

If you answered Yes to (a), (b), or (c) give the following information about each incident:

Date	Place (City) (State/Country)	Nature of offense	Outcome of case, if any
1)			
2)			
3)			
4)			
5)			

25. Have you ever received public assistance from any source, including the U.S. Government or any state, county, city or municipality?

☐ Yes ☐ No (If Yes, explain, including the name(s) and Social Security number(s) you used.)

26. Do any of the following relate to you? (Answer Yes or No to each)

A Have you been treated for a mental disorder, drug addiction, or alcoholism? ☐ Yes ☐ No

B Have you engaged in, or do you intend to engage in, any commercialized sexual activity? ☐ Yes ☐ No

C Are you or have you at any time been an anarchist, or a member of or affiliated with any Communist or other totalitarian party, including any subdivision or affiliate? ☐ Yes ☐ No

D Have you advocated or taught, by personal utterance, by written or printed matter, or through affiliation with an organization,
1) opposition to organized government ☐ Yes ☐ No
2) the overthrow of government by force or violence ☐ Yes ☐ No
3) the assaulting or killing of government officials because of their official character ☐ Yes ☐ No
4) the unlawful destruction of property ☐ Yes ☐ No
5) sabotage ☐ Yes ☐ No
6) the doctrines of world communism, or the establishment of a totalitarian dictatorship in the United States? ☐ Yes ☐ No

E Have you engaged or do you intend to engage in prejudicial activities or unlawful activities of a subversive nature? ☐ Yes ☐ No

F During the period beginning March 23, 1933, and ending May 8, 1945, did you order, incite, assist, or otherwise participate in persecuting any person because of race, religion, national origin, or political opinion, under the direction of, or in association with any of the following:
1) the Nazi government in Germany ☐ Yes ☐ No
2) any government in any area occupied by the military forces of the Nazi government in Germany ☐ Yes ☐ No
3) any government established with the assistance or cooperation of the Nazi government of Germany ☐ Yes ☐ No
4) any government that was an ally of the Nazi government of Germany ☐ Yes ☐ No

G Have you been convicted of a violation of any law or regulation relating to narcotic drugs or marijuana, or have you been an illicit trafficker in narcotic drugs or marijuana? ☐ Yes ☐ No

H. Have you been involved in assisting any other aliens to enter the United States in violation of the law? ☐ Yes ☐ No

I. Have you applied for exemption or discharge from training or service in the Armed Forces of the United States on the ground of alienage and have you been relieved or discharged from that training or service? ☐ Yes ☐ No

J. Are you mentally retarded, insane, or have you suffered one or more attacks of insanity? ☐ Yes ☐ No

K. Are you afflicted with psychopathic personality, sexual deviation, mental defect, narcotic drug addiction, chronic alcoholism, or any dangerous contagious disease? ☐ Yes ☐ No

L. Do you have a physical defect, disease, or disability affecting your ability to earn a living? ☐ Yes ☐ No

M. Are you a pauper, professional beggar, or vagrant? ☐ Yes ☐ No

N. Are you likely to become a public charge? ☐ Yes ☐ No

O. Are you a polygamist or do you advocate polygamy? ☐ Yes ☐ No

P. Have you been excluded from the United States within the past year, or have you at any time been deported from the United States, or have you at any time been removed from the United States at government expense? ☐ Yes ☐ No

Q. Have you procured or have you attempted to procure a visa by fraud or misrepresentation? ☐ Yes ☐ No

R. Are you a former exchange visitor who is subject to, but has not complied with, the two-year foreign residence requirement? ☐ Yes ☐ No

S. Are you a medical graduate coming principally to work as a member of the medical profession, without passing Parts I and II of the National Board of Medical Examiners Examination (or an equivalent examination)? ☐ Yes ☐ No

T. Have you left the United States to avoid military service in time of war or national emergency? ☐ Yes ☐ No

U. Have you committed or have you been convicted of a crime involving moral turpitude? ☐ Yes ☐ No

If you answered Yes to any question above, explain fully (Attach a continuation sheet if necessary):

_____
_____
_____
_____
_____

27. ☐ **Completed Form G-325A (Biographic Information) is signed, dated and attached as part of this application.** Print or type so that all copies are legible.

☐ **Completed form G-325A (Biographic Information) is not attached because applicant is under 14 or over 79 years of age.**

Penalties: You may, by law, be fined up to $10,000, imprisoned up to five years, or both, for knowingly and willfully falsifying or concealing a material fact or using any false document in submitting this application.

Your Certification

I certify, under penalty of perjury under the laws of the United States of America, that the above information is true and correct. Furthermore, I authorize the release of any information from my records which the Immigration and Naturalization Service needs to determine eligibility for the benefit that I am seeking.

Signature _____ Date _____ Phone Number _____

Signature of Person Preparing Form if Other than Above

I declare that I prepared this document at the request of the person above and that it is based on all information of which I have any knowledge.

(Print Name)　(Address)　(Signature)　(Date)

G-28 ID Number _____

Stop Here

Volag Number _____

*(Applicant is **not** to sign the application below until he or she appears before an officer of the Immigration and Naturalization Service for examination)*

I, _____ swear (affirm) that I know the contents of this application that I am signing including the attached documents, that they are true to the best of my knowledge, and that corrections numbered ( ) to ( ) were made by me or at my request, and that I signed this application with my full, true name:

_____
(Complete and true signature of applicant)

Signed and sworn to before me by the above-named applicant at _____ on _____
(Month) (Day) (Year)

_____
(Signature and title of officer)

U.S. Department of Justice
Immigration and Naturalization Service

OMB No. 1115-0081
Immigrant Petition by Alien Entrepreneur

START HERE - Please Type or Print

| | FOR INS USE ONLY |

Part 1. Information about you.

Family Name | Given Name | Middle Initial

Address - In Care of:

Street # and Name | Apt. #

City or town | State or Province

Country | Zip or Postal Code

Date of Birth (month/day/year) | Country of Birth

Social Security # | A#

If in the U.S. | Date of Arrival (month/day/year) | I-94#

Current Nonimmigrant Status | Expires on (month/day/year)

FOR INS USE ONLY

Returned | Receipt

Resubmitted

Reloc Sent

Reloc Rec'd

☐ Applicant Interviewed

Part 2. Application Type (check one).

a. ☐ This petition is based on an investment in a commercial enterprise in a targeted employment area for which the required amount of capital invested has been adjusted downward.

b. ☐ This petition is based on an investment in a commercial enterprise in an area for which the required amount of capital invested has been adjusted upward.

b. ☐ This petition is based on an investment in a commercial enterprise which is not in either a targeted area or in an upward adjustment area.

Part 3. Information about your investment.

Name of Commercial Enterprise Invested In

Street Address

Phone # | Business Organized as (Corporation, partnership, etc...)

Kind of Business (*Example: Furniture Manufacturer*)

Date established (month/day/year) | IRS Tax #

Date of your initial Investment(month/day/year) | Amount of your Initial Investment $

Your total Capital Investment in Enterprise to date $ | % of Enterprise you own

If you are not the sole investor in the new commercial enterprise, list on separate paper the names of all other parties (natural and non-natural) who hold a percentage share of ownership of the new enterprise and indicate whether any of these parties is seeking classifications as an alien entrepreneur. Include the name, percentage of ownership and whether or not the person is seeking classification under section 203(b)(5).

If you indicated in Part 2 that the enterprise was in a targeted employment area or in an upward adjustment area, give the location at right.   County   State

Action Block

To Be Completed by Attorney or Representative, if any
☐ Fill in box if G-28 is attached to represent the applicant
VOLAG#
ATTY State License #

Form I-526 (Rev. 12-2-91)   ***Continued on back.***

Part 4.   Additional Information about the enterprise.

Type of enterprise *(check one):*

☐ new commercial enterprise resulting from the creation of a new business
☐ new commercial enterprise resulting from the reorganization of an existing business.
☐ new commercial enterprise resulting from a captial investment in an existing business.

Assets: Total amount in U.S. bank account $ _____
Total value of all assets purchased for use in the enterprise $ _____
Total value of all property transferred from abroad to the new enterprise $ _____
Total of all debt financing $ _____
Total stock purchases $ _____
Other (explain on separate paper) $ _____
Total $ _____

Income: When you made investment   Gross $ _____   Net $ _____
Now   Gross $ _____   Net $ _____
Net worth When you made investment $ _____   Now $ _____

Part 5.   Employment creation information.

# of full-time employees in Enterprise in U.S. (excluding you, spouse, sons & daughters)

When you made your initial investment _____   Now _____   Difference _____

How many of these new jobs
were created by your investment? _____   How many additional new jobs will be
created by your additional investment? _____

What is your position, office or title with the new commercial enterprise?

_____

Briefly describe your duties, activities and responsibilities.

_____
_____
_____

Your Salary   Cost of Benefits

Part 6.   Processing Information.

Below give the U.S. Consulate you want notified if this petition is approved and if any requested adjustment of status cannot be granted.
American Consulate: **City**   **Country**

If you gave a U.S. address in Part 1, print your foreign address below. If your native alphabet does not use Roman letters, print your name and foreign address in the native alphabet.

Name   **Foreign Address**

Is an application for adjustment of status attached to this petition?   ☐ yes   ☐ no
Are you in exclusion or deportation proceedings?   ☐ yes (If yes, explain on separate paper)   ☐ no
Have you ever worked in the U.S. without permission?   ☐ yes (explain on separate paper)   ☐ no

Part 7.   Signature. *Read the information on penalties in the instructions before completing this section.*

I certify under penalty of perjury under the laws of the United States of America that this petition, and the evidence submitted with it, is all true and correct.   I authorize the release of any information from my records which the Immigration and Naturalization Service needs to determine eligibility for the benefit I am seeking.

Signature   Date

Please Note: *If you do not completely fill out this form, or fail to submit required documents listed in the instructions, you may not be found eligible for the requested document and this application may be denied.*

Part 8.   Signature of person preparing form if other than above. *(Sign below)*

I declare that I prepared this application at the request of the above person and it is based on all information of which I have knowledge.
Signature   Print Your Name   Date

Firm Name
and Address

*U.S. G.P.O: 1992 — 322-294/69055

For sale by the U.S. Government Printing Office
tendent of Documents, Mail Stop: SSOP, Washington, DC 2040\

U.S. Department of Justice
Immigration and Naturalization Service

Application to Extend/ChangeNonimmigrant Status

OMB #1115-0093

START HERE - Please Type or Print

Part 1. Information about you.

Family Name	Given Name	Middle Initial

Address - In
Care of:

Street # and Name		Apt. #

City	State

Zip Code

Date of Birth (month/day/year)	Country of Birth

Social Security # (if any)	A# (if any)

Date of Last Arrival Into the U.S.	I-94#

Current Nonimmigrant Status	Expires on (month/day/year)

Part 2. Application Type.   (See instructions for fee.)

1. **I am applying for:** (check one)
   a. ☐ an extension of stay in my current status
   b. ☐ a change of status. The new status I am requesting is: _____
2. **Number of people included in this application:** (check one)
   a. ☐ I am the only applicant
   b. ☐ Members of my family are filing this application with me.
       The Total number of people included in this application is _____
       (complete the supplement for each co-applicant)

Part 3. Processing information.

1. I/We request that my/our current or requested
   status be extended until (month/day/year)   _____

2. Is this application based on an extension or change of status already granted to your spouse,
   child or parent?
   ☐ No   ☐ Yes (receipt # _____)

3. Is this application being filed based on a separate petition or application to give your spouse,
   child or parent an extension or change of status?
   ☐ No   ☐ Yes, filed with this application   ☐ Yes, filed previously and pending with INS

4. If you answered yes to question 3, give the petitioner or applicant name:

   _____

   If the application is pending with INS, also give the following information.

   Office filed at_____ Filed on_____(date)

Part 4. Additional information.

1. For applicant #1, provide passport information: Country of issuance	Valid to: (month/day/year)

2. Foreign address: Street # and Name		Apt#

City or Town	State or Province

Country	Zip or Postal Code

Form I-539 (Rev. 12-2-91)   *Continued on back.*

Part 4.   Additional Information. *(continued)*

3. **Answer the following questions. If you answer yes to any question, explain on separate paper.**

	Yes	No
a. Are you, or any other person included in this application, an applicant for an immigrant visa or adjustment of status to permanent residence?		
b. Has an immigrant petition ever been filed for you, or for any other person included in this application?		
c. Have you, or any other person included in this application ever been arrested or convicted of any criminal offense since last entering the U.S.?		
d. Have you, or any other person included in this application done anything which violated the terms of the nonimmigrant status you now hold?		
e. Are you, or any other person included in this application, now in exclusion or deportation proceedings?		
f. Have you, or any other person included in this application, been employed in the U.S. since last admitted or granted an extension or change of status?		

If you answered YES to question 3f, give the following information on a separate paper: Name of person, name of employer, address of employer, weekly income, and whether specifically authorized by INS.

If you answered NO to question 3f, fully describe how you are supporting yourself on a separate paper. Include the source and the amount and basis for any income.

Part 5.   Signature.   *Read the information on penalties in the instructions before completing this section. You must file this application while in the United States.*

I certify under penalty of perjury under the laws of the United States of America that this application, and the evidence submitted with it, is all true and correct. I authorize the release of any information from my records which the Immigration and Naturalization Service needs to determine eligibility for the benefit I am seeking.

Signature	Print your name	Date

Please Note: If you do not completely fill out this form, or fail to submit required documents listed in the instructions, you cannot be found eligible for the requested document and this application will have to be denied.

Part 6.   Signature of person preparing form if other than above. *(Sign below)*

I declare that I prepared this application at the request of the above person and it is based on all information of which I have knowledge.

Signature	Print Your Name	Date

Firm Name and Address

(Please remember to enclose the mailing label with your application)

Form I-539 (Rev. 12-2-91)

Supplement-1

Attach to Form I-539 when more than one person is included in the petition or application. *(List each person separately. Do not include the person you named on the form).*

Family Name	Given Name	Middle Initial	Date of Birth (month/day/year)
Country of Birth	Social Security No.	A#	

IF IN THE U.S.	Date of Arrival (month/day/year)	I-94#	
	Current Nonimmigrant Status:	Expires on (month/day/year)	

| Country where passport issued | Expiration Date (month/day/year) | | |

Family Name	Given Name	Middle Initial	Date of Birth (month/day/year)
Country of Birth	Social Security No.	A#	

IF IN THE U.S.	Date of Arrival (month/day/year)	I-94#	
	Current Nonimmigrant Status:	Expires on (month/day/year)	

| Country where passport issued | Expiration Date (month/day/year) | | |

Family Name	Given Name	Middle Initial	Date of Birth (month/day/year)
Country of Birth	Social Security No.	A#	

IF IN THE U.S.	Date of Arrival (month/day/year)	I-94#	
	Current Nonimmigrant Status:	Expires on (month/day/year)	

| Country where passport issued | Expiration Date (month/day/year) | | |

Family Name	Given Name	Middle Initial	Date of Birth (month/day/year)
Country of Birth	Social Security No.	A#	

IF IN THE U.S.	Date of Arrival (month/day/year)	I-94#	
	Current Nonimmigrant Status:	Expires on (month/day/year)	

| Country where passport issued | Expiration Date (month/day/year) | | |

Family Name	Given Name	Middle Initial	Date of Birth (month/day/year)
Country of Birth	Social Security No.	A#	

IF IN THE U.S.	Date of Arrival (month/day/year)	I-94#	
	Current Nonimmigrant Status:	Expires on (month/day/year)	

| Country where passport issued | Expiration Date (month/day/year) | | |

U.S. Department of Justice
Immigraton and Naturalization Serv Application for Waiver of Groun f Excludability   OMB No. 1115-0048

DO NOT WRITE IN THIS BLOCK

☐ 212 (a) (1)   ☐ 212 (a) (10)   Fee Stamp
☐ 212 (a) (3)   ☐ 212 (a) (12)
☐ 212 (a) (6)   ☐ 212 (a) (19)
☐ 212 (a) (9)   ☐ 212 (a) (23)

A. Information about applicant -

1. Family Name (Surname in CAPS)   (First)   (Middle)

2. Address (Number and Street)   (Apartment Number)

3. (Town or City)   (State/Country)   (ZIP/Postal Code)

4. Date of Birth *(Month/Day/Year)*   5. I&N File Number
A-

6. City of Birth   7. Country of Birth

8. Date of visa application   9. Visa applied for at:

10. Applicant was declared inadmissible to the United States for the following reasons: (List acts, convictions, or physical or mental conditions. If applicant has active or suspected tuberculosis, the reverse of this page must be fully completed.)

_____

_____

_____

_____

_____

11. Applicant was previously in the United States, as follows:
City & State   From (Date)   To (Date)   I&NS Status

_____

_____

_____

_____

_____

12. Social Security Number

B. Information about relative, through whom applicant claims eligibility for a waiver -

1. Family Name (Surname in CAPS)   (First)   (Middle)

2. Address (Number and Street)   (Apartment Number)

3. (Town or City)   (State/Country)   (ZIP/Postal Code)

4. Relationship to applicant   5. I&NS Status

C. Information about applicant's other relatives in the U.S.
(List only U.S. citizens and permanent residents)

1. Family Name (Surname in CAPS)   (First)   (Middle)

2. Address (Number and Street)   (Apartment Number)

3. (Town or City)   (State/Country)   (ZIP/Postal Code)

4. Relationship to applicant   5. I&NS Status

1. Family Name (Surname in CAPS)   (First)   (Middle)

2. Address (Number and Street)   (Apartment Number)

3. (Town or City)   (State/Country)   (ZIP/Postal Code)

4. Relationship to applicant   5. I&NS Status

1. Family Name (Surname in CAPS)   (First)   (Middle)

2. Address (Number and Street)   (Apartment Number)

3. (Town or City)   (State/Country)   (ZIP/Postal Code)

4. Relationship to applicant   5. I&NS Status

Signature (of applicant or petitioning relative)

Relationship to applicant   *Date*

Signature (of person preparing application, if not the applicant or petitioning relative) I declare that this document was prepared by me at the request of the applicant, or petitioning relative, and is based on all information of which I have any knowledge.
Signature

Address   *Date*

	Initial receipt	Resubmitted	Relocated		Completed		
			Received	Sent	Approved	Denied	Returned

Form I-601 (04-24-85)N
Page 1

To be completed for applicants with
active tuberculosis or suspected tuberculosis

A. Statement by Applicant

Upon admission to the United States I will:

1. Go directly to the physician or health facility named in Section B;

2. Present all X-rays used in the visa medical examination to substantiate diagnosis;

3. Submit to such examinations, treatment, isolation, and medical regimen as may be required; and

4. Remain under the prescribed treatment or observation whether on inpatient or outpatient basis, until discharged.

Signature of Applicant

Date

B. Statement by Physician or Health Facility

(May be executed by a private physician, health department, other public or private health facility, or military hospital.)

I agree to supply any treatment or observation necessary for the proper management of the alien's tuberculous condition.

I agree to submit Form CDC 75.18 "Report on Alien with Tuberculosis Waiver" to the health officer named in Section D:

1. Within 30 days of the alien's reporting for care, indicating presumptive diagnosis, test results, and plans for future care of the alien; or

2. 30 days after receiving Form CDC 75.18 if the alien has not reported.

Satisfactory financial arrangements have been made. (This statement does not relieve the alien from submitting evidence, as required by consul, to establish that the alien is not likely to become a public charge.)

I represent (enter an "X" in the appropriate box and give the complete name and address of the facility below.)

☐ 1. Local Health Department
☐ 2. Other Public or Private Facility
☐ 3. Private Practice
☐ 4. Military Hospital

Name of Facility (please type or print)

Address (Number & Street)   (Apartment Number)

City, State & ZIP Code

Signature of Physician   Date

C. Applicant's Sponsor in the U.S.

Arrange for medical care of the applicant and have the physician complete Section B.

If medical care will be provided by a physician who checked box 2 or 3, in Section B., have Section D. completed by the local or State Health Officer who has jurisdiction in the area where the applicant plans to reside in the U.S.

If medical care will be provided by a physician who checked box 4., in Section B., forward this form directly to the military facility at the address provided in Section B.

Address where the alien plans to reside in the U.S.

Address (Number & Street)   (Apartment Number)

City, State & ZIP Code

D. Endorsement of Local or State Health Officer

Endorsement signifies recognition of the physician or facility for the purpose of providing care for tuberculosis. If the facility or physician who signed in Section B is not in your health jurisdiction and is not familiar to you, you may wish to contact the health officer responsible for the jurisdiction of the facility or physician prior to endorsing.

Endorsed by: *Signature of Health Officer*

Date

Enter below the name and address of the Local Health Department to which the "Notice of Arrival of Alien with Tuberculosis Waiver" should be sent when the alien arrives in the U. S.

Official Name of Department

Address (Number & Street)   (Apartment Number)

City, State & ZIP Code

Please read instructions with care.

If further assistance is needed, contact the office of the Immigration and Naturalization Service with jurisdiction over the intended place of U.S. residence of the applicant.

Form I-601 (04-24-85)N
Page 2

U.S. Department of Justice
Immigraton and Naturalization Serv ● ● **Application for Waiver of Grou** ● **of Excludability**   OMB No. 1115-0048

DO NOT WRITE IN THIS BLOCK

☐ 212 (a) (1)   ☐ 212 (a) (10)   Fee Stamp
☐ 212 (a) (3)   ☐ 212 (a) (12)
☐ 212 (a) (6)   ☐ 212 (a) (19)
☐ 212 (a) (9)   ☐ 212 (a) (23)

A. Information about applicant -

1. Family Name (Surname in CAPS)   (First)   (Middle)

2. Address (Number and Street)   (Apartment Number)

3. (Town or City)   (State/Country)   (ZIP/Postal Code)

4. Date of Birth *(Month/Day/Year)*   5. I&N File Number A-

6. City of Birth   7. Country of Birth

8. Date of visa application   9. Visa applied for at:

10. Applicant was declared inadmissible to the United States for the following reasons: (List acts, convictions, or physical or mental conditions. If applicant has active or suspected tuberculosis, the reverse of this page must be fully completed.)

11. Applicant was previously in the United States, as follows:
City & State   From (Date)   To (Date)   I&NS Status

12. Social Security Number

B. Information about relative, through whom applicant claims eligibility for a waiver -

1. Family Name (Surname in CAPS)   (First)   (Middle)

2. Address (Number and Street)   (Apartment Number)

3. (Town or City)   (State/Country)   (ZIP/Postal Code)

4. Relationship to applicant   5. I&NS Status

C. Information about applicant's other relatives in the U.S. *(List only U.S. citizens and permanent residents)*

1. Family Name (Surname in CAPS)   (First)   (Middle)

2. Address (Number and Street)   (Apartment Number)

3. (Town or City)   (State/Country)   (ZIP/Postal Code)

4. Relationship to applicant   5. I&NS Status

1. Family Name (Surname in CAPS)   (First)   (Middle)

2. Address (Number and Street)   (Apartment Number)

3. (Town or City)   (State/Country)   (ZIP/Postal Code)

4. Relationship to applicant   5. I&NS Status

1. Family Name (Surname in CAPS)   (First)   (Middle)

2. Address (Number and Street)   (Apartment Number)

3. (Town or City)   (State/Country)   (ZIP/Postal Code)

4. Relationship to applicant   5. I&NS Status

Additional Information and Instructions

Signature and Title of Requesting Officer

Address   *Date*

This office will maintain only a folder relating to the applicant pursuant to A.M. 2712.01

U.S. Department of Justice
Immigration and Naturalization Service

OMB No. 1115-0145
Petition to Remove the Conditions on Residence

START HERE - Please Type or Print

Part 1. Information about you.

Family Name	Given Name	Middle Initial

Address - C/O:

Street Number and Name		Apt. #
City	State or Province	
Country	ZIP/Postal Code	

Date of Birth (month/day/year)	Country of Birth
Social Security #	A #

Conditional residence expires on (month/day/year)

Mailing address if different from residence in C/O:

Street Number and Name		Apt #
City	State or Province	
Country	ZIP/Postal Code	

FOR INS USE ONLY

Returned	Receipt
Resubmitted	
Reloc Sent	
Reloc Rec'd	
☐ Applicant Interviewed	

Remarks

Action

Part 2. Basis for petition (check one).

a. ☐ My conditional residence is based on my marriage to a U.S. citizen or permanent resident, and we are filing this petition together.

b. ☐ I am a child who entered as a conditional permanent resident and I am unable to be included in a Joint Petition to Remove the Conditional Basis of Alien's Permanent Residence (Form I-751) filed by my parent(s).

My conditional residence is based on my marriage to a U.S. citizen or permanent resident, but I am unable to file a joint petition and I request a waiver because: (check one)

c. ☐ My spouse is deceased.

d. ☐ I entered into the marriage in good faith, but the marriage was terminated though divorce/annulment.

e. ☐ I am a conditional resident spouse who entered in to the marriage in good faith, or I am a conditional resident child, who has been battered or subjected to extreme mental cruelty by my citizen or permanent resident spouse or parent.

f. ☐ The termination of my status and deportation from the United States would result in an extreme hardship.

Part 3. Additional information about you.

Other names used (including maiden name):	Telephone #
Date of Marriage	Place of Marriage

If your spouse is deceased, give the date of death (month/day/year)

Are you in deportation or exclusion proceedings?	☐ Yes ☐ No
Was a fee paid to anyone other than an attorney in connection with this petition?	☐ Yes ☐ No

To Be Completed by Attorney or Representative, if any

☐ Fill in box if G-28 is attached to represent the applicant

VOLAG#

ATTY State License #

Form I-751 (Rev. 12-4-91)   *Continued on back.*

Part 3. Additional Information about you. (con't)

Since becoming a conditional resident, have you ever been arrested, cited, charged, indicted, convicted, fined or imprisoned for breaking or violating any law or ordinace (excluding traffic regulations), or committed any crime for which you were not arrested?

☐ Yes ☐ No

If you are married, is this a different marriage than the one through which conditional residence status was obtained?

☐ Yes ☐ No

Have you resided at any other address since you became a permanent resident?

☐ Yes ☐ No *(If yes. attach a list of all addresses and dates)*

Is your spouse currently serving employed by the U. S. government and serving outside the U.S.?

☐ Yes ☐ No

Part 4. Information about the spouse or parent through whom you gained your conditional residence

Family Name	Given Name	Middle Initial	Phone Number ( )
Address			

Date of Birth *(month/day/year)*	Social Security #	A#

Part 5. Information about your children. *List all your children.   Attach another sheet if necessary*

	Name	Date of Birth *(month/day/year)*	If in U.S., give A#, current immigration status and U.S. Address	Living with you?
1				☐ Yes ☐ No
2				☐ Yes ☐ No
3				☐ Yes ☐ No
4				☐ Yes ☐ No

Part 6. Complete if you are requesting a waiver of the joint filing petition requirement based on extreme mental cruelty.

Evaluator's ID Number:	State: ☐☐ Number: ☐☐☐☐☐☐☐	Expires on *(month/day/year)*	Occupation
Last Name	First Name		Address

Part 7. Signature. *Read the information on penalties in the instructions before completing this section. If you checked block "a" in Part 2 your spouse must also sign below.*

I certify, under penalty of perjury under the laws of the United States of America, that this petition, and the evidence submitted with it, is all true and correct. If conditional residence was based on a marriage, I further certify that the marriage was entered into in accordance with the laws of the place where the marriage took place, and was not for the purpose of procuring an immigration benefit. I also authorize the release of any information from my records which the Immigration and Naturalization Service needs to determine eligibility for the benefit being sought.

Signature	Print Name	Date
Signature of Spouse	Print Name	Date

Please note: If you do not completely fill out this form, or fail to submit any required documents listed in the instructions, then you cannot be found eligible for the requested benefit, and this petition may be denied.

Part 8. Signature of person preparing form if other than above.

I declare that I prepared this petition at the request of the above person and it is based on all information of which I have knowledge.

Signature	Print Name	Date
Firm Name and Address		

Form I-751 (Rev. 12-4-91)   * GPO : 1992 0 - 316-463

U. S. Department of Justice
Immigration and Naturalization Service

Application for Waiver of Requirement to
File Joint Petition for Removal of Conditions

OMB # 1115-0146

Do not write in this block

Case ID #	ACTION STAMP	FEE STAMP
A #		
G-28 or VOLAG #		

Remarks		Receipt	Resubmitted	Relocated Rec'd	Sent	Completed Ret	App	Den

A. Basis of Application for Waiver

I am applying for a waiver of the requirement to file a joint petition for removal of the conditional basis of my residence on the basis of (check one:

☐ A. The termination of my status and deportation from the United States would result in an extreme hardship.

☐ B. I entered into the marriage through which I obtained conditional permanent residence in good faith, but terminated the marriage through divorce or annulment for good cause.

☐ C. I am a child who entered as a conditional permanent resident and I am unable to be included in a Joint Petition to Remove the Conditional Basis of Alien's Permanent Residence (Form I-751) filed by my parent(s). (If Form I-751 was already filed by the applicant's parent(s), attach a copy of that petition or an explanation listing the parents' names and INS file numbers and the date of filing of the petition.)

(Note: Regardless of the reason on which your application is based, you must attach a statement of explanation and any documentation which you wish to be considered in support of your application. Please refer to the instructions.)

B. Information About Conditional Permanent Resident

1. Name (Family name in CAPS) (First) (Middle)
2. Other names used (including maiden name)
3. INS A#   4. Social Security #
5. Telephone #   6. Country of Citizenship
7. Address (Number and Street)
(Town or City) (State/Country) (ZIP/Postal Code)
8. Have you resided at any other address since becoming a permanent resident? (If yes, attach a list of all addresses and dates).
☐ Yes ☐ No
9. Date of Birth   10. Place of Birth
11. Current Employer (Name)
12. Employer's Address (Number and Street)
(Town or City) (State/Country) (ZIP/Postal Code)
13. Employer's Telephone #   14. Job Title
15. Supervisor's Name
16. Supervisor's Telephone #
17. Have you been employed anywhere else since becoming a conditional permanent resident? (If yes, attach a list including all information requested in items 9 through 14 for each.)
☐ Yes ☐ No

C. Information About (Former) Petitioning Spouse/ Parent

1. Name (Family name in CAPS) (First) (Middle)
2. Other names used (including maiden name)
3. INS A#   4. Social Security #
5. Telephone #   6. Country of Citizenship
6. Address (Number and Street)
(Town or City) (State/Country) (ZIP/Postal Code)
8. Has this person resided at any other address the applicant became a permanent resident? (If yes, attach a list of all addresses and dates).
☐ Yes ☐ No
9. Date of Birth   10. Place of Birth
11. Current Employer (Name)
12. Employer's Address (Number and Street)
(Town or City) (State/Country) (ZIP/Postal Code)
13. Employer's Telephone #   14. Job Title
15. Supervisor's Name
16. Supervisor's Telephone #
17. Has this person been employed anywhere else since the applicant became a conditional permanent resident? (If yes, attach a list including all information requested in items 9 through 14 for each.)
☐ Yes ☐ No

Form I-752 (4/15/88)

D. Information Pertaining to the Marriage Through Which You Obtained Conditional Permanent Resident

1.   Date of Marriage   2.   Place of Marriage

3.   Was a fee paid to anyone other than an attorney in connection with the filing of the petition through which status was obtained, or in connection with this application? (If yes, attach a statement of explanation.)   ☐ Yes   ☐ No

4.   Children of applicant. Attach an additional sheet if there are more than six children.

Name	Date of Birth	Place of Birth	INS File Number	Address of Child

Warning:

The INS investigates information claimed on petitions and verifies the authenticity of documents. The INS seek criminal prosecutions when information or documents are falsified to obtain benefits.

Documentation:

All supporting documentation must be submitted in accordance with parts A., B., and C., Item number 6, in the instructions of this form.

Penalties:

You may, by law, be fined up to $250,000 or imprisoned up to five years, or both, for entering into a marriage contract for the purpose of evading any provision of the immigration laws. Furthermore, you may be fined up to $10,000 or imprisoned up to five years, or both, for knowingly and willfully falsifying or concealing a material fact or using any false document in submitting this application.

E. Certification of Information and Authorization for Release of Information.

Your certification *(must be signed in ink)*:

I certify, under penalty of perjury under the laws of the United States of America, that the foregoing is true and correct. Furthermore, I authorize the release of any information from my records which the Immigration and Naturalization Service needs to determine eligibility for the benefit being sought.

_____   _____

Signature of Conditional Permanent Resident   *Date*

Signature of Person Preparing Form, if Other than Above:

I declare that I prepared this documents at the request of the persons above and that it is based on all information on which I have any knowledge.

_____   _____

Signature of Preparer   *Date*   Print Name and Address

U. S. Department of Justice
Immigration and Naturalization Service

OMB # 1115-0163
Application for Employment Authorization

Do Not Write in This Block   **Please Complete Both Sides of Form**

Remarks	Action Stamp	Fee Stamp
A#		

Applicant is filing under 274a.12 _____

☐ Application Approved. Employment Authorized / Extended (Circle One) _____ (Date).
until _____ (Date).

Subject to the following conditions: _____
☐ Application Denied.
　☐ Failed to establish eligibility under 8 CFR 274a.12 (a) or (c).
　☐ Failed to establish economic necessity as required in 8 CFR 274a.12(c) (13) (14) (18) and 8 CFR 214.2(f)

I am applying for:　☐ Permission to accept employment
　　　　　　　　　☐ Replacement (of lost employment authorization document).
　　　　　　　　　☐ Extension of my permission to accept employment (attach previous employment authorization document).

1. Name (Family Name in CAPS)　　(First)　　　　(Middle)

2. Other Names Used (Include Maiden Name)

3. Address in the United States (Number and Street)　(Apt. Number)

　(Town or City)　　(State/Country)　　(ZIP Code)

4. Country of Citizenship/Nationality

5. Place of Birth (Town or City) (State/Province)　(Country)

6. Date of Birth (Month/Day/Year)　　7. Sex
　　　　　　　　　　　　　　　　☐ Male ☐ Female

8. Marital Status　☐ Married　☐ Single
　　　　　　　　☐ Widowed　☐ Divorced

9. Social Security Number (Include all Numbers you have ever used)

10. Alien Registration Number (A-Number) or I-94 Number (if any)

11. Have you ever before applied for employment authorization from INS?
　　☐ Yes (If yes, complete below)　　☐ No
　　Which INS Office?　　　　Date(s)

　　Results (Granted or Denied - attach all documentation)

12. Date of Last Entry into the U.S. (Month/Day/Year)

13. Place of Last Entry into the U.S.

14. Manner of Last Entry (Visitor, Student, etc.)

15. Current Immigration Status (Visitor, Student, etc.)

16. Go to the Eligibility Section on the reverse of this form and check the box which applies to you. In the space below, place the letter and number of the box you selected from the reverse side:

Eligibility under 8 CFR 274a.12

(　　) (　　) (　　)

Complete the reverse of this form before signature.

Your Certification: I certify, under penalty of perjury under the laws of the United States of America, that the foregoing is true and correct. Furthermore, I authorize the release of any information which the Immigration and Naturalization Service needs to determine eligibility for the benefit I am seeking. I have read the reverse of this form and have checked the appropriate block, which is identified in item #16, above.

Signature　　　　　　　Telephone Number　　　　　　Date

Signature of Person Preparing Form If Other Than Above: I declare that this document was prepared by me at the request of the applicant and is based on all information of which I have any knowledge.

Print Name　　　　Address　　　　Signature　　　　Date

Initial Receipt	Resubmitted	Relocated		Completed		
		Rec'd	Sent	Approved	Denied	Returned

Form I-765 (Rev. 04/11/91) Y Page 2

Eligibility

GROUP A

The current immigration laws and regulations permit certain classes of aliens to work in the United States. If you are an alien described below, you do not need to request that employment authorization be granted to you, but you do need to request a document to show that you are able to work in the United States. For aliens in classes (a) (3) through (a) (11), **NO FEE** will be required for the original card or for extension cards. A **FEE** will be required if a replacement employment authorization document is needed. A **FEE IS REQUIRED** for aliens in item (a) (12) who are over the age of 14 years and under the age of 65 years.

Place an X in the box next to the number which applies to you.

- ☐ **(a) (3)** - I have been admitted to the United States as a refugee.
- ☐ **(a) (4)** - I have been paroled into the United States as a refugee.
- ☐ **(a) (5)** - My application for asylum has been granted.
- ☐ **(a) (6)** - I am the fiancé(e) of a United States citizen and I have K-1 nonimmigrant status; OR I am the dependent of a fiancé(e) of a United States citizen and I have K-2 nonimmigrant status.
- ☐ **(a) (7)** - I have N-8 or N-9 nonimmigrant status in the United States.
- ☐ **(a) (8)** - I am a citizen of the Federated States of Micronesia or of the Marshall Islands.
- ☐ **(a) (10)** - I have been granted withholding of deportation.
- ☐ **(a) (11)** - I have been granted extended voluntary departure by the Attorney General.
- ☐ **(a) (12)** - I am an alien who has been registered for Temporary Protected Status (TPS) and I want an employment authorization document. **FEE REQUIRED.**

GROUP C

The immigration law and regulations allow certain aliens to apply for employment authorization. If you are an alien described in one of the classes below you may request employment authorization from the INS and, if granted, you will receive an employment authorization document. The instruction **FEE REQUIRED** printed below refers to your initial document, replacement, and extension.

Place an X in the box next to the number which applies to you.

- ☐ **(c) (1)** - I am the dependent of a foreign government official (A-1 or A-2). I have attached certification from the Department of State recommending employment. **NO FEE.**
- ☐ **(c) (2)** - I am the dependent of an employee of the Coordination Council of North American Affairs and I have E-1 nonimmigrant status. I have attached certification of my status from the American Institute of Taiwan. **FEE REQUIRED.**
- ☐ **(c) (3) (i)** - I am a foreign student (F-1). I have attached certification from the designated school official recommending employment for economic necessity. I have also attached my INS Form I-20 ID copy. **FEE REQUIRED.**
- ☐ **(c) (3) (ii)** - I am a foreign student (F-1). I have attached certification from the designated school official recommending employment for practical training. I have also attached my INS Form I-20 ID copy. **FEE REQUIRED.**
- ☐ **(c) (3) (iii)** - I am a foreign student (F-1). I have attached certification from my designated school official and I have been offered employment under the sponsorship of an international organization within the meaning of the International Organization Immunities Act. I have certification from this sponsor and I have also attached my INS Form I-20 ID copy. **FEE REQUIRED**
- ☐ **(c) (4)** - I am the dependent of an officer or employee of an international organization (G-1 or G-4). I have attached certification from the Department of State recommending employment. **NO FEE.**
- ☐ **(c) (5)** - I am the dependent of an exchange visitor and I have J-2 nonimmigrant status. **FEE REQUIRED.**
- ☐ **(c) (6)** - I am a vocational foreign student (M-1). I have attached certification from the designated school official recommending employment for practical training. I have also attached my INS Form I-20 ID Copy. **FEE REQUIRED.**
- ☐ **(c) (7)** - I am the dependent of an individual classified as NATO-1 through NATO-7. **FEE REQUIRED.**
- ☐ **(c) (8)** - I have filed a non-frivolous application for asylum in the United States and the application is pending. **FEE REQUIRED FOR REPLACEMENT ONLY.**
- ☐ **(c) (9)** - I have filed an application for adjustment of status to lawful permanent resident status and the application is pending. **FEE REQUIRED.**
- ☐ **(c) (10)** - I have filed an application for suspension of deportation and the application is still pending. **FEE REQUIRED.**
- ☐ **(c) (11)** - I have been paroled into the United States for emergent reasons or for reasons in the public interest. **FEE REQUIRED.**
- ☐ **(c) (12)** - I am a deportable alien and I have been granted voluntary departure either prior to or after my hearing before the immigration judge. **FEE REQUIRED.**
- ☐ **(c) (13)** - I have been placed in exclusion or deportation proceedings. I have not received a final order of deportation or exclusion and I have not been detained. **I understand that I must show economic necessity and I will refer to the instructions concerning "Basic Criteria to Establish Economic Necessity."** **FEE REQUIRED.**
- ☐ **(c) (14)** - I have been granted deferred action by INS as an act of administrative convenience to the government. **I understand that I must show economic necessity and I will refer to the instructions concerning "Basic Criteria to Establish Economic Necessity."** **FEE REQUIRED.**
- ☐ **(c) (16)** - I entered the United States prior to January 1, 1972 and have been here since January 1, 1972. I have applied for registry as a lawful permanent resident alien and my application is pending. **FEE REQUIRED.**
- ☐ **(c) (17) (i)** - I am a (B-1) visitor for business. I am and have been (before coming to the United States) the domestic or personal servant for my employer who is temporarily in the United States. **FEE REQUIRED.**
- ☐ **(c) (17) (ii)** - I am a visitor for business (B-1) and am the employee of a foreign airline. I have B-1 nonimmigrant classification because I am unable to obtain visa classification as a treaty trader (E-1). **FEE REQUIRED.**
- ☐ **(c) (18)** - I am a deportable alien who has been placed under an order of supervision (OS). **I Understand that I must show economic necessity and I will refer to the instructions concerning "Basic Criteria to Establish Economic Necessity."** **FEE REQUIRED.**
- ☐ **(c) (19)** - I am an alien who is prima facie eligible for Temporary Protected Status (TPS) and (1) INS has not given me a reasonable chance to register during the first 30 days of the registration period [FEE REQUIRED], or (2) INS has not made a final decison as to my eligibility for TPS. **FEE REQUIRED.**

★U.S.GPO:1992-0-312-328/61844

PLEASE DO NOT STAPLE THIS FORM

ASSURE THAT IMPRESSIONS ON ALL COPIES ARE CLEAR

APPROVED OMB 3116-0006 EXP. 10/31/92
*Estimated Burden Hours: 15 mins. (See page 4).

United States Information Agency
EXCHANGE VISITOR FACILITATIVE STAFF GC/V
CERTIFICATE OF ELIGIBILITY FOR EXCHANGE VISITOR (J-1) STATUS

D

1. _____ ( ) Male ( ) Female

(FAMILY NAME OF EXCHANGE VISITOR) *(FIRST NAME)* *(MIDDLE NAME)*

born |___|___|___| in _____ , _____
(Mo.) *(Day)* *(Yr.)* *(City)* *(Country)*

a citizen of _____ |_____| a legal permanent resident of _____
(Country) *(Code)*

_____ |_____| , whose position in that country is _____
(Country) *(Code)*

_____ |_____|
(Pos. Code)

U.S. address _____

THE PURPOSE OF THIS FORM IS TO:

1 ( ) Begin a new program ( ) Accompanied by _____ immediate family members

2 ( ) Extend an on-going program.

3 ( ) Transfer to a different program

4 ( ) Replace a lost form.

5 ( ) Permit visitor's immediate family (_____ members) to enter U.S. separately.

2. will be sponsored by _____

_____ to participate in Exchange Visitor Program No. |_____|-|_____|-|_____|, which is still valid and is officially described as follows:

3. This form covers the period from |___|___|___| to |___|___|___| Students are permitted to travel abroad & maintain status (e.g. obtain a new visa)
(Mo.) *(Day)* *(Yr.)* *(Mo.)* *(Day)* *(Yr.)*
under duration of the program as indicated by the dates on this from.
If this form is for family travel or replaces a lost form, the expiration date on the exchange visitor's I-94 is _____ .

4. The category of this visitor is 1 ( ) Student, 2 ( ) Trainee, 3 ( ) Teacher, 4 ( ) Professor, Research Scholar or Specialist, 5 ( ) International Visitor, 6 ( ) Medical Trainee, 7 ( ) Alien employee of the USIA. The Specific field of study, research, training or professional activity is_____verbally described as follows:
(Subj/Field Code)

5. During the period covered by this form, it is estimated that the following financial support (in U.S. $) will be provided to this exchange visitor by:

a. ( ) The Program Sponsor in item 2 above $ _____

This Program Sponsor has ☐ has not ☐ (check one) received funding for international exchange from one or more U.S. Government Agency(ies) to support this exchange visitor. If any U.S. Government Agency(ies) provided funding, indicate the Agency(ies) by code ___ ___ ___ .

Financial support from organizations other than the sponsor will be provided by one or more of the following:

b1. ( ) U.S. Government Agency(ies): _____ (Agency Code), $ _____ ; b2. _____ (Agency Code), $ _____

c1. ( ) International Organization(s): _____ (Int. Org. Code), $ _____ ; c2. _____ (Int. Org. Code), $ _____

d. ( ) The Exchange Visitor's Government $ _____   (If necessary, use above spaces

e. ( ) The binational Commission of the visitor's Country $ _____   for funding by multiple U.S. Agencies or Intl. Organizations)

f. ( ) All other organizations providing support $ _____

g. ( ) Personal funds $ _____

6. I.N.S. USE

7. _____
(Name of Official Preparing Form) *(Title)*

_____
(Address)

_____
(Signature of Responsible Officer or Alternate R.O.) *(Date)*

PRELIMINARY ENDORSEMENT OF CONSULAR OR IMMIGRATION OFFICER REGARDING SECTION 212 (e) OF THE I.N.S.

I. *(Name)*

(Title)

have determined that this alien in the above program
1. ( ) is not subject to the two year residence requirement.
2. ( ) is subject based on: — A. ( ) government financing and/or
B. ( ) the Exchange visitor skills list and/or
C. ( ) PL 94 484 as amended
The United States Information Agency reserves the right to make the final determination.

_____
(Signature of Officer) *(Date)*

8. **STATEMENT OF RESPONSIBLE OFFICER FOR RELEASING SPONSOR (FOR TRANSFER OF PROGRAM)**

Date_____ , Transfer of this exchange visitor from program No. _____ sponsored by_____ to the program specified in item (2) is necessary or highly desirable and is in conformity with the objectives of the Mutual Educational and Cultural Exchange Act of 1961.

_____
(Signature of Officer) *(Date)*

IAP-66 (12-90)   **Copy 1-For Immigration and Naturalization Service**   PAGE 1

INSTRUCTIONS FOR AND CERTIFICATION BY the alien beneficiary named on page 1 of this Form:

Read and complete this page prior to presentation to a United States consular or imigration official.

1. I understand that the following conditions are applicable to exchange visitors:

    (a) *Extension of Stay and Program Transfers.* A completed form IAP-66 is required in order to apply for an extension or transfer and may be obtained from or with the assitance of the sponsor. It must be submitted to the appropriate office of the Immigration and Naturalization Service within fifteen to sixty days before the expiration of the authorized period of stay.

    (b) *Limitation on Stay:* STUDENTS -as long as they pursue a substantial scholastic program leading to recognized degrees or certificate. Students for whom the sponsor recommends practical training may be permitted to remain for such purpose for an additional period of up to 18 months after receiving their degree or certificate. BUSINESS AND INDUSTRIAL TRAINEES - 18 months, TEACHERS, PROFESSORS, RESEARCH SCHOLARS, and SPECIALISTS - 3 years. INTERNATIONAL VISITORS - 1 year. MEDICAL TRAINEES: Graduate nurses - 2 years, Medical Technologists, Medical Record Librarians, Medical Record Technicians, Radiologic Technicians, and other participants in similar categories - the length of the approved training program plus a maximum of 18 months for practical experience, not exceeding a total of 3 years. Medical Interns and Residents - the time typically required to complete the medical specialty involved but limited to 7 years with the possibility of extension if such extension is approved by the Director of the United States Information Agency.

    (c) *Documentation Required for Admission or Readmission as an Exchange Visitor:* To be eligible for admission or readmission to the United States, an exchange visitor must present the following at the port of entry: (1) A valid nonimmigrant visa bearing classification J-1, unless exempt from nonimmigrant visa requirements; (2) A passport valid for six months beyond the anticipated period of admission, unless exempt from passport requirements; (3) A properly executed Form IAP-66. Copies one and two of Form IAP-66 must be surrendered to a United States immigration officer upon arrival in the United States. Copy three may be retained for re-entries within a period of previously authorized stay.

    (d) *Change of Status:* Exchange visitors are expected to leave the United States upon completing their objective. An exchange visitor who is subject to the two-year home-country physical presence requirement is not eligible to change his/her status while in the United States to any other nonimmigrant category except, if applicable, that of official or employee of a foreign government (A) or of an international organization (G) or member of the family or attendant of either of these types of officials or employees.

    (e) *Two-Year Home-Country Physical Presence Requirement:* Any exchange visitor whose program is financed in whole or in part, directly or indirectly by either his/her own government or by the United States Government is required to reside in his/her own country for two years following completion of his/her program in the United States before he/she can become eligible for permanent residence (immigration) or for status as a temporary worker ("H") or as an intracompany transferee ("L"). Likewise, if an exchange visitor is acquiring a skill which is in short supply in his/her own country (these skills appear on the *Exchange Visitor Skills List*) he/she will be subject to this same two-year home-country residence requirement as well as alien physicians entering the U.S. to receive graduate medical education or training (Section 212(e) of the Immigration and Nationality Act and PL 94 484, as amended).

2. I seek to enter into, or remain temporarily in, the United States as an exchange visitor under Section 101(a)(15)(J) of the Immigration and Nationality Act, as amended, for a total maximum stay of _____ *(months or years)* for the purpose of (state type of degree, certificate, or other objective toward which your program participation will be directed. Doctors of medicine should indicate their medical specialty): _____

   _____ ,

   and I understand that I shall be permitted only those activities described in Item 2 and 4 on page 1 of this Form.

   I intend to return to (country) _____ where I am (check one) ☐ legal permanent resident ☐ citizen.

3. My passport numbered _____ issued by _____ *(Country)* expires on _____
   _____ *(Mo. Day/Yr.)*

4. I ☐ have ☐ have not *(check one)* been in the United States previously as an exchange visitor. (If you have been in the United States previously as an exchange visitor, show total length of time: _____, and dates: _____):

5. (To be completed only if application is being made for extension of stay or Program transfer. Use a continuation sheet if necessary.) I first entered the United Stated as an exchange visitor, or acquired exchange visitor status, on _____ *(Mo./Day/Yr.)* and have engaged in the following activities under the sponsorship of respective institutions listed for each activity *(include program numbers)*:

   _____

   _____

6. I understand that a counsular or Immigration Officer will make a preliminary determination on whether I am subject to the two-year home-country physical present requirement described in item 1(e) above. The United States Information Agency reserves the right to make a final determination. when determined subject, I will accept that determination and comply with the requirement.

7. I certify that I have read and I understand the foregoing.

   _____   _____   _____
   (Signature of Applicant)   *(Place)*   *(Date: Mo. Day. Yr.)*

INSTRUCTIONS FOR AND CERTIFICATION BY the alien beneficiary named on page 1 of this Form:

Read and complete this page prior to presentation to a United States consular or immigration official.

I. I understand that the following conditions are applicable to exchange visitors:

(a) *Extension of Stay and Program Transfers.* A completed form IAP-66 is required in order to effect an extension or transfer and may be obtained from or with the assistance of the sponsor. It must be submitted to the appropriate office of the Immigration and Naturalization Service within fifteen to sixty days before the expiration of the authorized period of stay.

(b) *Limitation on Stay:* STUDENTS -as long as they pursue a substantial scholastic program leading to recognized degrees or certificate. Students for whom the sponsor recommends practical training may be permitted to remain for such purpose for an additional period of up to 18 months after receiving their degree or certificate. BUSINESS AND INDUSTRIAL TRAINEES - 18 months. TEACHERS, PROFESSORS, RESEARCH SCHOLARS, and SPECIALISTS - 3 years. INTERNATIONAL VISI-TORS - 1 year. MEDICAL TRAINEES: Graduate Nurses - 2 years. Medical Technologists, Medical Record Librarians, Medical Record Technicians, Radiologic Technicians, and other participants in similar categories - the length of the approved training program plus a maximum of 18 months for practical experience, not exceeding a total of 3 years. Medical Interns and Residents - the time typically required to complete the medical specialty involved but limited to 7 years with the possibility of extension if such extension is approved by the Director of the United States Information Agency.

(c) *Documentation Required for Admission or Readmission as an Exchange Visitor:* To be eligible for admission or readmission to the United States, an exchange visitor must present the following at the port of entry: (1) A valid nonimmigrant visa bearing classification J-1, unless exempt from nonimmigrant visa requirements; (2) A passport valid for six months beyond the anticipated period of admission, unless exempt from passport requirements; (3) A properly executed Form IAP-66. Copies one and two of Form IAP-66 must be surrendered to a United States immigration officer upon arrival in the United States. Copy three may be retained for re-entries within a period of previously authorized stay.

(d) *Change of Status:* Exchange visitors are expected to leave the United States upon completing their objective. An exchange visitor who is subject to the two-year home-country physical presence requirement is not eligible to change his/her status while in the United States to any other nonimmigrant category except, if applicable, that of official or employee of a foreign government (A) or of an international organization (G) or member of the family or attendant of either of these types of officials or employees.

(e) *Two-Year Home Country Physical Presence Requirement:* Any exchange visitor whose program is financed in whole or in part, directly or indirectly by either his/her own government or by the United States Government is required to reside in his/her own country for two years following completion of his/her program in the United States before he/she can become eligible for permanent residence (immigration) or for status as a temporary worker ("H") or as an intracompany transferee ("L"). Likewise, if an exchange visitor is acquiring a skill which is in short supply in his/her own country (these skills appear on the *Exchange Visitor Skills List*) he/she will be subject to this same two-year home-country residence requirement as well as alien physicians entering the U.S. to receive graduate medical education or training (Section 212(e) of the Immigration and Nationality Act and Pl. 94 484, as amended).

_____	_____	_____
(Signature of Applicant)	*(Place)*	*(Date: Mo., Day, Yr.)*

IAP-66 (12-85)

VALIDATION BY RESPONSIBLE OFFICER

(1) Exchange visitor is in good standing from _____ to _____

_____
Signature of Responsible Officer

NOTICE TO ALL EXCHANGE VISITORS

To facilitate your readmission to the United States after a visit to another country other than a contiguous territory or adjacent islands you should have the Responsible Officer of your sponsoring organization indicate that you continue to be in good standing on this copy of the IAP-66 form.

(2) Exchange visitor is in good standing from _____ to _____

_____
Signature of Responsible Officer

(3) Exchange visitor is in good standing from _____ to _____

_____
Signature of Responsible Officer

(4) Exchange visitor is in good standing from _____ to _____

_____
Signature of Responsible Officer

(5) Exchange visitor is in good standing from _____ to _____

_____
Signature of Responsible Officer

U.S. Department of Justice
Immigration and Naturalization Service

OMB #1115-0009

Application for Naturalization

START HERE - Please Type or Print

Part 1. Information about you.

Family Name	Given Name	Middle Initial

U.S. Mailing Address - Care of

Street Number and Name		Apt. #
City	County	
State	ZIP Code	

Date of Birth (month/day/year)	Country of Birth
Social Security #	A #

Part 2. Basis for Eligibility *(check one).*

a. ☐ I have been a permanent resident for at least five (5) years .

b. ☐ I have been a permanent resident for at least three (3) years and have been married to a United States Citizen for those three years.

c. ☐ I am a permanent resident child of United States citizen parent(s) .

d. ☐ I am applying on the basis of qualifying military service in the Armed Forces of the U.S. and have attached completed Forms N-426 and G-325B

e. ☐ Other. (Please specify section of law) _____

Part 3. Additional information about you.

Date you became a permanent resident (month/day/year)	Port admitted with an immigrant visa or INS Office where granted adjustment of status.

Citizenship

Name on alien registration card (if different than in Part 1)

Other names used since you became a permanent resident (including maiden name)

Sex ☐ Male ☐ Female	Height	Marital Status: ☐ Single ☐ Married	☐ Divorced ☐ Widowed

Can you speak, read and write English ?   ☐No ☐Yes.

Absences from the U.S.:

Have you been absent from the U.S. since becoming a permanent resident?   ☐ No ☐Yes.

If you answered **"Yes"** , complete the following, Begin with your most recent absence. If you need more room to explain the reason for an absence or to list more trips, continue on separate paper.

Date left U.S.	Date returned	Did absence last 6 months or more?	Destination	Reason for trip
		☐ Yes ☐ No		
		☐ Yes ☐ No		
		☐ Yes ☐ No		
		☐ Yes ☐ No		
		☐ Yes ☐ No		
		☐ Yes ☐ No		

Form N-400 (Rev. 07/17/91)N   *Continued on back.*

FOR INS USE ONLY

Returned	Receipt
Resubmitted	
Reloc Sent	
Reloc Rec'd	
☐ Applicant Interviewed	

At interview

☐ request naturalization ceremony at court

Remarks

Action

To Be Completed by
Attorney or Representative, if any
☐ Fill in box if G-28 is attached to represent the applicant

VOLAG#

ATTY State License #

Part 4. Information about your residences and employment.

A. List your addresses during the last five (5) years or since you became a permanent resident, whichever is less. Begin with your current address. If you need more space, continue on separate paper:

Street Number and Name, City, State, Country, and Zip Code	Dates (month/day/year)	
	From	To

B. List your employers during the last five (5) years. List your present or most recent employer first. If none, write "None". If you need more space, continue on separate paper.

Employer's Name	Employer's Address	Dates Employed (month/day/year)		Occupation/position
	Street Name and Number - City, State and ZIP Code	From	To	

Part 5. Information about your marital history.

A. Total number of times you have been married _____ If you are now married, complete the following regarding your husband or wife.

Family name	Given name	Middle initial

Address

Date of birth (month/day/year)	Country of birth	Citizenship
Social Security#	A# *(if applicable)*	Immigration status (If not a U.S. citizen)

Naturalization (If applicable) (month/day/year)   Place   (City, State)

If you have ever previously been married or if your current spouse has been previously married, please provide the following on separate paper: Name of prior spouse, date of marriage, date marriage ended, how marriage ended and immigration status of prior spouse.

Part 6. Information about your children.

B. Total Number of Children _____ . Complete the following information for each of your children. If the child lives with you, state "with me" in the address column; otherwise give city/state/country of child's current residence. If deceased, write "deceased" in the address column. If you need more space, continue on separate paper.

Full name of child	Date of birth	Country of birth	Citizenship	A - Number	Address

Form N-400 (Rev 07/17/91)N   ***Continued on next page***

Part 7. Additional eligibility factors.

Please answer each of the following questions. If your answer is **"Yes"**, explain on a separate paper.

1. Are you now, or have you ever been a member of, or in any way connected or associated with the Communist Party, or ever knowingly aided or supported the Communist Party directly, or indirectly through another organization, group or person, or ever advocated, taught, believed in, or knowingly supported or furthered the interests of communism?   ☐ Yes ☐ No
2. During the period March 23, 1933 to May 8, 1945, did you serve in, or were you in any way affiliated with, either directly or indirectly, any military unit, paramilitary unit, police unit, self-defense unit, vigilante unit, citizen unit of the Nazi party or SS, government agency or office, extermination camp, concentration camp, prisoner of war camp, prison, labor camp, detention camp or transit camp, under the control or affiliated with:
    a. The Nazi Government of Germany?   ☐ Yes ☐ No
    b. Any government in any area occupied by, allied with, or established with the assistance or cooperation of, the Nazi Government of Germany?   ☐ Yes ☐ No
3. Have you at any time, anywhere, ever ordered, incited, assisted, or otherwise participated in the persecution of any person because of race, religion, national origin, or political opinion?   ☐ Yes ☐ No
4. Have you ever left the United States to avoid being drafted into the U.S. Armed Forces?   ☐ Yes ☐ No
5. Have you ever failed to comply with Selective Service laws?   ☐ Yes ☐ No
    If you have registered under the Selective Service laws, complete the following information:
    Selective Service Number:_____ Date Registered:_____
    If you registered before 1978, also provide the following:
    Local Board Number:_____ Classification:_____
6. Did you ever apply for exemption from military service because of alienage, conscientious objections or other reasons?   ☐ Yes ☐ No
7. Have you ever deserted from the military, air or naval forces of the United States?   ☐ Yes ☐ No
8. Since becoming a permanent resident, have you ever failed to file a federal income tax return?   ☐ Yes ☐ No
9. Since becoming a permanent resident, have you filed a federal income tax return as a nonresident or failed to file a federal return because you considered yourself to be a nonresident?   ☐ Yes ☐ No
10 Are deportation proceedings pending against you, or have you ever been deported, or ordered deported, or have you ever applied for suspension of deportation?   ☐ Yes ☐ No
11. Have you ever claimed in writing, or in any way, to be a United States citizen?   ☐ Yes ☐ No
12. Have you ever:
    a. been a habitual drunkard?   ☐ Yes ☐ No
    b. advocated or practiced polygamy?   ☐ Yes ☐ No
    c. been a prostitute or procured anyone for prostitution?   ☐ Yes ☐ No
    d. knowingly and for gain helped any alien to enter the U.S. illegally?   ☐ Yes ☐ No
    e. been an illicit trafficker in narcotic drugs or marijuana?   ☐ Yes ☐ No
    f. received income from illegal gambling?   ☐ Yes ☐ No
    g. given false testimony for the purpose of obtaining any immigration benefit?   ☐ Yes ☐ No
13. Have you ever been declared legally incompetent or have you ever been confined as a patient in a mental institution?   ☐ Yes ☐ No
14. Were you born with, or have you acquired in same way, any title or order of nobility in any foreign State?   ☐ Yes ☐ No
15. Have you ever:
    a. knowingly committed any crime for which you have not been arrested?   ☐ Yes ☐ No
    b. been arrested, cited, charged, indicted, convicted, fined or imprisoned for breaking or violating any law or ordinance excluding traffic regulations?   ☐ Yes ☐ No

(If you answer yes to 15 , in your explanation give the following information for each incident or occurrence the **city**, **state**, and **country**, where the offense took place, the **date** and **nature** of the offense, and the **outcome** or **disposition** of the case).

Part 8. Allegiance to the U.S.

If your answer to any of the following questions is **"NO"**, attach a full explanation:
1. Do you believe in the Constitution and form of government of the U.S.?   ☐ Yes ☐ No
2. Are you willing to take the full Oath of Allegiance to the U.S.? (see instructions)   ☐ Yes ☐ No
3. If the law requires it, are you willing to bear arms on behalf of the U.S.?   ☐ Yes ☐ No
4. If the law requires it, are you willing to perform noncombatant services in the Armed Forces of the U.S.?   ☐ Yes ☐ No
5. If the law requires it, are you willing to perform work of national importance under civilian direction?   ☐ Yes ☐ No

Form N-400 (Rev 07/17/91)N   ***Continued on back***

Part 9. Memberships and organizations.

A.   List your present and past membership in or affiliation with every organization, association, fund, foundation, party, club, society, or similar group in the United States or in any other place. Include any military service in this part. If none, write "none". Include the name of organization, location, dates of membership and the nature of the organization. If additional space is needed, use separate paper.

_____

_____

_____

_____

_____

Part 10. Complete only if you checked block " C " in Part 2.

How many of your parents are U.S. citizens?   ☐ One   ☐ Both   (Give the following about one U.S. citizen parent:)

Family Name	Given Name	Middle Name

Address

Basis for citizenship: Relationship to you (check one):   ☐ natural parent   ☐ adoptive parent
☐ Birth
☐ Naturalization Cert. No.   ☐ parent of child legitimated after birth

If adopted or legitimated after birth, give date of adoption or, legitimation: (month, day, year)_____

Does this parent have legal custody of you?   ☐ Yes   ☐ No

(Attach a copy of relating evidence to establish that you are the child of this U.S. citizen and evidence of this parent's citizenship.)

Part 11. Signature.   *(Read the information on penalties in the instructions before completing this section).*

I certify or, if outside the United States, I swear or affirm, under penalty of perjury under the laws of the United States of America that this application, and the evidence submitted with it, is all true and correct. I authorize the release of any information from my records which the Immigration and Naturalization Service needs to determine eligibility for the benefit I am seeking.

Signature   **Date**

Please Note: If you do not completely fill out this form, or fail to submit required documents listed in the instructions, you may not be found eligible for naturalization and this application may be denied.

Part 12. Signature of person preparing form if other than above. *(Sign below)*

I declare that I prepared this application at the request of the above person and it is based on all information of which I have knowledge.

Signature   **Print Your Name**   **Date**

Firm Name
and Address

DO NOT COMPLETE THE FOLLOWING UNTIL INSTRUCTED TO DO SO AT THE INTERVIEW

I swear that I know the contents of this application, and supplemental pages 1 through_____, that the corrections, numbered 1 through_____, were made at my request, and that this amended application, is true to the best of my knowledge and belief.

Subscribed and sworn to before me by the applicant.

_____
(Complete and true signature of applicant)

_____
(Examiner's Signature)   Date

1. SURNAMES OR FAMILY NAMES *(Exactly as in Passport)*

2. FIRST NAME AND MIDDLE NAME *(Exactly as in Passport)*

3. OTHER NAMES *(Maiden, Professional, Aliases)*

DO NOT WRITE IN THIS SPACE

4. DATE OF BIRTH			7. PASSPORT NUMBER
DAY	MONTH (letters)	YEAR	

5. PLACE OF BIRTH *(City, Province, Country)*

DATE PASSPORT ISSUED

6. NATIONALITY

DATE PASSPORT EXPIRES

8. HOME ADDRESS *(Include apartment no., street, city, province and postal zone)*

9. NAME AND PRESENT ADDRESS OF PRESENT EMPLOYER OR SCHOOL *(Postal box number unacceptable)*

10. HOME TELEPHONE NO.   11. BUSINESS TELEPHONE NO.

12. SEX
☐ Female
☐ Male

13. COLOR OF HAIR

14. COLOR OF EYES

15. COMPLEXION

16. HEIGHT

17. MARITAL STATUS
☐ Married
☐ Single
☐ Widowed
☐ Divorced
☐ Separated

18. MARKS OF IDENTIFICATION

19. NAMES AND RELATIONSHIPS OF PERSONS TRAVELING WITH YOU
(NOTE; A separate application must be made for a visa for each traveler, including children and infants.)

20. HAVE YOU EVER APPLIED FOR AN IMMIGRANT OR NONIMMIGRANT U.S. VISA BEFORE?
☐ No   ☐ Yes Where?
☐ Visa was issued   When?
☐ Visa was refused   Type of visa?

21. HAS YOUR U.S. VISA EVER BEEN CANCELED?
☐ No   ☐ Yes

22. Bearers of visitors visa may not work or study in the U.S.
DO YOU INTEND TO WORK IN THE U.S.? ☐ No ☐ Yes
If YES, explain.

23. DO YOU INTEND TO STUDY IN THE U.S.? ☐ No ☐ Yes
If YES, write name and address of school as it appears on form I-20.

24. WHO WILL FURNISH FINANCIAL SUPPORT INCLUDING TICKETS?

25. PRESENT OCCUPATION *(If retired, state past occupation)*

26. AT WHAT ADDRESS WILL YOU STAY IN THE U.S.A.?

27. WHAT IS THE PURPOSE OF YOUR TRIP?

28. WHEN DO YOU INTEND TO ARRIVE IN THE U.S.A.?

29. HOW LONG DO YOU PLAN TO STAY IN U.S.A?

30. DO YOU PLAN FUTURE TRIPS TO THE U.S.A. IF SO, WHEN?

31. HAVE YOU EVER BEEN IN THE U.S.A.?
☐ No   ☐ Yes When? For how long?

NONIMMIGRANT VISA APPLICATION

COMPLETE ALL QUESTIONS ON REVERSE OF FORM

OPTIONAL FORM 156 (Rev. 6/88) PAGE 1

32. (a) HAS ANYONE EVER FILED AN IMMIGRANT VISA PETITION ON YOUR BEHALF? ☐ No ☐ Yes
(b) HAS LABOR CERTIFICATION FOR EMPLOYMENT IN THE UNITED STATES EVER BEEN REQUESTED BY YOU OR ON YOUR BEHALF? ☐ No ☐ Yes
(c) HAVE YOU OR ANYONE ACTING FOR YOU EVER INDICATED TO A U.S. CONSULAR OR IMMIGRATION EMPLOYEE A DESIRE TO IMMIGRATE TO THE U.S.? ☐ No ☐ Yes

33. ARE ANY OF THE FOLLOWING IN THE U.S.? *(If YES, circle appropriate relationship and indicate what that person is doing in the U.S., i.e. studying, working, etc.)*

HUSBAND/WIFE _____   FIANCE/FIANCEE _____   BROTHER/SISTER_____

FATHER/MOTHER_____   SON/DAUGHTER _____

34. PLEASE LIST THE COUNTRIES WHERE YOU HAVE LIVED FOR MORE THAN SIX MONTHS DURING THE PAST FIVE YEARS

COUNTRIES   CITIES   APPROXIMATE DATES

35. **IMPORTANT: ALL APPLICANTS MUST READ AND ANSWER THE FOLLOWING:**

A visa may not be issued to persons who are within specific categories defined by law as inadmissible to the United States (except when a waiver is obtained in advance). Complete information regarding these categories and whether any may be applicable to you can be obtained from this office. Generally, they include persons:

— Afflicted with contagious diseases (e.g. tuberculosis) or who have suffered serious mental illness;

— Arrested, convicted for any offense or crime even though subject of a pardon, amnesty, or other such legal action;

— Believed to be narcotic addicts or traffickers;

— Deported from the U.S.A. within the last 5 years;

— Who have sought to obtain a visa by misrepresentation or fraud;

— Who are or have been members of certain organizations including Communist organizations and those affiliated therewith;

— Who ordered, incited, assisted, or otherwise participated in the persecution of any person because of race, religion, national origin, or political opinion under the control, direct or indirect, of the Nazi Government of Germany, or of the government of any area occupied by, or allied with, the Nazi Government of Germany.

DO ANY OF THESE APPEAR TO APPLY TO YOU?

NO ☐   **YES** ☐

If YES, or if you have any question in this regard, personal appearance at this office is recommended. If it is not possible at this time, attach a statement of facts in your case to this application.

36. I certify that I have read and understood all these questions set forth in this application, and the answers I have furnished on this form are true and correct to the best of my knowlegde and belief. I understand that possession of a visa does not entitle the bearer to enter the United States of America upon arrival at a port of entry if he or she is found inadmissible.

DATE OF APPLICATION _____

APPLICANT'S SIGNATURE _____

If this application has been prepared by a travel agency or another person on your behalf, the agent should indicate name and address of agency or person with appropriate signature of individual preparing form.

SIGNATURE OF PERSON PREPARING FORM _____

DO NOT WRITE IN THIS SPACE

HAVE YOU COMPLIED WITH THE FOLLOWING?

1. Answered ALL 35 questions completely
2. SIGNED and DATED the form
3. Affixed ONE PHOTO
4. DETACHED and RETAINED information sheet
5. Included ADDRESSED STAMPED ENVELOPE

37 mm × 37 mm
1½ inches × 1½ inches

——————— PHOTO ———————

Glue or staple photo here

POST SYMBOL:	**BIOGRAPHIC DATA FOR VISA PURPOSES**	Form Approved OMB No. 1405–0016 Approval Expires 12/31/86

INSTRUCTIONS

Complete this form for your entire family (yourself, spouse and unmarried children under 21 years of age).

If space below is insufficient to answer any questions properly, the additional information may be printed below or on a separate sheet of paper and attached to this form.

1. NAME	(Family name)	(First name)	(Middle names)

OTHER NAMES, ALIASES (If married woman, maiden name and surname of any previous spouses)

NAME IN NATIVE LETTERS OR CHARACTERS IF DIFFERENT FROM ABOVE

2. PRESENT ADDRESS

3. PLACE OF BIRTH (City)	(State or province)	(Country)	DATE OF BIRTH (Day) (Month) (Year)

4. SEX ☐ Male ☐ Female	PRESENT NATIONALITY	PAST NATIONALITY

5. NAME OF FATHER	6. MAIDEN NAME OF MOTHER

7. FATHER'S BIRTHPLACE (City) (State or province) (Country)	8. MOTHER'S BIRTHPLACE (City) (State or province) (Country)

9. NAME OF SPOUSE (Maiden or family name)	(First name)	(Middle names)

10. SPOUSE'S BIRTHPLACE (City) (State or province) (Country)	11. SPOUSE'S BIRTHDATE (Month) (Day) (Year)	12. WILL SPOUSE IMMIGRATE WITH YOU? ☐ Yes ☐ No

13. NAME OF SPOUSE'S FATHER	14. NAME OF SPOUSE'S MOTHER

15. BIRTHPLACE OF SPOUSE'S FATHER (City) (State or province) (Country)	16. BIRTHPLACE OF SPOUSE'S MOTHER (City) (State or province) (Country)

17. LIST UNMARRIED CHILDREN UNDER 21 YEARS, NOT U.S. CITIZENS, WHO WILL ACCOMPANY YOU

NAME OF CHILD	PLACE OF BIRTH (City, state or province, country)	BIRTHDATE

18. IF YOU OR YOUR SPOUSE ARE NOW, OR HAVE BEEN, IN THE UNITED STATES, INDICATE:

☐ APPLICANT ☐ SPOUSE	CHECK TYPE OF VISA USED FOR SUCH ENTRY: ☐ Immigrant ☐ Exchange Visitor ☐ Other nonimmigrant Specify

50179-102
NSN 7540-00-130-8317

(over)

OPTIONAL FORM 179
REVISED 8-85
DEPT. OF STATE

19. LIST BELOW IN DATE ORDER ALL PLACES WHERE YOU, YOUR SPOUSE AND UNMARRIED CHILDREN NAMED ON THE OTHER SIDE HAVE LIVED SINCE REACHING THE AGE OF 16. (It is not necessary to list the places where you have lived less than six months.)

FIRST NAME OF FAMILY MEMBER	SEX	CITY OR TOWN, PROVINCE, COUNTRY	OCCUPATION	FROM (Month, Year)	TO (Month, Year)

20. MEMBERSHIP OR AFFILIATION IN ORGANIZATIONS IN EACH COUNTRY NAMED IN ITEM 19: CULTURAL, SOCIAL, LABOR OR POLITICAL

ORGANIZATION	FROM	TO

I certify that all information given is complete and correct.

DATE	SIGNATURE AND PRESENT ADDRESS

OMB APPROVAL NO. 1405-0015
EXPIRES: 8-31-92
* ESTIMATED BURDEN: 1 HOUR

APPLICATION FOR IMMIGRANT VISA AND ALIEN REGISTRATION

PART I – BIOGRAPHIC DATA

INSTRUCTIONS: Complete one copy of this form for yourself and each member of your family, regardless of age. who will immigrate with you. Please print or type your answer to all questions. Questions that are **Not Applicable** should be so marked. If there is insufficient room on the form, answer on a separate sheet using the same numbers as appear on the form. Attach the sheet to this form.

WARNING: Any false statement or concealment of a material fact may result in your permanent explusion from the United States.

This form is Part I of two parts which, together with Optional Form OF–230 PART II, constitute the complete Application for Immigrant Visa and Alien Registration.

1. FAMILY NAME	FIRST NAME	MIDDLE NAME

2. OTHER NAMES USED OR BY WHICH KNOWN *(If married woman, give maiden name)*

3. FULL NAME IN NATIVE ALPHABET *(If Roman letters not used)*

4. DATE OF BIRTH (Day) (Month) (Year)	5. AGE	6. PLACE OF BIRTH (City or town) (Province) (Country)

7. NATIONALITY *(If dual national, give both)*

8. SEX
☐ Male
☐ Female

9. MARITAL STATUS
☐ Single *(Never married)*   ☐ Married   ☐ Widowed   ☐ Divorced   ☐ Separated

Including my present marriage. I have been married_____ times.

10. PERSONAL DESCRIPTION
a. Color of hair _____   c. Height _____
b. Color of eyes _____   d. Complexion _____

11. OCCUPATION

12. MARKS OF IDENTIFICATION

13. PRESENT ADDRESS

Telephone number: Home _____   Office _____

14. NAME OF SPOUSE *(Maiden or family name)*   *(First name)*   *(Middle name)*

Date and place of birth of spouse:

Address of spouse *(If different from your own)*:

15. LIST NAME, DATE AND PLACE OF BIRTH, AND ADDRESSES OF ALL CHILDREN

NAME	DATE AND PLACE OF BIRTH	ADDRESS *(If different from your own)*
_____	_____	_____
_____	_____	_____
_____	_____	_____
_____	_____	_____
_____	_____	_____

THIS FORM MAY BE OBTAINED GRATIS AT CONSULAR OFFICES OF THE UNITED STATES OF AMERICA

NSN 7540-00-149-0919
50230-106

Previous editions obsolete

OPTIONAL FORM 230 I (ENGLISH)
REVISED 4-91
DEPT. OF STATE

PAGE 2

16. PERSON(S) NAMED IN 14 AND 15 WHO WILL ACCOMPANY OR FOLLOW ME TO THE UNITED STATES.

17. NAME OF FATHER, DATE AND PLACE OF BIRTH, AND ADDRESS *If deceased, so state, giving year of death)*

18. MAIDEN NAME OF MOTHER, DATE AND PLACE OF BIRTH, AND ADDRESS *(If deceased, so state, giving year of death)*

19. IF NEITHER PARENT IS LIVING PROVIDE NAME AND ADDRESS OF NEXT OF KIN *(nearest relative)* **IN YOUR HOME COUNTRY.**

20. LIST ALL LANGUAGES YOU CAN SPEAK, READ, AND WRITE

LANGUAGE	SPEAK	READ	WRITE

21. LIST BELOW ALL PLACES YOU HAVE LIVED FOR SIX MONTHS OR LONGER SINCE REACHING THE AGE OF 16. BEGIN WITH YOUR PRESENT RESIDENCE.

CITY OR TOWN	PROVINCE	COUNTRY	OCCUPATION	DATES (FROM – TO)

22. LIST ANY POLITICAL, PROFESSIONAL, OR SOCIAL ORGANIZATIONS AFFILIATED WITH COMMUNIST, TOTALITARIAN, TERRORIST OR NAZI ORGANIZATIONS WHICH YOU ARE NOW OR HAVE BEEN A MEMBER OF OR AFFILIATED WITH SINCE YOUR 16TH BIRTHDAY.

NAME AND ADDRESS	FROM/TO	TYPE OF MEMBERSHIP

23. LIST DATES OF ALL PREVIOUS RESIDENCE IN OR VISITS TO THE UNITED STATES. *(If never, so state)* **GIVE TYPE OF VISA STATUS IF ANY. GIVE I.N.S. "A" NUMBER IF ANY.**

LOCATION	FROM/TO	VISA	I.N.S. FILE NO. *(If known)*

SIGNATURE OF APPLICANT	DATE

NOTE: Return this completed form immediately to the consular office address on the covering letter. This form will become part of your immigrant visa and your visa application cannot be processed until this form is complete.

*Public reporting burden for this collection of information is estimated to average 24 hours per response, including time required for searching existing data sources, gathering the necessary data, providing the information required, and reviewing the final collection. Send comments on the accuracy of this estimate of the burden and recommendations for reducing it to: Department of State (OIS/RA/DR) Washington, D.C. 20520–0264, and to the Office of Information and Regulatory Affairs, Office of Management and Budget, Paperwork Reduction Project (1405–0015), Washington, D. C. 20503.

FORM APPROVED
O.M.B. No. 1405-0015

OPTIONAL FORM 230 (English) (Rev. 6-82)
DEPT. OF STATE
50230—105

APPLICATION FOR IMMIGRANT VISA AND ALIEN REGISTRATION

INSTRUCTIONS: This form must be filled out by typewriter, or if by hand in legible block letters. All questions must be answered, if applicable. Questions which are not applicable should be so marked. *If there is insufficient room on the form, answer on separate sheets, in duplicate, using the same numbers as appear on the form.* Attach the sheets to the forms. DO NOT SIGN this form until instructed to do so by the consular officer. The fee for filing this application for an immigrant visa [varies]. The fee should be paid in United States dollars or local currency equivalent or by bank draft, when you appear before the consular officer.

WARNING: Any false statement or concealment of a material fact may result in your permanent exclusion from the United States. Even though you should be admitted to the United States, a fraudulent entry could be grounds for your prosecution and/or deportation.

1. Family name   First name   Middle name

2. Other names used or by which known *(If married woman, give maiden name)*

3. Full name in native alphabet *(If Roman letters not used)*

4. Date of birth
(Day)   (Month)   (Year) | **5. Age** | **6. Place of birth**
(City or town)   (Province)   (Country)

7. Nationality | **8. Sex** ☐ Male ☐ Female | **9. Marital status**
☐ Single *(never married)* ☐ Married ☐ Widowed ☐ Divorced ☐ Separated
Including my present marriage, I have been married .... times.

10. Occupation | **11. Present address**

12. Name, address, date and place of birth of wife/husband *(Give maiden name of wife)*

Date and place of marriage

13. Names, addresses, dates and places of birth of all children

14. Person(s) named in 12 and 13 who will accompany or follow me to the United States | **15. Final address in the United States**

16. Person you intend to join *(Give name, address, and relationship, if any)* | **17. Name and address of sponsoring person or organization** *(If different from 16)*

18. Personal description
(a) Color of hair   (c) Height ....feet ....inches | **19. Marks of identification**

(b) Color of eyes   (d) Complexion | **20. Purpose in going to the United States**

21. Length of intended stay *(If permanently, so state)* | **22. Intended port of entry** | **23. Do you have a ticket to final destination?**

THIS FORM MAY BE OBTAINED GRATIS AT CONSULAR OFFICES OF THE UNITED STATES OF AMERICA

NSN 7540-00-149-0919   Previous edition not usable

OPTIONAL FORM 230 (English) (Rev. 6-82)   Page 2

24. Personal financial resources
   (a) Cash ....
   (c) Real estate (value) ....
   (b) Bank deposits ....
   (d) Other (describe) ....

25. Father's name, address, date and place of birth *(If deceased, so state giving year of death)*

26. Mother's maiden name, address, date and place of birth *(If deceased, so state giving year of death)*

27. Name, address, and relationship of next of kin in home country *(If neither parent is living)*

28. List all places of residence for 6 months or more since your 16th birthday

City or town	*Province*	*Country*	*Dates (From-To)*	*Calling or occupation*

29. List all organizations you are now or have been a member of or affiliated with since your 16th birthday *(Include professional, vocational, social, and political organizations)*

Name and address	*Dates (From-To)*	*Type of membership and office held, if any*

30. List all languages, including your own, that you can speak, read, and write

Language	*Speak*	*Read*	*Write*

31. Inclusive dates of previous residence in or visits to the United States *(Give type of visa or status) (If never, so state)*

32. Have you ever been treated in a hospital, institution, or elsewhere for a mental disorder, drug addiction, or alcoholism? *(If answer is Yes, explain)*   Yes ☐ No ☐

33. Have you ever been arrested, convicted, or confined in a prison, or have you ever been placed in a poorhouse or other charitable institution? *(If answer is Yes, explain)*   Yes ☐ No ☐

34. Have you ever been the beneficiary of a pardon, amnesty, rehabilitation decree, other act of clemency, or similar action? *(If answer is Yes, explain)*   Yes ☐ No ☐

35. Have you ever applied for a visa to enter the United States? *(If answer is Yes, state where and when, whether you applied for a nonimmigrant or an immigrant visa, and whether the visa was issued or refused)*   Yes ☐ No ☐

36. Have you been refused admission to the United States during the last 12 months? *(If answer is Yes, explain)*   Yes ☐ No ☐

37. Have you ever registered with a draft board under United States Selective Service Laws? *(If answer is Yes, explain)*   Yes ☐ No ☐

38. Have you ever applied for relief from training and service in the United States Armed Forces or departed from or remained outside the United States to avoid or evade military service? *(If answer is Yes, explain)*   Yes ☐ No ☐

39. Do you intend to enter the United States from Canada, Mexico, or an island adjacent to the United States within 2 years after arrival in Canada, Mexico, or such adjacent island? *(If answer is Yes, give the name of the transportation company by which you entered or intend to enter Canada, Mexico, or such island)*   Yes ☐ No ☐

40. United States laws governing the issuance of visas require each applicant to state whether or not he or she is a member of any class of individuals excluded from admission into the United States. The excludable classes are described below. You should read carefully the following paragraphs; your understanding of their content and the answers you give the questions that follow will assist the consular officer to reach a decision on your eligibility to receive a visa.

EXCEPT AS OTHERWISE PROVIDED BY LAW, ALIENS WITHIN ANY OF THE FOLLOWING CLASSES ARE INELIGIBLE TO RECEIVE AN IMMIGRANT VISA:

(a) Aliens who are mentally retarded, insane, or who have suffered one or more attacks of insanity; aliens afflicted with psychopathic personality, sexual deviation, a mental defect, narcotic drug addition, chronic alcoholism, or any communicable disease; aliens who have a physical defect, disease, or disability affecting their ability to earn a living; aliens who are paupers, professional beggars, or vagrants; aliens convicted of a crime involving moral turpitude or who admit committing the essential elements of such a crime, or who have been sentenced to confinement for at least 5 years in the aggregate for conviction of two or more crimes; aliens who are polygamists, or who practice or advocate polygamy; aliens who are prostitutes, or who have engaged in, benefited financially from, procured, or imported persons for the purpose of prostitution, or who seek entry to the United States to engage in prostitution or other commercialized vice, or any immoral sexual act; aliens who seek entry to perform skilled or unskilled labor and who have not been certified by the Secretary of Labor; and aliens likely to become a public charge in the United States.

Do any of the foregoing classes apply to you?   Yes ☐   No ☐   *(If answer is Yes, explain)*

(b) Aliens who seek re-entry within 1 year of their exclusion from the United States, or who, within the past 5 years, have been arrested and deported from the United States, or removed at Government expense in lieu of deportation, or removed as an alien in distress or as an alien enemy; aliens who procure or attempt to procure a visa or other documentation by fraud or willful misrepresentation; aliens who are not eligible to acquire United States citizenship, or who have departed from or remained outside the United States to avoid United States military service in time of war or national emergency; aliens who have been convicted for violating or for conspiring to violate certain laws or regulations relating to narcotic drugs or marihuana, or who are known or believed to be, or to have been, an illicit trafficker in narcotic drugs or marihuana; aliens who are unable to read and understand some language or dialect; aliens who, knowingly and for gain, have encouraged or assisted any other alien to enter, or attempt to enter, the United States in violation of law; aliens who are former exchange visitors who have not fulfilled the 2-year foreign residence requirement; and aliens who are graduates of foreign medical schools destined to the United States to perform medical services are ineligible for a visa unless they have passed parts I and II of the NBME Exam or an equivalent exam as determined by the Department of Health and Human Services.

Do any of the foregoing classes apply to you?   Yes ☐   No ☐   *(If answer is Yes, explain)*

(c) Aliens who are, or at any time have been, anarchists, or members of or affiliated with any Communist or other totalitarian party, including any subdivision or affiliate thereof; aliens who advocate or teach, or who have advocated or taught, either by personal utterance, or by means of any written or printed matter, or through affiliation with an organization, (1) opposition to organized government, (2) the overthrow of government by force and violence, (3) the assaulting or killing of government officials because of their official character, (4) the unlawful destruction of property, (5) sabotage, or (6) the doctrines of world communism, or the establishment of a totalitarian dictatorship in the United States; aliens who seek to enter the United States to engage in prejudicial activities or unlawful activities of a subversive nature.

Do any of the foregoing classes apply to you?   Yes ☐   No ☐   *(If answer is Yes, explain)*

(d) Aliens who during the period beginning on March 23, 1933, and ending on May 8, 1945, under the control, direct or indirect, of the Nazi Government of Germany or of the government of any area occupied by, or allied with, the Nazi Government of Germany, ordered, incited, assisted, or otherwise participated in the persecution of any person because of race, religion, national origin, or political opinion.

Does the foregoing class apply to you?   Yes ☐   No ☐   *(If answer is Yes, explain)*

41. Were you assisted in completing this application? *(If answer is Yes, give name and address of person assisting you indicating whether relative, friend, travel agent, attorney, or other)*   Yes ☐   No ☐

Name	*Address*	*Relationship*

OPTIONAL FORM 230 (English) (Rev. 6-82) Page 4

42. The following documents are submitted in support of this application:

- ☐ Passport
- ☐ Birth certificate
- ☐ Police certificate(s)
- ☐ Marriage certificate
- ☐ Death certificate
- ☐ Divorce decree
- ☐ Military record

- ☐ Evidence of own assets
- ☐ Affidavit of support
- ☐ Offer of employment
- ☐ Medical record(s)
- ☐ Photographs
- ☐ Other (describe)
- ☐ Birth certificate of spouse

☐ Birth certificates of unmarried children under age 21 who will not be immigrating at this time *(List those for whom birth certificates are not available or whose birth certificates are being submitted at this time in connection with a visa application.)*

DO NOT WRITE BELOW THE FOLLOWING LINE
The consular officer will assist you in answering parts 43 and 44

---

43. I claim to be exempt from ineligibility to receive a visa and exclusion under item.............. in part 40 for the following reasons:

212(a)(5)   Beneficiary of Waiver under ☐ 212(a)(28)(I)(i)   ☐ 212(e)
    ☐ Not applicable   ☐ 212(a)(28)(I)(ii)   ☐ 212(g)
    ☐ Attached   ☐ 212(b)(1)   ☐ 212(h)
                      ☐ 212(b)(2)   ☐ 212(i)

---

44. I claim to be a

☐ .... preference immigrant subject to the numerical limitation for ....
                                                                         (Foreign state or dependent area)

☐ Special immigrant not subject to limitation

☐ Immediate relative of a United States citizen

    My claim is based on the following facts:

☐ I am (my .... is) the beneficiary of a .... petition.

☐ I am a returning resident alien.

☐ I derive foreign state chargeability under Section 202(b) through my ....

☐ Other (specify)

I understand that I am required to surrender my visa to the United States Immigration Officer at the place where I apply to enter the United States, and that the possession of a visa does not entitle me to enter the United States if at that time I am found to be inadmissible under the immigration laws.

I understand that any willfully false or misleading statement or willful concealment of a material fact made by me herein may subject me to permanent exclusion from the United States and, if I am admitted to the United States, may subject me to criminal prosecution and/or deportation.

I, the undersigned applicant for a United States immigrant visa, do solemnly swear (or affirm) that all statements which appear in this application have been made by me, including the answers to parts 32 through 41 inclusive, and are true and complete to the best of my knowledge and belief. I do further swear (or affirm) that, if admitted into the United States, I will not engage in activities which would be prejudicial to the public interest, or endanger the welfare, safety, or security of the United States; in activities which would be prohibited by the laws of the United States relating to espionage, sabotage, public disorder, or in other activities subversive to the national security; in any activity a purpose of which is the opposition to, or the control, or overthrow of, the Government of the United States, by force, violence, or other unconstitutional means.

I understand all the foregoing statements, having asked for and obtained an explanation on every point which was not clear to me.

(Signature of Applicant)

The relationships claimed in items 12 and 13 verified by
documentation submitted to consular officer except as noted:

Subscribed and sworn to before me this .... day of............................, 19......... at...

(Consular Officer)

TARIFF ITEM NO. 20

List of Visa Waiver Countries

Countries whose nationals do not require visas to enter the United States if they are coming as tourists for 90 days or less

Belgium	Germany	Luxembourg
Britain	Holland	Norway
Denmark	Iceland	Spain
Finland	Italy	Sweden
France	Japan	Switzerland

List of Treaty Trader/Investor Countries

Countries that have E-1 Treaty Trader Agreements with the United States

Argentina	Ethiopia	Israel
Australia	Finland	Italy
Austria	France (including the	Japan
Belgium	departments of	Korea
Bolivia	Martinique, Guadeloupe,	Latvia
Brunei	French Guiana, and	Liberia
Canada	Reunion)	Luxembourg
China (Taiwan)	Germany	Netherlands (including
Colombia	Greece	Aruba and the
Costa Rica	Honduras	Netherlands Antilles)
Denmark	Iran	Norway
Estonia	Ireland	Oman

Pakistan
Paraguay
Philippines
Spain

Suriname
Sweden
Switzerland
Thailand

Togo
Turkey
United Kingdom
Yugoslavia

Countries that have E-2 Bilateral Investment Treaties with the United States

Argentina
Australia
Austria
Bangladesh
Belgium
Cameroon
Canada
China (Taiwan)
Colombia
Costa Rica
Egypt
Ethiopia
France (including the
    departments of
    Martinique, Guadeloupe,

French Guiana, and
    Reunion)
Germany
Grenada
Honduras
Iran
Italy
Japan
Korea
Liberia
Luxembourg
Netherlands (including
    Aruba and Netherlands
    Antilles)
Norway

Oman
Pakistan
Panama
Paraguay
Philippines
Senegal
Spain
Suriname
Sweden
Switzerland
Thailand
Togo
United Kingdom
Yugoslavia
Zaire

Naturalization Eligibility Charts

Chart Number 1: For determining whether LEGITIMATE CHILDREN BORN OUTSIDE THE UNITED STATES acquired United States citizenship at birth

PERIOD	PARENTS	RESIDENCE REQUIRED OF U.S. CITIZEN PARENT	CHILD
Step 1 Select period in which child was born	*Step 2* Select applicable parentage	*Step 3* Measure citizen parent's residence against the requirements for the period in which the child was born. (The child acquires U.S. citizenship at birth if, at the time of birth, the citizen parent had met the applicable residence requirements.)	*Step 4* Determine whether child has since lost U.S. citizenship.
Prior to 5/24/34	Father citizen	Citizen father resided in the United States (Only father could transmit citizenship in this period.)	None
5/24/34 to 1/13/41	Both parents citizens	If both parents citizens, one must have resided in the United States.	None
	One parent citizen, one not	If one parent citizen, that parent must have resided in the United States.	same requirements as below
1/13/41 to 12/24/52	One parent citizen and one not	If one parent citizen, that parent must have resided in the United States or outlying possession for ten years, at least five of which must have been after age 16; or if parent served in the United States armed forces: (a) from 12/7/41 to 12/31/46, five of these years had to be after age 12; (b) from 12/31/46 to 12/24/52, 10 years	5 years' residence in the United States or outlying possessions between ages 13 and 21, or 2 years continuous presence in the United States between ages

PERIOD	PARENTS	RESIDENCE REQUIRED OF U.S. CITIZEN PARENT	CHILD
		physical presence needed, five of these after age 14.	14 and 28. (NONE, if at time of birth, citizen parent was employed by U.S. organization abroad.)
	Both parents citizens	One parent must have resided in the United States or outlying possessions.	None
12/24/52 to 11/14/86	Both parents citizens; or one citizen and one not	One citizen parent must have resided in the United States or outlying area; or citizen parent must have been physically present in the United States or outlying possession for ten years, five of them after age 14.	None
On/after 11/14/86	Both parents citizens; or one citizen and one not	One citizen parent must have resided in the United States or outlying possessions; citizen parent must have been physically present in the United States or outlying possession 5 years, at least 2 of which were after age 14.	None

NOTE: It is advisable to check with the United States consulate or embassy if you are unclear about any of the above information or if you need additional information regarding your claim to citizenship.

Chart Number 2: For determining whether ILLEGITIMATE CHILDREN BORN OUTSIDE THE UNITED STATES acquired United States citizenship at birth

PART 1 - Child not legitimated
PART 2 - Child legitimated by an alien father
PART 3 - Child legitimated by U.S. citizen father
PART 4 - Child legitimated or acknowledged by U.S. citizen father

PART 1	CHILD NOT LEGITIMATED
Prior to 12/24/52	Mother was a U.S. citizen who had resided in the United States or outlying possessions prior to birth of child. NOTE: Children born before 5/24/34 acquired U.S. citizenship retroactively when the Nationality Act of 1940 went into effect, to date of birth on 1/13/41.
On/after 12/24/52	Mother was U.S. citizen who was physically present in the United States or outlying possessions for continuous period of one year prior to birth of child.

PART 2	CHILD LEGITIMATED BY AN ALIEN FATHER

An illegitimate child did not acquire U.S. citizenship through its U.S. citizen mother if he/she was legitimated by an alien father and all three of the following elements were present:

1. Child was born before 5/24/34
2. Child was legitimated before age 21
3. This legitimation took place before 1/13/41

PART 3	CHILD LEGITIMATED BY U.S. CITIZEN FATHER
Date of child's birth	If the child did not acquire citizenship through its mother, but was legitimated by a U.S. citizen father under the following conditions, apply the law pertinent to legitimate children born in a foreign country (according to Chart 1)
Prior to 1/13/41	1. Child legitimated at any time after birth under law of father's domicile. 2. Father had the required residence at time of birth. 3. No residence required for child to retain U.S. citizenship.

1/13/41 to 12/24/52	1. Child legitimated before age 21 under law of father's domicile. 2. Father had the required residence at time of child's birth. 3. Child complies with residence requirements for retention.
On/after 12/24/52	1. Child legitimated before age 21 under law of father's domicile. 2. Father had the required residence at time of child's birth. 3. Child must be unmarried.

PART 4	CHILD LEGITIMATED/ACKNOWLEDGED BY U.S. CITIZEN FATHER
Relationship established on/after 11/14/86	1. Child/father blood relationship established. 2. Father, if alive, must provide written statement under oath that he will provide financial support for child until child turns 18. 3. Child must be legitimated under the law of child's residence or domicile, or father must acknowledge paternity of child in writing under oath, or paternity must be established by competent court. 4. Father must have been the U.S. citizen and met the required residence requirements at time of child's birth. 5. Child must be under age 18.

Chart Number 3: Derivative Citizenship of Children

If child was under statutory age during any specified time period and one or both parents became naturalized United States citizens and the child is a legal permanent resident, the child will derive citizenship except as noted in the Remarks column.

PERIOD IN WHICH LAST CONDITION WAS FULFILLED	STATUTORY AGE BEFORE WHICH LAST CONDITION MUST BE FULFILLED	IMMIGRA-TION STATUS OF CHILD	NATURAL-IZATION OF PARENTS	REMARKS
Prior to 5/24/34	21 years	LEGAL PERMANENT RESIDENT OF THE UNITED STATES	Either parent	
5/24/34 to 1/13/41	21 years		Either parent	U.S. citizenship began 5 years after child began to live perma-nently in the United States
			Both parents[1]	None
1/13/41 to 12/24/52	18 years		Both parents[1]	Illegitimate child did not derive in this period
On or after 12/24/52	16 years		Both parents[1]	Marriage bars derivation in this period
On or after 10/5/78	18 years		Both parents[1]	Marriage bars derivation in this period

ADMINISTRATIVE NATURALIZATION				
On or after 11/14/86	18 years	LEGAL PERMANENT RESIDENT OF U.S.	Both parents[1]	Marriage bars citizenship in this period

[1]Includes surviving parent, parent having legal custody over child, alien parent, when other parent is U.S. citizen, or, except during the period 1/13/41 to 12/23/52, the mother of an illegitimate child.

Immigration and Naturalization Service Regional Service Centers

EASTERN SERVICE CENTER
INS
75 Lower Welden Street
St. Albans, VT 05479-0001

NORTHERN SERVICE CENTER
INS
P.O. Box 82521
Lincoln, NE 68501-2521

SOUTHERN SERVICE CENTER
INS
P.O. Box 152122, Dept. A
Irving, TX 75015-2122

WESTERN SERVICE CENTER
INS
P.O. Box 30111
Laguna Niguel, CA 92607-0113

United States Embassies and Consulates Abroad

ALBANIA
Rruga Labinoti 103
Room 2921
Tirana
Tel. 355-42-32875

ALGERIA
4 Chemin Cheikh Bachir
  El-Ibrahimi
Algiers
Tel. 213/2-601-425

14 Square de Bemako
Oran
Tel. 213/6-334-509

**ANTIGUA AND
  BARBUDA**
St. John's
Tel. 809/462-3505

ARGENTINA
4300 Colombia, 1425
Unit 4334
Buenos Aires
Tel. 54/1-774-7611

ARMENIA
Hotel Hrazdan
Yerevan
Tel. 7-885/253-5332

AUSTRALIA
Moonah Place
Canberra, ACT 2600
Tel. 61/6-270-5000

553 St. Kilda Road
Melbourne, Victoria 3004
Tel. 61/3-526-5900

Electricity House
Park and Elizabeth Streets
36th Floor
Sydney, NSW 2000
Tel. 61/2-261-9200

16 St. Georges Terrace
13th Floor
Perth, WA 6800
Tel. 61/9-231-9400

383 Wickham Terrace
Brisbane, Queensland 4000
Tel. 61/7-839-8955

AUSTRIA
Boltzmanngasse 16
A-1091, Unit 27937
Vienna
Tel. 43/1-31-55-11

AZERBAIJAN
Hotel Intourist
Baku
Tel. 7-8922/91-79-56

BAHAMAS
Mosmar Building
Queen Street
Nassau
Tel. 809/322-1181

BAHRAIN
Road No. 3119
Zinj, Manama
Tel. 973/273-300

BANGLADESH
Madani Avenue
Baridhara, Dhaka
Tel. 880/2-884700-22

BARBADOS
P.O. Box 302
Bridgetown
Tel. 809/436-4950

BELGIUM
27 Boulevard de Regent
B-1000 Brussels
Tel. 32/2-513-3830

Rubens Center
Nationalestraat 5,
B-2000 Antwerp
Tel. 32/03-225-0071

BELIZE
Gabourel Lane and Hutson
  Street
Belize City
Tel. 501/2-77161

BENIN
Rue Caporal Anani Bernard
BP 2012, Cotonou
Tel. 229/30-06-50

BERMUDA
Crown Hill
16 Middle Road
Devonshire, Hamilton
Tel. 809/295-1342

BOLIVIA
Banco Popular Del Peru
    Building
Corner of Calles Mercado
    and Colon
La Paz
Tel. 591/2-350251

BOTSWANA
P.O. Box 90
Gaborone
Tel. 267/353-982

BRAZIL
Avenida das Nacoes
Lote 3, Unit 3500
Brasilia
Tel. 55/61-321-7272

Avenida Presidente
    Wilson 147
Rio de Janeiro
Tel. 55/21-292-7117

Rua Padre Joao Manoel 933
Sao Paulo
Tel. 55/11-881-6511

BRUNEI
3rd Floor, Teck Guan Plaza
Jalan Sultan
Bandar Seri Begawan
Tel. 673/2-229-670

BULGARIA
1 A. Stamboliski Boulevard
Unit 25402
Sofia
Tel. 359/2-88-48-01

BURKINA FASO
01 BP 35
Ouagadougou
Tel. 226/30-67-23

BURMA
581 Merchant Street
Rangoon
Tel. 95/1-82055

BURUNDI
BP 1720
Avenue des Etats-Unis
Burumbura
Tel. 257/222-454

BYELARUS
Storovilenskaya 6
Minsk
Tel. 7-0172/69-08-02

CAMBODIA
27 EO Street 240
Phnom Penh
Tel. 855/23-26436

CAMEROON
Rue Nachtigal
Yaounde
Tel. 237/234014

CANADA
100 Wellington Street
Ottawa, Ontario K1P 5T1
Tel. 613/238-5335

615 MacLeod Trail SE
Suite 1050
Calgary, Alberta T2G 4T8
Tel. 403/266-8962

Cogswell Tower, Suite 910
Scotia Square
Halifax, Nova Scotia
    B3J 3K1
Tel. 902/429-2480

P.O. Box 65
Postal Station Desjardins
Montreal, Quebec H5B 1G1
Tel. 514/398-9695

2 Place Terasse Dufferin
Quebec, Quebec G1R 4T9
Tel. 418/692-2095

360 University Avenue
Toronto, Ontario M5G 1S4
Tel. 416/595-1700

1095 West Pender Street
Vancouver, British
    Columbia V6E 2M6
Tel. 604/685-4311

**REPUBLIC OF CAPE
    VERDE**
Rua Hoji Ya Henda 81
Praia
Tel. 238/61-56-16

**CENTRAL AFRICAN
    REPUBLIC**
Avenue David Dacko
Bangui
Tel. 236/61-02-00

CHAD
Avenue Felix Eboue
N'Djamena
Tel. 235/51-62-18

CHILE
Codina Building
1343 Agustinas
Unit 4127
Santiago
Tel. 56/2-671-0133

CHINA
Xiu Shui Bei Jei 3
Beijing 100600
Tel. 86/1-532-3831

1 South Shamian Street
Shamian Island, Guanghzou
   20031
Tel. 86/20-888911

1469 Huai Hai Middle Road
Shanghai
Tel. 86/21-433-6880

40 Lane 4, Section 5
Sanjing Street, Heping
   District
Shenyang
Tel. 86/24-220000

Jinjiang Hotel
180 Renmin Road
Chengdu, Sichuan
Tel. 86/28-582222

COLOMBIA
Calle 38, No. 8-61
Bogota
Tel. 57/1-285-1300

Calle 77 Carrera 68
Centro Comercial
   Mayorista
Barranquilla
Tel. 57/58-45-7088

COMOROS
Boite Postale 1318
Moroni
Tel. 269/73-22-03

**PEOPLE'S REPUBLIC
  OF THE CONGO**
Avenue Amilcar Cabral
Brazzaville
Tel. 242/83-20-70

COSTA RICA
Pavas
San Jose
Tel. 506/20-39-39

COTE D'IVOIRE
5 Rue Jesse Owens
Abidjan
Tel. 225/21-09-79

CUBA
Swiss Embassy
Calzada Entre LYM
Vedado, Havana
Tel. 33/3550

CYPRUS
Therissos and Dositheos
   Streets
Nicosia
Tel. 357/2-465151

CZECHOSLOVAKIA
Trziste 15
125 48 Prague 1
Tel. 42/2-536-641

Hviezdoslavovo Namesite 4
81102 Bratislava
Tel. 42/7-330861

DENMARK
Dag Hammarskjolds Alle
  24
2100 Copenhagen
Tel. 45/31-42-31-44

**REPUBLIC OF
  DJIBOUTI**
Plateau du Serpent
Blvcd. Marechal Joffre
Djibouti
Tel. 253/35-39-95

DOMINICAN REPUBLIC
Calles Cesar Nicolas
   Penson and
Leopoldo Navarro, Unit
  5500
Santo Domingo
Tel. 809/541-2171

ECUADOR
Avenidas 12 de Octubre y
   Patria
Quito
Tel. 593/2-562-890

9 de Octubre y Garcia
   Moreno
Guayaquil
Tel. 593/4-323-570

**EGYPT (ARAB
  REPUBLIC OF)**
North Gate 8
Kamal El-Din Salah Street
Cairo
Tel. 20/2-355-7371

110 Horreya Avenue
Alexandria
Tel. 20/3-482-1911

EL SALVADOR
25 Avenida Norte No. 1230
San Salvador
Tel. 503/26-7100

EQUATORIAL GUINEA
Calle de Los Ministros
Malabo
Tel. 240/9-2185

ESTONIA
Kentmanni 20
Tallinn
Tel. 011/358-49-303-182

ETHIOPIA
Entoto Street
Addis Ababa
Tel. 251/1-550-666

FIJI
31 Loftus Street
Suva
Tel. 679/314-466

FINLAND
Itainen Puistotie 14A
Helsinki
Tel. 358/0-171931

FRANCE
2 Avenue Gabriel
75382 Paris
Tel. 33/1-42-96-12-02

GABON
Blvd. de la Mer
Libreville
Tel. 241/762003

THE GAMBIA
Kairaba Avenue
Banjul
Tel. 220/92856

GEORGIA
Metechi Palace Hotel
Tbilisi
Tel. 7-8832/74-46-23

FEDERAL REPUBLIC OF GERMANY
Deichmanns Aue
5300 Bonn 2
Tel. 49/228-3391

Neustaedtische Kirchstrasse 4-5
Berlin
Tel. 49/30-238-5174

Siesmayerstrasse 21
6000 Frankfurt
Tel. 49/69-7535-0

Alsterufer 27/28
2000 Hamburg 36
Tel. 49/40-411710

Koeniginstrasse 5
8000 Muenchen 22
Tel. 49/89-28881

Urbanstrasse 7
7000 Stuttgart
Tel. 49/711-214-5224

Karl Tauchnitz Strasse 15/151
0-7010 Leipzig
Tel. 37/41-211-7866

GHANA
Ring Road East
Accra
Tel. 233/21-775348

GREECE
91 Vasilissis Sophias Boulevard
10160 Athens
Tel. 30/1-721-2951

GRENADA
P.O. Box 54
St. George's
Tel. 809/444-1173

GUATEMALA
7-01 Avenida de la Reforma
Guatemala City
Tel. 502/2-31-15-41

GUINEA
2d Boulevard and 9th Avenue
Conakry
Tel. 224/44-15-20

GUINEA-BISSAU
Avenida Domingos Ramos
Bissau
Tel. 245/20-1139

GUYANA
99-100 Young and Duke Streets
Kingston, Georgetown
Tel. 592/2-54900-9

HAITI
Harry Truman Boulevard
Port-Au-Prince
Tel. 509/22-0354

THE HOLY SEE
Vatican City
Villino Pacelli
Via Aurelia 294
00165 Rome
Tel. 396/639-0558

HONDURAS
Avenido La Paz
Tegucigalpa
Tel. 504/32-3120

HONG KONG
26 Garden Road
Hong Kong
Tel. 852/523-9011

HUNGARY
V. Szabadsag Ter. 12
Budapest
Tel. 36/1-112-6450

ICELAND
Laufasvegur 21 Box 40
Reykjavik
Tel. 354/1-29100

INDIA
Shanti Path
Chanakyapuri
New Delhi 110021
Tel. 91/11-600651

Lincoln House
78 Bhulabhai Desai Road
Bombay 400026
Tel. 91/22-363-3611

5/1 Ho Chi Minh Sarani
Calcutta 700071
Tel. 91/033-22-3611

264 United States Embassies and Consulates Abroad

Mount Road
Madras 600006
Tel. 91/44-473-040

INDONESIA
Medan Merdeka Selatan 5
Jakarta
Tel. 62/21-360-360

Jalan Imam Bonhol 13
Medan
Tel. 62/61-322200

Jalan Raya Dr. Sutomo 33
Surabaya
Tel. 62/31-69287

IRAQ
Opp. Foreign Ministry Club
Masbah Quarter
Baghdad
Tel. 964/1-719-6138

IRELAND
42 Elgin Road
Ballsbridge, Dublin
Tel. 353/1-688777

ISRAEL
71 Hayarkon Street
Tel Aviv
Tel. 972/3-517-4338

ITALY
Via Veneto 119/A
00187 Rome
Tel. 39/6-46741

Banca d'America e d'Italia
  Building
Piazza Portello 6
16124 Genoa
Tel. 39/10-282-741

Via Principe Amedeo 2/10
20121 Milan
Tel. 39/2-290-351

Piazza della Repubblica
80122 Naple
Tel. 39/81-761-4303

Via Vaccarini 1
90143 Palermo
Tel. 39/91-343-532

Lungarno Amerigo
  Vespucci 38
50123 Firenze
Tel. 39/55-239-8276

JAMAICA
Jamaica Mutual Life
  Center
2 Oxford Road, 3rd Floor
Kingston
Tel. 809/929-4850

JAPAN
10-5 Akasaka 1-chrome
Minato-ku 107
Tokyo
Tel. 81/3-3224-5000

2564 Nishihara
Urasoe City
Okinawa 90121
Tel. 81/98-876-4211

11-5 Nishitenma 2-chrome
Kita-ku
Osaka 530
Tel. 81/6-315-5900

Kita 1-Jo Nishi 28-chrome
Chuo-ku
Sapporo 064
Tel. 81/11-641-1115

5-26 Ohori 2-chrome
Chuo-ku
Fukuoka-810
Tel. 81/92-751-9331

JERUSALEM
18 Agron Road
Jerusalem 94190
Tel. 972/2-253288

JORDAN
Jabel Amman
Amman
Tel. 962/6-644-371

KAZAKHSTAN
Hotel Kazakhstan
Alma-Ata
Tel. 3272/61-90-56

KENYA
Moi/Haile Selassie Avenue
Nairobi
Tel. 254/2-334141

KOREA
82 Sejong-Ro
Chongro-ku
Seoul
Tel. 82/2-732-2601

24 2-Ka
Daechung Dong, Chung-ku
Pusan
Tel. 82/51-246-7791

KUWAIT
P.O. Box 77 Safat, 13001
  Safat
Kuwait
Tel. 965/242-4151

KYRGYZSTAN
Derzhinskiy Prospek 66
Bishkek
Tel. 3313/22-22-70

LAOS
Rue Bartholonie
Vientiane
Tel. 856/2220

LATVIA
Raina Boulevard 7
Riga 226050
Tel. 0-11-358/49-311-348

LEBANON
Antelias, P.O. Box 70-840
Beirut
Tel. 961/417774

LESOTHO
P.O. Box 333
Maseru 100
Tel. 266/312-666

LIBERIA
111 United Nations Drive
Monrovia
Tel. 231/222991

LITHUANIA
Akmenu 6
Vilnius 232600
Tel. 011/7-012-2-222-724

LUXEMBOURG
22 Bovd. Emmanuel
    Servais
2535 Luxembourg
Tel. 352/460123

MADAGASCAR
14-16 Rue Rainitovo
Antsahavola
Antananarivo
Tel. 261/2-212-57

MALAWI
P.O. Box 30016
Lilongwe
Tel. 265/730-166

MALAYSIA
376 Jalan Tun Razak
50400 Kuala Lumpur
Tel. 60/3-248-9011

MALI
Rue Rochester NY and Rue
    Mohamed V
Bamako
Tel. 223/225470

MALTA
2nd Floor, Development
    House
St. Anne Street, Floriana
Valletta
Tel. 356/240424

MARSHALL ISLANDS
P.O. Box 1379
Majuro
Tel. 011/692-4011

MAURITANIA
BP 222
Nouakchott
Tel. 222/2-526-60

MAURITIUS
Rogers House, 4th Floor
John Kennedy Street
Port Louis
Tel. 230/208/9763

MEXICO
Paseo de la Reforma 305
Colonia Cuahtemoc
Mexico City, 06500
Tel. 52/5-211-0042

Avenue Lopez Mateos 924N
Ciudad Juarex, Chihuahua
Tel. 52/16-134048

Progreso 175
Guadalajara
Tel. 52/36-25-2998

Avenida Constitucion 411
Poniente 64000
Monterrey, Nuevo Leon
Tel. 52/83-45-2120

Tapachula 96
Tijuana
Tel. 52/66-81-7400

Monterrey 141
Hermosillo, Son
Tel. 52/62-172375

Ave. Primera 2002
Matamoros, Tamaulipas
Tel. 52/891-6-72-70

Circunvalacion 120
    Centro
Mazatlan, Sinaloa
Tel. 52/69-85-22-05-7

Paseo Montejo 453
Merida, Yucatan
Tel. 52/99-25-5011

Calle Allenda 3330
Col. Jardin
88260 Nuevo Laredo,
    Tamps

MICRONESIA
P.O. Box 1286
Pohnpei, Kolonia
Tel. 691/320-2187

MOLDAVIA
Strada Alexei Mateevich
    103
Chisinau
Tel. 7-0422-233-894

**PEOPLE'S REPUBLIC
    OF MONGOLIA**
c/o American Embassy
    Beijing
PSC 461, Box 300, FPO AP
    95921-0002
Ulaanbaatar
Tel. 800/29095

MOROCCO
2 Ave. de Marrakech
Rabat
Tel. 212/7-76-22-65

8 Blvd. Moulay Youssef
Casablanca
Tel. 212/2-26-45-50

MOZAMBIQUE
Avenida Kenneth Kaunda
    193
Maputo
Tel. 258/1-49-27-97

NAMIBIA
Ausplan Building
14 Lossen Street
Windhoek
Tel. 264/61-221-601

NEPAL
Pani Pokhari
Kathmandu
Tel. 977/1-411179

NETHERLANDS
Lange Voorhout 102
The Hague
Tel. 31/70-310-9209

Museumplein 19
Amsterdam
Tel. 31/20-664-5661

**NETHERLANDS
    ANTILLES**
St. Anna Boulevard 19
Willemstad, Curacao
Tel. 599/9-613066

NEW ZEALAND
29 Fitzherbert Terrace
Thorndon, Wellington
Tel. 64/4-472-2068

Yorkshire General Bldg.,
    4th Floor
Shortland and O'Connell
    Streets
Auckland
Tel. 64/9-303-2724

NICARAGUA
Km. 4 1/2 Carretera Sur
Managua
Tel. 505/2-666010

NIGER
Rue Des Ambassades
Naimey
Tel. 227/72-26-61

NIGERIA
2 Eleke Crescent
Lagos
Tel. 234/1-610097

9 Maska Road
Kaduna
Tel. 234/62-201070

NORWAY
Drammensveien 18
0244 Oslo 2
Tel. 47/2-44-85-50

OMAN
P.O. Box 50202 Madinat
    Qaboos
Muscat
Tel. 968/698-989

PAKISTAN
Diplomatic Enclave
Ramna 5
Islamabad
Tel. 92/51-826161

8 Abdullah Haroon Road
Karachi
Tel. 92/21-5685170

Shara-E-Bin-Badees
50 Empress Road
New Simla Hills
Lahore
Tel. 92/42-365530

11 Hospital Road
Unit 62217
Peshawar
Tel. 92/521-79801

REPUBLIC OF PALAU
P.O. Box 6028
Koror
Tel. 680/488-2920

PANAMA
Unit 0945, Apartado 6959
Panama City
Tel. 507/27-1777

PAPUA NEW GUINEA
Armit Street
Port Moresby
Tel. 675/211-455

PARAGUAY
1776 Mariscal Lopez Avenue
Asuncion
Tel. 595/21-213-715

PERU
Corner of Avenidas Inca
    Garcilas de la Vega and
    España
Lima
Tel. 51/14-33-8000

PHILIPPINES
1201 Roxas Boulevard
Manila
Tel. 63/2-521-7116

PCI Bank, Gorordo Avenue,
    3rd Floor
Lahug, Cebu
Tel. 63/32-311-261

POLAND
Aleje Ujazdowskie 29/31
Warsaw
Tel. 48/2-828-3041

Ulica Stolarska 9
31043 Krakow
Tel. 48/12-229764

Ulica Chopina 4
Poznan
Tel. 48/61-529586

PORTUGAL
Avenida das Forcas
    Armadas
1600 Lisbon
Tel. 351/1-726-6600

Avenida D. Henrique
Ponta Delgada, Sao Miguel,
    Azores
Tel. 351/96-22216

QATAR
149 Ali Bin Ahmed Street
Farig Bin Omran
Doha
Tel. 0974/864701

ROMANIA
Strada Tudor Arghezi 7-9
Bucharest
Tel. 40/0-10-40-40

RUSSIA
Ulitsa Chaykovskogo
    19/21/23
Moscow
Tel. 7-095/252-2450

Ulitsa, Petra Lavrova Street
15
St. Petersburg
Tel. 812/274-8235

RWANDA
Blvd. de la Revolution
Kigali
Tel. 250/75601

SAUDI ARABIA
Collector Road M
Riyadh Diplomatic Quarter
Tel. 966/1-488-3800

Between Aramco HQ and
    Dhahram Airport
P.O. Box 81, Dhahram
    Airport 31932
Dhahram
Tel. 966/3-891-3200

Palestine Road
Ruwais, Jeddah
Tel. 966/2-667-0080

SENEGAL
BP 49, Avenue Jean XXIII
Dakar
Tel. 221/23-42-96

SEYCHELLES
Victoria House, Box 251
Victoria, Mahe
Tel. 248/25256

SIERRA LEONE
Walpole and Siaka Stevens
    Streets
Freetown
Tel. 232/22-226-481

SINGAPORE
30 Hill Street
Singapore 0617
Tel. 65/338-0251

SOLOMON ISLANDS
Mud Alley
Honiara
Tel. 677/23890

SOUTH AFRICA
Thibault House
225 Pretorius Street
Pretoria
Tel. 27/12-28-4266

Broadway Industries
    Center
Heerengracht, Foreshore
Cape Town
Tel. 27/21-214-280

Durban Bay House, 29th
    Floor
333 Smith Street
Durban 4001
Tel. 27/31-304-4737

Kine Center, 11th Floor
Commissioner and Kruis
    Streets
Johannesburg
Tel. 27/11-331-1681

SPAIN
Serano 75
28006 Madrid
Tel. 34/1-577-4000

Via Layetana 33
08003 Barcelona
Tel. 34/3-319-9550

Lehendakari Agirre 11-3
48014 Bilbao
Tel. 34/4-475-8300

SRI LANKA
210 Galle Road
Colombo 3
Tel. 94/1-44-80-07

SUDAN
Sharia Ali Abdul Latif
Khartoum
Tel. 74700

SURINAME
Dr. Sophie Redmondstraat
   129
Paramaribo
Tel. 597/472900

SWAZILAND
Central Bank Building
Warner Street
Mbabane
Tel. 268/46441

SWEDEN
Strandvagen 101
Stockholm
Tel. 46/8-783-5300

SWITZERLAND
Jubilaeumstrasse 93
3005 Bern
Tel. 41/31-437-011

Botanic Building
1-3 Avenue de la Paix
1202 Geneva
Tel. 41/22-738-7613

Zollikerstrasse 141
8008 Zurich
Tel. 41/1-422-25-66

SYRIA
Abu Roumaneh
al-Mansur Street, No. 2
Damascus
Tel. 963/11-333052

TAJIKISTAN
Interim Chancery
39 Ainii Street
Dushanbe
Tel. 7/3772-24-82-33

TANZANIA
36 Laibon Road
Dar Es Salaam
Tel. 255/51-66010

THAILAND
95 Wireless Road
Bangkok
Tel. 66/2-252-5040

Vidhayanond Road
Chiang Mai
Tel. 66/53-252-629

9 Sadao Road
Songkhla
Tel. 66/74-321-441

35/6 Supakitjanya Road
Udorn
Tel. 66/42-244-270

TOGO
Rue Pelletier Caventou and
   Rue Vauban
Lome
Tel. 228/21-77-17

**TRINIDAD AND
   TOBAGO**
15 Queen's Park West
Port-of-Spain
Tel. 809/622-6372

TUNISIA
144 Ave. de la Liberte
1001 Tunis-Belvedere
Tel. 216/1-782-566

TURKEY
110 Ataturk Boulevard
Ankura
Tel. 90/4-426-54-70

104-108 Mesrutiyet Caddesi
Tepebasl, Istanbul
Tel. 90/1-251-36-02

92 Ataturk Caddesi, 3rd
   Floor
Izmir
Tel. 90/51-149426

Ataturk Caddesi
Adana
Tel. 90/71-139106

TURKMENISTAN
Yubilenaya Hotel
Ashkhabad
Tel. 7/36320-24-49-08

UGANDA
Parliament Avenue
Kampala
Tel. 256/41-259792

UKRAINE
10 Yuria Kotsyubinskovo
252053 Kiev
Tel. 7/044-279-0188

**UNITED ARAB
   EMIRATE**
Al-Sudan Street
Abu Dhabi
Tel. 971/2-336691

Dubai International Trade
   Center
Dubai
Tel. 971/4-371115

UNITED KINGDOM
24/31 Grosvenor Square
London, England W1A
   1AE
Tel. 44-71/499-9000

Queen's House
14 Queen Street
Belfast, Northern Ireland
   BT1 6EQ
Tel. 44-232/328239

3 Regent Terrace
Edinburgh, Scotland EH7
   5B
Tel. 44-31/556-8315

UNITED STATES
799 United Nations Plaza
New York, NY 10017
Tel. 212/415-4050

URUGUAY
Lauro Muller 1776
Montevideo
Tel. 598/2-23-60-61

UZBEKISTAN
55 Chelanzanskaya
Tashkent
Tel. 7-3217/77-14-07

VENEZUELA
Avenida Francisco de
    Miranda and Avenida
    Principal de la floresta
Caracas 1060-A
Tel. 58/2-285-2222

Edificio Sofimara
Piso 3, Calle 77 Con
    Avenida 13
Maracaibo
Tel. 58/61-83054

WESTERN SAMOA
P.O. Box 3430
Apia
Tel. 685/21-631

REPUBLIC OF YEMEN
Dhahr Himyar Zone
Sheraton Hotel District
Sanaa
Tel. 967/1-238-842

YUGOSLAVIA
Box 5070, Unit 25402
Belgrade
Tel. 38/11-645-655

Brace Kavurica 2
Zagreb
Tel. 38/41-444-800

ZAIRE
310 Avenue des Aviateurs
Kinshasa
Tel. 243/12-21532

1029 Blvd. Kamanyola
Lubumbashi
Tel. 243/011-222324

ZAMBIA
Independence and United
    Nations Avenue
Lusaka
Tel. 260-1/228-595

ZIMBABWE
172 Herbert Chitapo Avenue
Harare
Tel. 263/4-794-521

Companies that do Professional Evaluations of Foreign University Degrees and Diplomas

Credentials Evaluation Service
International Education Research
   Foundation
P.O. Box 66940
Los Angeles, California 90066
Tel. (213) 390-6276

Education Credential Evaluators, Inc.
P.O. Box 17499
Milwaukee, Wisconsin 53217
Tel. (414) 964-0477

Schedule 1 Occupations/Professions that Qualify for B-1/Business Visas in Terms of the Canada-United States Free Trade Agreement (FTA)

There are seven broad areas in which Canadians will be granted B-1 business visas to enter the United States and Americans will be granted the equivalent business visas to enter Canada in terms of the FTA. Only Canadian and United States citizens are eligible for these visas that will be granted at the border without prior application and without the necessity of acquiring employment authorization or labor clearance. These areas are as follows:

1. **Research and design**
   - Technical, scientific, and statistical researchers conducting independent research, or research for an enterprise located in Canada/the United States;

2. **Growth, manufacture, and production**
   - Harvestor owner supervising a harvesting crew admitted under applicable law;
   - Purchasing and production management personnel conducting commercial transactions for an enterprise located in Canada/the United States;

3. **Marketing**
   - Market researchers and analysts conducting independent research or analysis, or research or analysis for an enterprise located in Canada/the United States;
   - Trade fair and promotional personnel attending a trade convention;

4. **Sales**
   - Sales representatives and agents taking orders or negotiating contracts for goods or services but not delivering goods or providing services;
   - Buyers purchasing for an enterprise located in Canada/the United States;

5. **Distribution**
   - Transportation operators delivering to the United States/Canada or loading and transporting back to Canada/the United States, with no intermediate loading or delivery within the United States/Canada;
   - Customs brokers performing brokerage duties associated with the export of goods from the United States/Canada to or through Canada/the United States;

6. After-sales service

- Installers, repair and maintenance personnel, and supervisors, possessing specialized knowledge essential to the seller's contractual obligation, performing services or training workers to perform such services, pursuant to a warranty or other service contract incidental to the sale of commercial or industrial equipment or machinery, including computer software, purchased from an enterprise located outside the United States/Canada, during the life of the warranty or service agreement;

7. General service

- Professionals, with respect to entry into the United States of America, otherwise classifiable under section 101 (a) (15) (H) (i) of the Immigration and Nationality Act, but receiving no salary or other remuneration from a United States source; and, with respect to entry into Canada, exempt from the requirement to obtain an employment authorization pursuant to subsection 19 (1) of the Immigration Regulations, 1978, but receiving no salary or other remuneration from a Canadian source;

- Management and supervisory personnel engaging in commercial transactions for an enterprise located in Canada/the United States;

- Computer specialists, with respect to entry into the United States of America, otherwise classifiable under section 101 (a) (15) (H) (i) of the Immigration and Nationality Act, but receiving no salary or other remuneration from a United States source; and, with respect to entry into Canada, exempt from the requirement to obtain an employment authorization pursuant to subsection 19 (1) of the Immigration Regulations, 1978, but receiving no salary or other remuneration from a Canadian source;

- Financial services personnel (insurers, bankers, or investment brokers) engaging in commercial transactions for an enterprise located in Canada/ the United States;

- Public relations and advertising personnel consulting with business associates, or attending or participating in conventions;

- Tourism personnel (tour and travel agents, tour guides, or tour operators) attending or participating in conventions or conducting a tour that has begun in Canada/the United States;

- Translators or interpreters performing services as employees of an enterprise located in Canada/the United States.

Schedule 2 Professions that Qualify for TC Visas in Terms of the Canada-United States Free Trade Agreement (FTA)

accountant
engineer
scientist.
- biologist
- biochemist
- physicist
- geneticist
- zoologist
- entomologist
- geophysicist
- epidemiologist
- pharmacologist
- animal scientist
- agriculturalist (agronomist)
- dairy scientist
- poultry scientist
- soil scientist

research assistant (working in a postsecondary educational institution)
management consultant (bachelor's degree or equivalent professional experience required)
medical/allied professional:
- physician (teaching and/or research only)
- dentist
- registered nurse
- veterinarian
- medical technologist
- clinical laboratory technologist

psychologist
scientific technician/technologist who:

1. works in direct support of professional in the following disciplines: chemistry, geology, geophysics, meteorology, physics, astronomy, agricultural sciences, biology, or forestry
2. has theoretical knowledge of the discipline
3. solves practical problems in the discipline
4. applies principles of the discipline to basic or applied research

disaster relief insurance claims adjustor
architect
lawyer
teacher: college
                   university
seminary
economist
social worker
vocational counselor
mathematician
hotel manager (bachelor's degree plus three years of experience required)
librarian (master's degree in library science required)
animal breeder
plant breeder
horticulturalist
sylviculturalist (forestry specialist)
journalist (bachelor's degree plus three years of experience required)
nutritionist
dietician
technical publications writer
computer systems analyst

Countries Whose Nationals
Do Not Require Visitors' Visas
to Enter Canada

Andorra	Ireland	Saudi Arabia
Antiqua	Israel	Seychelles
Argentina	Italy	Singapore
Australia	Japan	Solomon Islands
Austria	Kenya	Spain
Bahamas	Kiribati	St. Kitts and Nevis
Barbados	Lesotho	St. Lucia
Belgium	Liechtenstein	St. Vincent
Belize	Luxembourg	Surinam
Botswana	Malawi	Swaziland
Brunei	Malaysia	Sweden
Costa Rica	Malta	Switzerland
Cyprus	Mexico	Tonga
Denmark	Monaco	Tuvalu
Dominica	Nauru	United States
Federal Republic of Germany	Netherlands	Uruguay
Finland	New Guinea	Vanuatu
France	New Zealand	Venezuela
Greece	Norway	Western Samoa
Grenada	Paraguay	Zambia
Iceland	San Marino	Zimbabwe

ABOUT THE AUTHOR

Howard David Deutsch, a specialist in the fields of immigration and international law received his LLB/JD at Yale Law School and also studied international law at the University of Cambridge in England. Mr. Deutsch is admitted to the Bar in the states of New York and California. He counsels individual clients and corporations from the law offices of Deutsch & Salberg in New York City.

Mr. Deutsch is also the author of *Getting into America*, 1984, *Employer's Complete Guide to Immigration*, 1987, and the *Deutsch & Salberg Immigration Law and Business Newsletter*. He has lectured and taught seminars on U.S. immigration law in Canada, the Republic of South Africa, the United Kingdom, and Ireland, and has been invited to lecture in Moscow.

INDEX